Rental Houses for the Successful Small Investor

Second Edition

Suzanne P. Thomas

Gemstone House Publishing
PO Box 19948
Boulder, CO 80308

The following trademarks appear in this book
Monopoly and QuickBooks

Rental Houses for the Successful Small Investor, 2nd edition

Copyright 2006
First Printing 2006

Publisher's Cataloguing-in-Publication
(Provided by Quality Books, Inc.)

Thomas, Suzanne Patricia, 1965-
    Rental houses for the successful small investor /
Suzanne P. Thomas. -- 2nd ed.
    p. cm.
    Includes index
    Preassigned LCCN:2005908580
    ISBN: 0-9664691-4-3 (paperback)
        978-0-9664691-4-1

    1. Real estate investment. 2. Real estate
investment-- Finance. 3. Real estate
management 4. Rental housing --United States.
I. Title.

HD1382.5.T46 2006   332.63'24
                              QBI98-1264

Gemstone House Publishing
P.O. Box 19948
Boulder, CO 80308

Acknowledgments:

Many people helped to make the material in this book as accurate as possible.

Rich Levy and Linda Levy from 1031 Solutions, LLC, reviewed the 1031 tax deferred exchange chapter (they can be reached toll free at 1-866-440-1031).

Over the years the staff at World Savings and Washington Mutual have kept me updated on the material relating to adjustable mortgages and portfolio lenders. Any mistakes that slipped into this edition are mine, not theirs.

Rich Schad of Farmers Insurance in Lousiville, CO, continues to enlighten me as to how insurance coverage works.

David Stein at Stein & Co with Metro Brokers is a great real estate agent and mortgage broker. He's professional, trustworthy, and knowledgable. Plus I enjoy working with him.

Although family members supposedly will love anything written by a member of the clan, my father and sister care more about clarity and good writing. Thanks so much for the many tedious hours of critiquing and copy editing.

Also thanks to other investors. Whether we've met at adult education classes, investor meetings, or book discussions, your questions have taught me what you wanted to learn. Your feedback has made this book so much more effective.

Finally, thanks to my tenants. Some have occasionally driven me nuts, others have made my world a brighter place, all have taught me so much. Without them, my career in rental real estate wouldn't have been possible.

Table of Contents

Return • When to Restructure Your Investments • Cash Flow Versus Appreciation • Ignoring Rates of Return

Chapter Three

Building Up Equity • Saving Money • It's Impossible to Save • Unexpected Money • Get a Partner • Borrowing Money • Taking a Breather • Moving • Potential for Appreciation • Local Regulations • Taxes and Insurance • Inheriting Money • Life Insurance • Settlements • Lease Options

Chapter Four

Single Family Homes • Different Types of Single Family Homes • Brand New Houses • Overly Expensive Houses •Location and Appreciation • Negative Cash Flow • Fixer Uppers • Getting a Discount • Condominiums and Townhouses • Duplexes, Triplexes and Four-plexes • Apartment Houses • Functional Obsolescence • Falling in Love • Comparing Properties • Deciding Between Two Available Properties - The Shortcut Method • Magic Price Point • Properties with Two Bathrooms • Speculative Markets • Moving to a Different City or State • Buying in a Different State • Looking with an Agent • Helping Your Agent • Buyer's Agent • What If Your Agent Doesn't Do a Good Job? • Feeling Nervous • Making an Offer

Chapter Five

Conventional Lenders • Secondary Loan Market • Fannie Mae Limit on Number of Loans • Fannie Mae Limits on Loan Amounts •Portfolio Lenders • Qualifying Ratios • Portfolio Lender Ratios

• Minimizing Monthly Debt • Rental Income • Conventional Lenders & Investment Loans • Portfolio Lenders & Investment Loans • Credit Scores • Owner Occupant Versus Investor Loans • Leap Frogging from Home to Home • Loan Terms • Forty Year Mortgages • Bi-Weekly Mortgage Payments • Prepayment Penalties

• Bad and Good Tenants • Adequate Incomes and Good Credit • The Wheedlers • Maintaining a Property • Long Term Tenants • Questionable Credit Versus a Soft Heart • Accepting Pets • The Trouble with Smokers • Argumentative Tenants • Perfect and Good Enough Tenants • Option to Rent • Renting Multiple Properties • Fair Housing Laws a Qualified Intermediary • Identifying Your Replacement Properties • How Many Replacement Properties • 180 Days to Close • Reinvesting All of Your Proceeds • Minimizing Additional Cash Invested • Carrying Over Your Basis • The Reverse Exchange • The Improvement Exchange • Combining the Principal Residence Gain Exclusion with a 1031 Exchange • Contract Provisions • Summary

Introduction

This book is meant to help beginning and small investors achieve financial independence through owning a handful of rental properties. Perhaps you are just beginning to explore the idea of investing in real estate or you already own a couple of rentals. In either case, this book will help you to succeed. Small fortunes and big fortunes are made in real estate by thousands of people every year in America. You can be one of these people.

Yes, you'll have to learn a lot. You will need to know how to decide if a property is a good one to buy, how to choose the best loan, and how to manage tenants. But even if you aren't a wheeler and dealer type of person, you can make money investing in real estate. This book is designed for the average person who is interested in owning a small number of properties for at least ten years.

Buying and owning real estate can be fun and profitable. I'll share my guidelines for minimizing the headaches so you can relax and enjoy the financial rewards. For example, you don't have to spend weeks searching for distressed sellers or investigating foreclosures in order to do well in real estate. In many markets it is possible to pay market prices for single family homes in good to great condition yet still be able to rent them for a positive cash flow. Or, if the cash flow is negative, your overall rate of return can be strongly positive because of appreciation or paying down the loan.

No matter who you are or where you live, investing in real estate is one of the best second jobs you can create for yourself. Eventually, when you've acquired enough properties and owned them long enough for your cash flow to increase, being a part-time landlord can become your main job. Say good-bye to working nine to five!

Owning and managing a few rental houses is also a great career for the stay-at-home parent who wants to contribute substantially to the family's financial future. Compared to starting most small businesses, owning rental properties involves a low amount of risk. Financing is readily available, rents are relatively easy to predict, and properties can be sold relatively quickly if you change your mind or move. Compared to other small businesses, it's easier to start off on a small scale by buying just one or two properties.

Investing in rental properties requires only a modest investment of your time. Each property, if bought according to the suggestions in this book, will require an average of two to three hours per month including time spent driving and doing paperwork. Though you may spend eight or ten hours in a month when you are showing a property to prospective tenants or staining a deck, other months you'll do nothing except collect the rent and pay the mortgage. Shopping for properties to buy is actually the most time-consuming activity, and you can opt to do that only when you have extra time in your schedule.

Owning real estate involves more than investing your time. You also need to know how to handle tenants, evaluate properties, stay on the correct side of the law, and more. Besides covering all these basics, this book also contains valuable tips.

For example, did you know that you can insure yourself against the possibility of a tenant maliciously trashing one of your properties? In some instances insurance companies consider damage to be vandalism. The insurance company will reimburse you for your costs, including any lost rent during the time it takes to have your property repaired. I'll tell you what type of policy provides this coverage, and what type of damage may qualify.

Perhaps you would like to make some money when you buy by getting a house at a discount. I'll tell you about the type of sellers who will almost always give you a break in the price if you'll do one small favor for them. In addition, I'll tell you how to get a builder to give you a five to seven percent discount off the price of a brand new house, even if your local market is hot.

Since we all know the real estate market can go down as well as up, I'll tell you what you can do to protect yourself against the downturns. You'll find out how much equity you need as a cushion, what happens when you prepay an adjustable rate mortgage versus a fixed mortgage, and how to decide if the rent-to-property value ratios in your area are attractive.

Real estate investing can be your ticket to early retirement. Only five properties may be enough to provide you with a core income within five to ten years. You'll then be able to devote the majority of your energy to other interests besides a regular job.

Perhaps owning rental real estate will allow you to become a full-time volunteer who makes a difference in your community. Maybe you want the chance to write or paint without worrying about whether or not you'll earn enough to support yourself. Perhaps you'll decide to turn your rentals over to a management company and take off to travel the world.

Or maybe you'll enjoy real estate investing so much that you'll decide to move up to commercial property such as office or apartment buildings. You could 1031 tax defer exchange the equity in your first few condos or houses into larger properties.

Whatever your goals are or may become, this book can help you realize your dreams by helping you to set your goals, select properties and tenants, understand mortgages, develop a lease, or exchange your properties. Each chapter stands alone so you can flip immediately to the topic that interests you the most. Or you can start at page one and read straight through.

Owning a handful of rental houses gave me the freedom to do what I wanted to do in my thirties, and I'm eager to share how I did it so you can become as successful as you want to be, too.

Chapter One

As Rich as You Want to Be

People like to invest in real estate for many reasons. It's an investment they can see and literally touch. They can choose what properties to buy, who to rent to, and when to sell. They like this sense of control. Many people also know someone who has made money in real estate. If they can do it, why not them? And although investing in real estate can be done on a grand scale, it can also be successfully accomplished on a very modest basis with a handful of single family condominiums or houses.

It's possible, depending on your ambition, intelligence, and a bit of luck to make millions as a real estate investor. But before you decide to be a multimillionaire, you may want to give some thought to exactly why you want to make money. What do you want to do with it? What would give your life the most meaning? Do you want time to spend with your kids or in volunteer activities? Have the opportunity to live abroad? The financial wherewithal to send your kids to a private college? The possibilities are vast and the answers are different for each person or family.

It's easier to tolerate the occasional not-so-great tenants and to paint the same wall for the third time in ten years when you know that these real estate hassles will eventually give you the most important things in life: time with family and friends, an opportunity to learn and be creative, and a chance to spend your life doing what matters the most to you. It would be a shame to wait to devote more time to your dreams because you overestimated how much money your realistic dream life would actually cost. If your goals require a net worth of $1,200,000, why waste five extra years to make $1,450,000 instead?

A Dream Income

In the early nineties my dream income was $40,000 per year. I was single, twenty-five-years-old, and my income had never exceeded $20,000 per year. Therefore $40,000 seemed like a lot of money to me. While this goal may seem modest today, at that time it would have been enough for me to pay for all the necessities of life as well as a few nice luxuries such as fresh flowers and monthly massages. I wouldn't have to work at a job unless I wanted extra money to pay for something special.

I yearned for a quiet, reflective life with plenty of time to read books, visit with friends and relatives, plus the leisure to write romance novels without worrying about whether they would ever sell. I wanted a small garden and the time to learn to paint watercolor pictures of cats and flowers. I longed to be able to sleep late in the mornings, take naps in the sunshine in the afternoon, and stay up past midnight without having to suffer the next morning when the alarm clock went off. As a matter of fact, I wanted never again to be woken by the nasty buzzing of an alarm. If I didn't see the sun rise for the rest of my life, that would be fine with me. Sunsets and moonrises would suffice, thank you.

One afternoon I thought about how much income my personal residence would produce if the mortgage were paid off and the house rented for the current fair market rent. I multiplied this rent amount by twelve months, subtracted expenses such as taxes, vacancy, insurance and maintenance costs, and came up with $8,000. If I owned five rental houses, each producing an $8,000 yearly income, then I would receive my $40,000 dream income.

It seemed remarkably simple. All I had to do was buy five more houses like the modest 1,300 square foot house I already owned, concentrate on paying off the mortgages, and I could retire. I thought it would take me quite a while to pay off my loans, maybe twenty years, but even so I would be retiring in my forties. That sounded more appealing than waiting until I was sixty-five or seventy.

What Is Your Goal?

Your financial goal is inextricably tied up with your dream life. Do you want to live near the beach? In the mountains? Devote yourself to volunteer activities? Run for political office? Become an artist? Learn to play a musical instrument? Stay home with your children? Start a business?

Draw up a budget that matches your dream life. What is the minimal amount of income you would need to live the way you want to live? Don't worry, I'm not saying that you can't increase your goal later; indeed that's what I did. But wouldn't it be nice to know the smallest amount it would cost for you to have a satisfying lifestyle? To discover that maybe you are only five or eight years away from retiring if the rat race gets to be too much? You can always choose to work longer, but having a goal that can be reached in a relatively short time is more motivating.

Maybe you would like to continue working on a part-time basis, perhaps doing something entirely different from what you do now. How much money would that contribute to your annual budget? How much income will you need to earn from your investments?

Suppose you and your spouse determine you will need a $75,000 income to live a dream life. You are both willing to work part-time as part of your dream life; together you would bring in $23,000 per year. You also own stocks which would produce $7,000 in dividends per year. Subtracting your part-time work income and stock dividends from your target income of $75,000 leaves $45,000 in income that must come from new investments.

How Much Is Enough?

How much money is enough to fulfill your needs and allow for the extras that make life fun? Where do you get the most happiness for each dollar earned and spent?

The book *Your Money or Your Life* by Joe Dominguez and Vicki Robin teaches people how to evaluate their spending habits. If you need help getting the maximum personal return for every dollar you spend, as well as learning how much income would be enough for you and your family, you should read this book. Although I doubt you would choose a lifestyle as minimalist as the authors', their approach will work for anyone.

Another book you might want to read was written by two of Joe and Vicki's students, *Getting a Life* by Jacque Blix and David Heitmiller. Unlike Joe and Vicki who enjoyed a life so frugal that many Americans may have difficulty imagining it for themselves, Jacque and David take a more middle-of-the-road path. In this book they share their multi-year process of deciding what they most valued and how much income they needed to live personally fulfilling lives.

Evaluating value received per dollar spent can yield some surprising revelations. Not only may you discover that you are spending too much in some areas, you may also be spending too little in others. For example, I used to spend only $50 per year on books. But I love books! Yet while I rarely splurged at the bookstore, I thought nothing of going out to dinner with my husband three times a month and spending $60 each time.

After reading *Your Money or Your Life* I decided to increase my spending on books from $50 per year to $1,200, and cut back on dinners out. Spending my money on books instead of restaurant meals more accurately reflected my love of reading compared to my relative indifference to food. For less money spent I felt far more satisfaction.

Becoming Self-Employed

Many people dream of self-employment, either because they are the independent type or they are tired of being transferred by a big corporation. They decide to start a business from scratch or buy a franchise. Either choice involves a degree of risk and usually quite a bit of capital. The investment of time can be all consuming. New business owners tend to work many more hours for themselves than they ever did for a past employer.

Becoming a business owner poses enough problems to cause any sensible person to reconsider the idea. Investing in a business is tantamount to buying a job, but unlike a normal job, it's not possible to easily quit. Someone must be located to buy the business. Otherwise the invested capital is at risk of being lost.

Self-employment can turn out to be less flexible than regular employment. In a tight job market it can be a struggle to find good employees, and once found and hired they must be trained, managed and retained. If someone quits or doesn't show up for work, the owner is the backup staff.

Buying a franchise is supposed to protect the new business owner from many of the risks of owning a business, but franchise opportunities can be part of fads which sweep the country. Remember when yogurt shops were all the rage? Then came bagel stores and coffee shops. Some other businesses will be hot in the future. Meanwhile a number of the old businesses will have closed their doors without ever becoming financially successful.

The problems of the small business owner put the problems of a property owner into pleasant perspective. Instead of employees who must be dealt with every day, the property owner has a limited number of tenants. Besides doing occasional maintenance, screening new tenants, showing properties, and reminding tenants to pay the rent on time and water the lawns, the property owner has little contact with the people who are paying money to him or her every month. Based on my personal experience the average single family rental property requires an average of only two to three hours per month to manage and maintain.

Investing in real estate can be done one small step at a time. Instead of quitting a steady job to open a business, you can keep your regular job and buy your first rental property. If that goes well, a second property can be purchased and so on. If at any time you decide real estate is not for you, it is relatively easy to sell your investments. It is much easier to dispose of unwanted real estate than it is to sell a small business. Single family rental properties can be sold to homeowners as well as to investors.

A Great Home Business

You may want to work out of your home. Books exist which describe the various types of services and products that are suitable to sell from the home, but owning rental properties is usually overlooked. This is a mistake.

Managing a rental property requires very little in terms of space. Mortgages can be paid each month when you pay your other bills. A notebook can hold your receipts and records. An extra can or two of matching paint for the rental properties can be stashed in the garage. Your personal telephone will be adequate for the limited number of calls you will receive on "For Rent" ads and signs. Even if you include a computer for record keeping, your total space requirements will be less than two cubic yards.

Despite requiring so little room in your house, your rental property business can be worth a lot of money. Five houses that are worth $200,000 apiece add up to a million dollars together. This fact is especially important to the parent who chooses to stay at home with children. While the other spouse is out in the work force gaining new skills and earning promotions, the at-home spouse is also developing new skills and making a significant contribution to the family's financial picture.

Figuring Out How to Succeed in Real Estate

Until the key moment when I set my goal of acquiring five inexpensive houses (a goal I surpassed far sooner than I would have imagined possible), I wasn't entirely convinced I wanted to invest in real estate. Sure, I had been reading books on how to do it for years, but finding great deals and desperate sellers was considerably more difficult than the authors of these books made it sound. I did buy a couple of HUD and VA foreclosures, fixed them up and resold them, but the profits were soon spent on my living expenses.

Then I purchased a foreclosure house for a great price, more than 30% below market value, and I used no money of my own to buy the house. It was a no money down deal with a catch. My partners with the cash received part of the profits. So did the previous owner of the house since I felt she deserved some of the equity. My final share of the proceeds when the house sold was less than $15,000. That money, too, soon disappeared as I spent it toward living expenses. Not to mention that it required over a year and a half to find this one foreclosure deal.

During this time period I became a licensed real estate agent, thinking that maybe all the good deals were being snapped up by the people in the business. As an agent I did learn about marketing houses, negotiating contracts, and prospecting for clients, but I did not find any great deals.

The Power of a Goal

Once I set my goal to own five houses, I realized I had to stop buying and selling properties for a short term profit. Holding them for the long term was what would gain me my financial freedom. During the next seven years I managed to buy an average of one house per year. Once I learned what to do, it was easy to surpass my goal of five houses.

I also was able to change my target retirement age. In order to buy my first five investment houses, I had to get investor loans with adjustable interest rates because fixed interest rate loans for self-employed investors weren't available in the early 1990s. I was concerned about interest rates going up so I protected myself against this possibility by prepaying a bit extra each month on all of my mortgages.

Prepaying an Adjustable Rate Mortgage Versus a Fixed Rate Mortgage

That's when I learned something marvelous about adjustable rate mortgages. The required payments for adjustable rate mortgages are usually adjusted once per year. When the lenders do the adjustments, they change more than the interest rates. They also adjust the monthly payments so they will pay off the loans at the end of the original thirty year loan period.

If you have an adjustable rate mortgage and interest rates are stable, then the required principal and interest payment will stay the same when your payment is recalculated. (This assumes that you are paying the thirty year amortization payment, not an interest only or smaller option payment). If you have prepaid extra principal, then the lender must reduce the required mortgage payment amount in order to make the loan last the full thirty years of its original term.

This is different than the way it works with fixed rate mortgages. If you prepay on a fixed rate mortgage, the principal and interest payment stays the same (though the portion for taxes and insurance may change as the years go by) while the time period for the loan is shortened. If you make one extra principal and interest payment every year, your loan becomes a twenty-three year mortgage instead of a thirty year mortgage. Your principal and interest payment never becomes smaller.

Because I prepaid on my adjustable rate mortgages during the 1990s and into the next century, a time of stable or dropping interest rates, the lenders reduced my mortgage payments for my adjustable rate loans each year to keep me on the full thirty year loan schedule. In the meantime my rents slowly increased. Higher rents and smaller mortgage payments resulted in an increasing monthly cash flow. I used that additional cash flow to pay down my loans even faster.

It didn't take very big prepayments to set this wonderful cycle of decreasing mortgage payments into motion. For example, if my rent was $1,000 and my required minimum mortgage payment was $660, I would pay $750, or an extra $90. Five years of prepaying a little every month can add up to a big increase in monthly cash flow.

For example, let's say you have purchased five rental houses using adjustable rate mortgages. If interest rates stay relatively constant and your prepayments on the adjustable rate loans cause each payment to drop by only $20 each year, the total cash flow increase is substantial. Twenty dollars multiplied by five houses equals $100 per month or $1,200 per year. If each of your monthly principal and interest payments continue to drop by $20 every year, in five years your annual cash flow will increase by $6,000. And this doesn't take into account any rent increases!

When to Avoid Adjustable Rate Mortgages

You may not feel comfortable with adjustable rate mortgages. Especially when interest rates are already low, adjustable rate mortgages expose you to the risk of rising interest rates. If rents in your city fail to rise along with interest rates, your annual cash flow could decrease! This risk makes fixed rate mortgages the safest type of loan to get for your first few properties, and they are especially attractive if you can lock in a low interest rate for a property you intend to own for many years.

As you gain experience and financial stability, having a few adjustable rate mortgages will not be as risky. Instead of prepaying on your fixed mortgages, you can focus on prepaying on one of your adjustable rate mortgages.

By prepaying on an adjustable rate mortgage, you reap several benefits. First you'll protect yourself against rising interest rates by reducing the principal balance. If interest rates stay the same or drop, you'll experience increasing cash flow as your required payment falls. Plus focusing your prepaying efforts on one mortgage instead of spreading it between many mortgages will make it easier to accumulate enough equity in one property to refinance and pull out cash to buy something else.

Interest Only or Minimum Payment Options

Many adjustable rate mortgages now offer borrowers the opportunity to make interest only payments. Other loans start off with required minimum payments that pay only part of the interest. The unpaid interest is added to the loan balance. To pay off these loans in thirty years, the payments will eventually have to rise sharply. And if interest rates are rising at the same time, the payments could end up being much larger than they were at the start.

While I love loans that give me the option of making a lower payment if I hit a tough spot financially, I believe it's too risky to buy a property knowing that I can't afford to make the thirty year amortization payment. What if rents don't go up, or even go down? Or I lose my job? Or I need to sell my property, except I owe more money than the house is worth?

Yet in a rapidly appreciating market, many buyers figure that the yearly increase on their loan balance will be easily offset by the appreciation on a property. They could be right. People across the country made fabulous returns during the early 2000s. Just remember that there is a difference between investing and speculating. Speculators need to get out before the market tanks, and this can be difficult to time correctly. Investors have a long term plan that can handle ups AND downs.

Why Doesn't Everyone Buy Real Estate?

I believe the average person can retire or at least semi-retire in less than ten years by investing in real estate. Maybe it won't be a luxurious retirement, but it will be enjoyable. I retired the first time in my mid-thirties, helped by the fact that my husband and I paid off the mortgage on our small home in roughly ten years and we had no car payments. With a modest household budget, we didn't need large monthly cash flow to make ends meet. The cash flow from our partially paid off rentals was enough.

Many people would like to have an income that is independent of whether or not they work, but obstacles stand in their way. One is the lack of a clear financial goal. You should have started working on that earlier in this chapter. Having a definite financial goal helps motivate you to save and invest to achieve that goal.

The next obstacle is fear. Fear comes from a lack of knowledge. Fortunately, by reading books, looking at properties, talking with real estate agents and mortgage brokers, and meeting other investors you can teach yourself. It may take a few years before you feel ready to buy a rental property, but real estate will always be there waiting.

The biggest obstacle, however, for long term success as a real estate investor is a lack of patience. Many people are seduced by the speed with which appreciation can reward a property owner. When appreciation is slow or nonexistent, many investors aren't interested. If you want fast rewards, you'll be in and out of real estate. But the people who eventually build up sizeable equity in multiple properties are those who are patient. They buy good properties and hold them. Patience is required if you want to take advantage of compounding interest.

Compounding Interest

It's difficult to understand the power of compounding interest. Even though I'm good at math, it took me years to fully comprehend how compounding interest can make a person rich and why so few people take advantage of this power. I'm going to try to help you understand why it's easy to make choices that make it difficult for you to reach your financial goals.

Let's say a woman offers you a job. This job will last for thirty-five days. She will pay you one of two ways. Either she will pay you $1,000 per day or she will pay you a penny the first day, two pennies the second day, four pennies the third day, and so forth. Every day you will be paid twice as much as the day before. Which method of payment would you choose?

If you are like most people you can recognize a trick question when you see one. You want to be paid by the second method, of course. But here's the tough question: how much more will the second method pay you?

It's easy to calculate your total pay if you choose the first payment option. Thirty-five days multiplied by $1,000 equals $35,000. Calculating the total pay for the second option is not as simple. Before you write down your pay for each of the thirty-five days and add it up, guess the second amount off the top of your head. Will it be twice as much as $35,000? Ten times as much? One hundred times as much?

The second method pays a grand total of $343,597,363.21. If you find this difficult to believe, get out a piece of paper and write down the numbers in a row, then add them up with your calculator. You probably substantially underestimated how much income the second option would generate.

But even more importantly, notice how slowly the pay increases are in the beginning. Doubling your money seems inconsequential when we are talking about only a few pennies. If you were at a cocktail party after the fifth day of your job, you could let it slip that you earned sixteen cents that day. Is anyone going to be impressed? Or think what a smart cookie you are?

Let's say the guy you are talking with at the party accepted the same type of job but chose the first payment option. When he tells you he's making $1,000 a day, how are you going to feel? Not too clever. Probably you'll decide you selected the wrong payment plan. Without a solid understanding of how compounding interest can eventually make you rich, you might quit your job and get one like his.

Intellectually, you may understand that you will eventually do better financially than this man because your income is doubling every day while his remains stable, but that's hard to remember when currently he's out-earning and out-spending you.

Getting rich requires some upfront sacrifices. You look and feel poor because you are being frugal and saving while everyone else around you, including your tenants, are buying fancy consumer items. It seems easier to chase after a high paying job rather than plan for the future through investing. But a high paying job won't give you security; you can be downsized by a company with hardly any notice or severance pay.

Of course it can be easier to get ahead if you have a high-paying job, but that won't necessarily make you financially independent in the long run. You must also save your money and invest it. I read about a study that compared how much wealth people managed to acquire compared to their incomes. The researchers found very little correlation between a high income and a high net worth. What actually made the difference in accumulating wealth? The willingness to save something instead of spending every penny. Even low income people who were dedicated savers were able to achieve large nest eggs.

The first years you follow your investment plan will likely be the hardest ones. Even if you are making a good rate of return on your invested money, it won't look like much at the beginning. Can you stick to your plan for four to seven years, long enough to see how much progress you've made? Or will you be like many small real estate investors and jump ship after only two or three years? You should make at least a five year commitment to real estate if you want the chance to experience substantial financial rewards. If you keep at it for ten years, you'll probably be way ahead of the average person.

Your Fellow Investor

In your early days as a real estate investor, it helps to know fellow investors who can encourage you along the way. My twin sister, Shelley, and her husband, Brandon, adopted a five house goal at the same time as I did. They began to buy rental houses. Much of their free time and a high percentage of their income was earmarked for their investment activities. Instead of buying new cars, furniture or clothes, they saved to buy houses.

When Shelley reached the fourth year of her investment career she sometimes complained to me. "Is this really worth it? I'm so tired of being poor. All Brandon and I do is put our money and our time into our rentals. Will this really pay off someday?"

Since I was still a novice investor myself, I did my best to reassure her. The numbers made sense, and if we held tight we would all do well. We just had to be patient.

Less than two years later my sister was singing a different tune. She and her husband had a rental cash flow of over $18,000 per year. They needed to buy only one more property to reach their goal of five houses. After that purchase they could focus on paying off some of their fixed mortgages. They figured it would take another two and a half years to pay off the first of their mortgages and then their cash flow would jump to almost twenty-five thousand dollars per year. In less than nine years they would have created a substantial independent income that would keep growing as they paid off additional properties.

Another investor I met when I was starting off was Milt. Milt never liked debt. When he bought his home he furnished it with items from the Salvation Army store. He also concentrated on paying down his mortgage with what he describes as a neurotic fixation. With the birth of a daughter he realized he needed to earn more money, but due to his lack of credentials he didn't see any possibility of qualifying for a lucrative job.

Because the value of his home had increased substantially, Milt did have equity he could use as collateral for numerous small loans from his extensive network of friends. He had never before considered investing in real estate, but the appreciation on his home encouraged him to explore buying another property. His research convinced him that real estate was his best bet for achieving financial freedom.

For a few years being a landlord involved a lot of work with very little reward. Milt invested the majority of his cash flow and a lot of his spare time into improving his three investment properties, adding such items as dishwashers and decks.

But when Milt reached his fifth year as a real estate investor, he started to see the payoff for all his hard work. Due to his past fix up work his maintenance costs were low on his properties. His spendable cash flow ranged up to $800 a month, a fabulous amount as far as Milt was concerned. He decided he liked being a landlord.

How Many Properties Will You Need?

How many properties will you need to own to achieve your goals? The quick answer is you'll need enough to generate the cash flow for your retirement or semi-retirement target income. The number of properties required to produce a given amount of income varies across the country because properties in different areas earn widely varying rates of cash flow.

For example, a paid off four bedroom house worth $155,000 located in north Austin, Texas, may rent for $1,450 per month and throw off $1,000 of spendable cash flow after expenses. That's $12,000 per year. Divided by $155,000, that's a 7.742% rate of return from cash flow. If your annual income target from real estate was $75,000, you'd need to own properties worth $968,742 free and clear.

In a higher priced area a comparable home may sell for $500,000 and rent for $2,250. After expenses, the net monthly income may be $1,750, or $21,000 annually. That's a 4.2% cash flow rate of return if this property is also paid off. To achieve the same target income of $75,000, you would need to own properties worth $1,785,714 free and clear.

Of course, the investor in the area with the smaller cash flow rate of return could wait until his or her equity equals $968,742 after selling costs and 1031 tax defer exchange those properties into properties located in the first area where properties generated better cash flow. If the investor doesn't want to move to that other area, a manager could be hired. If the property manager charged 10%, then the investor would need paid off properties worth $1,076,380 instead of $968,742 to generate the target income ($1,076,380 X 7.742% X .90 = $75,000).

An alternative to keeping your equity invested in real estate is to accumulate enough equity so you can sell your properties, pay the taxes, and have enough left to reinvest in something like bonds or certificates of deposit to generate your desired annual income. By selling your real estate you would lose the protection against inflation provided by potential appreciation, but on the other hand you would substantially simplify your life. It's much easier to verify that you received your interest payments than it is to manage rental properties.

Because so much can change between the time you make your original retirement plan and when you retire or semi-retire, calculating the number of properties you want to buy is not an essential step. Yet for many people it provides a useful starting goal. If you would like to calculate how many properties you will need to generate your target income, here's how to do it.

First figure out how much income a target rental property will generate in the area where you want to invest, probably a neighborhood close to where you live or work. A blank worksheet is provided in Appendix A for you to use as you figure out the rental numbers for your area. The bottom half of the worksheet is filled out with the numbers from the example we are about to do. You may want to make a copy of it so you can refer to it easily as you read through the example.

If you don't like math, you may not want to do these calculations. You may decide that owning three to five properties sounds fine to you, and you'll find out later if you need buy more to meet your income goal. If you are this type of person, you can skim the next section, but you should still read the sections later in this chapter which talk about estimating maintenance costs and personal situation. When you are evaluating properties, comparing anticipated maintenance costs can help you choose which one you want to own. And recognizing your strengths and weaknesses can help you become a stronger investor.

Because we're going to pretend that your target property is owned free and clear, don't worry about mortgage rates or loan payments. However you will have to determine the market value for your target property, estimate the property taxes and insurance, and determine market rent for your target property plus home owner fees if applicable.

Doing this type of research takes time, yet even if you decide that your first choice of a target property isn't what you want to own, everything you learn will make you more knowledgable about your local real estate market. You'll improve your ability to correctly estimate the costs for any given property. Also, as you learn your market, you'll be more likely to quickly recognize an attractively priced property, which is the first step to finding and buying a good deal.

How Much Will Your Target Property Cost?

You need to find out the sales price for your target property. Depending where you live, your initial target property could be a downtown condo, a family sized house in the suburbs, or a townhouse. Cash flow rates of return will likely vary for different types of properties so you may want to do this exercise for more than one kind of property. But for now pick one type and gather the necessary information to calculate its cash flow rate of return.

What Is the Market Value?

Look for "For Sale" signs in your target neighborhood. Call the listing agents to find out prices and square footage. Attend open houses on the weekends. Your goal is to find out an average sale price for the type of property you hope to buy. Remember, focus on a particular type of property. Narrow your research until you are looking at properties that are approximately the same age, located in the same neighborhood with similar square footage, same number of bedrooms and baths, and same garage facilities.

Determining Property Taxes and Insurance

When you do your research on property taxes, remember that you may live in a state where investors are charged higher taxes than homeowners. You must always ask for and use the investor tax amount. To learn about taxes, call the tax assessor and find out what the investor taxes would be for some of the properties you've seen. Ask them what property values have been used to calculate these tax amounts. It's very common for taxes to rise when a sale demonstrates a new and usually higher value.

Also call your insurance agent to get an approximate idea of what landlord's insurance would cost for these properties. Agents will want to know the square footage, roofing material, presence of a fireplace, whether the garage is attached or detached, and possibly additional information.

Rental Rates for Your Target Property

Next you need to determine what your rents would be for your target property. Look in the newspaper again and call on ads which describe similar properties. Ask real estate agents, professional property managers or other investors what rent amount they think is realistic. Make sure you get rents for properties that are comparable to your target property. A three bedroom house built in the fifties will not rent for the same amount as a three bedroom house with the same square footage built ten years ago.

When you have a monthly rent figure you believe is accurate, multiple it by 11.5 months instead of 12 months to get the yearly rent. Why not the full year? Because you will experience occasional vacancies. For this example we'll assume your average vacancy rate will be half a month per year. (If vacancy rates in your area are much higher according to local property managers or the newspaper reports, you should adjust this. Maybe one month's vacancy would be more accurate if your area is in a slump). Let's say the anticipated rent is $1,350 per month. Multiplying this by 11.5 months gives us $15,525 for the yearly rent.

Projecting Maintenance Costs

Maintenance costs can be tricky to predict. You'll have to guesstimate what your average annual maintenance costs will be. Perhaps you will budget $250 for all the small stuff such as replacing heating elements in the oven, repairing broken gate latches or running "For Rent" ads in the newspaper. Any major expenditures such as new carpeting, a new roof, or repainting inside and out will need to be amortized over a period of years to give you an anticipated average yearly cost. You can predict which of these costs will occur in the next ten years. Use the worksheet provided in Appendix B, Average Annual Maintenance. Make several photocopies so you have plenty to use.

As an example of projecting maintenance costs, let's say you are thinking of buying an eight-year-old frame house. Let's look at the exterior paint first. If the paint job is two years old, in my part of the country you can count on repainting the exterior at least once in the next ten years. If you don't have personal experience to help you make this type of assessment, think who else would know the answer. Other homeowners you know? The staff at the local paint stores? Realtors you talk with at open houses? Ask any and all of these people how long they think paint jobs last, and pick the answer that makes the most sense to you.

The furnace probably won't last another ten years, especially if it is a horizontal furnace in a crawl space or attic. It will need to be replaced. The roof will most likely need a new layer of shingles, the hot water heater will die, and you'll have to repaint and recarpet the interior.

Let's add up the anticipated ten year costs for maintenance assuming that you will be too busy or unwilling to do any of the work yourself. The costs here may be completely different in your area so these are for the purpose of illustration only. You'll need to do some research to find out current prices in your area when you do a maintenance cost analysis for any property you are thinking of buying.

Repainting exterior	**$2,700**
New furnace	**$1,800**
New roof	**$3,500**
New hot water heater	**$650**
Repaint interior	**$2,000**
New carpet	**$2,400**
New vinyl	**$1,800**
Total	**$14,850**

$14,850 divided by ten years gives you $1,485 each year for long term maintenance items. Add to this the $250 for the annual small expenses. This gives you an average annual maintenance cost of $1,735.

Add your taxes and insurance to get your total annual costs. Let's say taxes would be $1,600 and insurance $950 for the sample property. Then the total annual costs would be $4,285. (In general older houses will have higher average annual maintenance costs, but will have better rent-to-property value ratios compared to newer houses.)

Keep in mind that all condominiums and townhomes will have part or all of their exterior maintenance included as part of the homeowners association fee. This can make predicting your expenses a bit more predictable, but do check the association's reserves for roofs, paving, painting and any other long term maintenance item such as pools. If the monthly fees are insufficient to build up the necessary reserves by the time repairs need to be made, you could face pricey special assessments in the future.

How Much Cash Flow Per Property?

Next subtract your total average annual costs from the anticipated rent. Using the numbers from this example we have $15,525 in rent and $4,285 for the average yearly maintenance expense. When you subtract the expense amount from the rent you get $11,240. This is the annual spendable cash flow you would receive if you owned the property free and clear today.

Remember that the cash flow number you calculate for your target property will not be the same as in this example unless your area magically has the same type of rents and anticipated costs. You must use the information you collect about your local rental market and repair costs to determine an annual cash flow for your target property.

How Many Properties?

Knowing how much income one property will produce is the first step. The next question to answer is how many similar properties you will need to own to earn your target income. Divide the annual income you want by the cash flow produced by your target property and you'll know how many properties you need.

For this example let's assume your annual income goal is $60,000. Since our target property generates an $11,240 annual cash flow, we'll divide $60,000 by $11,240. This gives us 5.34.

Since it's difficult to buy .34 of a property, you have a small problem. The easy answer is to settle for five properties. Five properties producing $11,240 per year equals a $56,200 annual income. Or you could buy five properties that are just a little bit more expensive than your target property, and that could allow you to hit your income goal. Or you could decide to buy six properties like your target property. Doing that would produce an annual income of $67,440.

If You Want to Be Exact

For people who enjoy doing math, you can figure out how many thousands worth of real estate will produce your dream income. Let's say your target property happened to cost $180,000. $180,000 is $1,000 multiplied by 180. Divide the cash flow for your target property, in this example $11,240, by 180. You get $62.44. This means that for every $1,000 your properties are worth, you'll receive $62.44 in cash flow each year.

We can use this number to calculate the total amount your target houses must be worth to generate your income goal of $60,000. First divide $60,000 by $62.44. This gives you 961. This is how many thousands of dollars worth of houses you'll need to own free and clear to generate your target income, or properties worth a total of $961,000 for this example.

180,000/1,000	**180**
$11,240/180	**$62.44**
$60,000/$62.44	**961**
961 X $1,000	**$961,000**

After you've been an investor for awhile, you may enjoy doing a different variation of this calculation. If bonds are paying 5% interest, and my total federal, state, and local capital gains taxes add up to 25%, how much would my properties have to be worth so I could sell them, pay my taxes, buy bonds, and enjoy my dream income without tenants in my life anymore? This game is especially fun on days when a tenant is causing you trouble. Of course, investing in bonds means you lose protection against inflation. But as you get older, you may be willing to dip into your principal to make up income shortfalls. Retirement books and web sites offer formulas for how much principal you can spend based on your age, your predictions about inflation, and how long you think you'll live.

Different Rental Ratios for Different Properties

Calculating how many thousands of dollars of properties you need to own to earn your target income isn't 100% accurate if you buy properties at price points that differ from your target property. Why not? Because the rent-to-property value ratio is not the same in all price ranges. The amount of cash flow generated by each thousand dollars worth of properties you own will vary depending on the price point of those properties. In our example we calculated the cash flow on a property worth $180,000. If you buy a property worth substantially more, you will receive less rent for each dollar you have invested. Properties in the upper price ranges for any given area rent for less compared to their market value than do lower priced houses.

For example, in 2005 a Denver house located in Stapleton worth $300,000 rented for $1,550, a 51.7% ratio of monthly rent to the property value. However a house worth $475,000 in that same neighborhood rented for $1,950, or a 41% ratio. That's almost a 21% decrease in the rent-to-value ratio.

Clearly you can get a better rent-to-value ratio if you buy properties at the low end of the market. You can drop the price per unit even more by buying multi-unit properties such as fourplexes and apartment buildings. The downside is that you will earn part of this additional money. with additional work. I discuss the pros and cons of different properties in more detail in Chapter 4, Selecting Properties.

How Long Until Retirement?

After you've determined the net worth of the properties you want to own, you can calculate how long it will take you to acquire these properties and pay them off. We'll assume for this example that you are shooting for full retirement with the understanding that you can decide to semi-retire anywhere along the way.

For this step you'll need to either use your financial calculator or find someone who has one and knows how to use it. Most real estate agents own a financial calculator and can help you. I'll tell you how to use a Texas Instrument BA II Plus Business Analyst financial calculator as we go through this example. Stores such as Target sell this calculator for thirty dollars. Another option is to go on-line and use one of the many financial calculators provided by a variety of web sites.

Here are the numbers you'll need before you can predict when you'll be financially independent.

a) What is the combined target value of the properties you plan to buy? (your net worth goal)
b) What is the value of your current assets available to invest in real estate (or already invested in real estate)?
c) How much money can you save for investing each year out of your regular income?
d) How many years are you willing to wait to reach your goal?

With these four numbers you can compute the missing fifth number which is the rate of return you will need to earn on an annual basis in order to reach your goal. If the required rate of return is a reasonable number, one you think you can earn, fine. Full steam ahead. If it's too high, a rate you don't believe is possible, you'll have to adjust your goal, your savings, or your timetable. If the rate is ridiculously low, you may be able to increase your goal or get there faster than you thought you could.

Let's say you have a goal of owning properties worth $1,200,000. This is your net worth goal. You have $40,000 either available in savings to invest in real estate or you have already invested that same $40,000 in a rental property. You are saving $5,000 per year from your regular income. You are willing to wait twelve years before you retire.

Turn on your calculator by pressing the ON/OFF button at the top right. To reset all variables to the normal defaults, press the yellow 2nd button and then the gray Reset button (+/-) at the bottom right of the calculator. The display will say <u>RST?</u>. Press the black ENTER button at the top left of the calculator. Now the display will say <u>RST 0.00</u> to confirm that you've reset the calculator. Because the calculator remembers the values for each of the time-value-of-money keys we are working with, you may want to reset between calculations as well.

Now enter 1,200,000, your net worth goal, and press the gray FV, future value, button

Keep in mind that the calculator wants your present value and your annual contributions to be entered as negative numbers. So enter 40,000, your current savings available for real estate investment, then the gray +/- button to make it negative, and hit the gray PV, present value, button. Enter 5,000, your annual savings, the +/- button to make it negative, then press the gray PMT, payment, button.

Enter 12 for the number of years before you want to retire and press the gray N, number of years, button.

Finally, press the CPT, compute, button at the top left of the calculator and the gray I/Y (interest per year), button. The calculator will calculate the annual interest rate you need to earn based on the numbers you entered.

In this example the display will show you I/Y = 29.02. So you'll have to earn a 29.02% rate of return on your invested money each year for the next twelve years to reach your retirement goal of $1,200,000 assuming that you start with $40,000 and add $5,000 per year. While this rate of return is possible, you'll have to use leverage in an appreciating market or create forced appreciation, perhaps by fixing up a property or converting a property to a higher use such as changing a tri-plex into three condominiums, to get a rate of return this high.

If you aren't willing to count on a quickly appreciating market and you are not a sophisticated investor who can take advantage of forced appreciation opportunities (at least, not yet!) you have some other options. You can change a few of your figures. You may be willing to increase the amount you currently have to invest by selling your boat, record collection, or other asset you don't use. Increasing your initial investment can be very powerful. That money will have many years to compound in value.

If getting more money to invest at the beginning is not possible then you may decide you are willing to wait longer. Giving yourself extra time can make a big difference in the rate of return you need to earn. In this example, waiting fifteen years to retire instead of twelve years drops the annual interest rate you need to earn to 21.88%. (Instead of re-entering all your numbers, just enter 15 and press the N key, then hit the CPT and I/Y buttons to do the same calculation changing only the one variable.) 21.88% would be much easier to earn over many years than 29.66%.

But maybe you really want to retire in twelve years. You could get a second job that pays you $10,000 after taxes. This would give you $15,000 to invest each year instead of $5,000. This would reduce the annual interest rate you need to earn to 23.04%.

Possibly none of these compromises appeals to you or is possible. The last figure you can change is your net worth goal. If you are willing to retire with a net worth of $800,000 invested in real estate instead of $1,200,000, you would need to earn only a 24.25% annual rate of return. Perhaps you are counting on a pension or IRA to start paying out at the same time you retire. Those payments could make up the difference in your income. Or maybe you could work part-time after you retire.

The options become endless when you start to change more than one variable at a time. The bottom line is that it is very possible for most of us to fully retire in less than twenty years. And semi-retirement can be much sooner. By doing some calculations you can create a financial game plan that can be adjusted as the years go by.

The Real World

The above example is simplified. In the real world while you are saving up your extra cash flow for the down payment on the next property, you won't get a great rate of return on that money. If you are saving your money in a money market fund, you may receive only 3% instead of the 20-30% you can receive once you buy your next property. This period of time when your money earns a smaller rate of return will slow down your progress to your goal.

In addition our example assumes that you won't lose any of your equity through the costs of selling one or more of your properties if you decide to exchange them into different properties. Money spent on commissions, closing costs, and exchange fees will no longer be compounding in your favor. Once spent, it will be gone. This is why you should try to avoid selling properties if possible.

Despite these real world problems, this method of planning the future will give you a rough idea of how long it will take you to reach your goal. Since life is full of surprises, things will happen which will both help and hinder you on your journey. That's okay. Adjust to your changing circumstances and keep on taking action to achieve your goal. If you are persistent you will reach it, probably sooner than you anticipated.

Personal Advantages and Disadvantages

Some would-be investors compare themselves to others in order to find an excuse for why they won't be able to succeed. Sure enough, everyone else has some advantage that they don't, and that's why these investors can't and never will be able to successfully invest in real estate.

It's one thing to realize that you aren't ready to invest in real estate at a particular point in your life. For example, you may be planning to move in the next few years, or you need to repair your credit, want to spend a year learning more about real estate, or finish your degree first. Lots of good, solid reasons exist for postponing buying your first investment property. But envying others for what they have won't get us any closer to success. To reach your goals you need to focus on your strengths, shore up your weaknesses, and ignore what you don't have the power to change. Success depends far more on your attitude than on what you have initially.

When I started off, I had youth, good credit, few debts, a supportive family, and affordable properties in nearby cities as advantages. On the downside I was single, made a pitiful income, had no experience doing anything with real estate, interest rates were 10%, and I had no contacts or work relationships with people in the real estate world.

While it wasn't within my control to instantly find a supportive spouse or to make interest rates drop, I could and did increase my income, learn to fix up properties, develop relationships with roofers and plumbers and other contractors, discover all sorts of useful loans, learn about landlord/tenant laws, find a great Realtor, and become familiar with many types of properties and neighborhoods in my city. This process of learning and meeting useful people continues. Every year I become a stronger investor, and so can you.

Take a look at the following list and see what factors you have working to your advantage.

Advantages:

You have a good paying job.

You have a significant other who is supportive.

You are married and your spouse is supportive.

You are married and your spouse makes good money.

You have family who will loan you money.

You have friends who will loan you money.

You are young and have plenty of time for your money to compound.

You are older and have money to invest.

The rent-to-property value ratio is high where you live so you can get a positive cash flow easily.

The rent-to-property value ratio is low where you live, but the appreciation rate is double the inflation rate.

Landlord-tenant laws are landlord friendly in your state and city.

You have experience fixing up properties.

You have inherited money.

You have exercised lucrative stock options.

You know someone in the mortgage business who will give you better-than-market rates.

You have enjoyed appreciation on your home and can refinance out some money to invest.

You have good credit.

You have few or no debts.

You know the local real estate market very well (perhaps because you are a Realtor or appraiser).

You have decided to buy just as your local real estate market takes off and begins to appreciate dramatically.

You meet people who are willing to sell their house to you at a discount from fair market value.

Properties are cheap where you live so it's easy to buy them.

Properties are expensive where you live so you only have to buy and manage a couple of properties to achieve your goals.

Interest rates are low so your mortgage payments are reasonable.

Interest rates are high so many people have to rent instead of buy, providing you with a plentiful pool of qualified tenants.

Some of these advantages are unlikely or even impossible to have at the same time. For example, youth is great because of the time you have to compound money, but on the other hand you probably don't have a lot of money to invest. Older people have the advantage there.

Older people are also more likely to have equity in their personal homes, better paying jobs, and know more people who can help them. They probably have experience maintaining properties because they've owned one or more personal homes.

Some of these factors are unchangeable. If your job and/or family ties you to a community with low rent-to-property value ratios, moving may not be an option. And if interest rates are high, you don't have much control over that. Nor can you conjure generous relatives or trusting friends out of thin air.

You can, however, keep your credit clean or improve it if you've had money troubles in the past. You can make friends with people who will invest with you or loan you money, learn about your local real estate market, join real estate investor groups, pay down your debts, learn more about mortgages, or get a higher paying job.

What's most important is to keep learning. Which neighborhoods offer opportunities to investors? Who are the best contractors to hire? How could you replicate another investor's success? What lenders offer the types of loans you need to do the deals you want to do? Which contractors will wait until the closing to be paid for their work?

Learn to keep your eyes open and your brain thinking. Nothing frustrates me more than when I tell people how I recently capitalized on an investment opportunity only to have them sigh and say, "But now it's too late for us to do the exact same thing." True enough, but they're acting as if that was the only opportunity out there. In contrast, I'm trying to show them how new opportunities constantly appear.

Year after year I recognize different ways to make money in my local real estate market. Whether interest rates go up or down, home prices stall or soar, the rental market is soft or fantastic, I see great investments. You can learn to see them, too, in any sort of market. The biggest advantage any investor can have is the willingness to learn and pay attention. And this advantage is something you can give to yourself.

Chapter Two

Rate of Return on Rental Real Estate

To achieve your financial goals within a particular time frame, you'll need to earn a minimum rate of return on your real estate investments. To find out if you are on track toward reaching your goal, you'll need to know what rate of return you are receiving.

You can also use projected rates of return to compare properties. If you find two properties you would like to buy, but can only afford to purchase one, projecting their anticipated rates of return will allow you to compare them against each other. Even if one is a condominium and the other is a house, you'll be able to compare them in terms of their projected rates of return.

You may also want to compare potential rates of return on real estate investments against the rates of return you think you could earn on other investments. Would real estate be a better investment than buying stocks or bonds or a share in your brother's new computer software company?

Your predictions will be best guesses. You'll become more accurate with experience. Yet some people don't care about rates of return. They know they love real estate and that's where they want to invest their money. They also know that if they buy properties and pay off the mortgages, they will eventually be able to retire and live their dream lives.

So if you want to skip this chapter and go straight to selecting properties and handling tenants, that's fine. If you don't do the rate of return numbers, your properties will still probably appreciate, you'll save money on taxes by depreciating your properties, your mortgages will gradually be paid off, and you'll eventually receive cash flow each month. You can profit handsomely by investing in real estate even if you never learn how to calculate your annual rates of return.

Calculating Your Rate of Return

If you want to analyze relative rates of return for different real estate investment opportunities, you must add together the multiple ways a property can make money for you. You'll receive appreciation (or depreciation) in the value of your properties, cash flow, principal paydown on your mortgages, plus tax savings. In order to determine your total annual rate of return, you'll have to figure out the rates of return for each of these four areas.

Appreciation

The fastest way to make money in real estate is through appreciation. If you are fortunate enough to buy in an up market, your gains can add up to impressive numbers in just a few years. Suppose you own a house worth $250,000. If it goes up 4% in value next year, that's a gain of $10,000. If your house, now worth $260,000, goes up 4% again the following year, you'll make an additional $10,400. By adding these gains together, your house would increase in value by over $20,400 in just two years. And if your market is appreciating by 8% or 13% or more each year, the gain is even more dramatic.

Appreciation is wonderful when you own a house free and clear, but it becomes even more amazing when you use leverage to increase your rate of return. Leverage is when you combine your money with someone else's money to make investments.

The Amazing Power of Leverage

Let's say you buy two houses. Each house costs $200,000. You buy the first one using all cash and the second one by putting down 20%, or $40,000, and getting a mortgage for $160,000. What happens if the real estate market appreciates 3% the next year? What will be your rate of return from appreciation on each of these houses?

You invested $200,000 cash in the first house. At the end of the year it is worth $206,000. When you divide the $6,000 gain by the $200,000 you have invested, you get a 3% rate of return.

But you invested only $40,000 of your own money in the second house. It also went up in value $6,000. When you divide the $6,000 gain by the $40,000 invested, you get a 15% rate of return. By using leverage you have multiplied your rate of return on your invested money by five. Clearly, you will reach your goal much faster if you use the power of leverage.

Let's suppose you really leverage your money. What would your rate of return be if you bought a $200,000 house with no money down and the house appreciated $6,000 in one year? You couldn't even calculate your rate of return due to appreciation. A $3,000 gain divided by zero is infinity!

Getting Into Trouble

Yet using leverage is how a lot of investors get into trouble. Leveraging your money is a smart thing to do, but within prudent limits. Why? Because although you will be a fantastic success in an appreciating market, you may lose everything in a depreciating market.

Let's say you buy a $200,000 house with no money down, and the market depreciates by 3%. Instead of having an infinite gain, you have an infinite loss. If instead you had $40,000 invested in the house, your loss on your invested money would be reduced to 15%. And if you owned the house free and clear, you would lose only 3% of your invested money.

So while you can use leverage to increase your rate of return dramatically in the good years, it will also magnify your losses in the down years. The less leverage you have the less dramatic the results.

Does this mean you should avoid leverage? Not at all. Using leverage is essential if you want to reach your goals within a relatively short period of time. The key is to find a good balance point between using leverage and controlling your risk.

While there is no magic number, I feel that a 20-30% equity position, as well as monthly payments that you can afford to make, is prudent. And even though real estate markets fall occasionally, historically property values go up. The key is to make sure you can ride out the bad times as well as enjoy the good times.

The Future of Appreciation

Just because real estate has appreciated in the past does not automatically mean it will continue to appreciate in the future. So why am I confident real estate will continue to rise in value?

Real estate will continue to appreciate for two reasons. The first is inflation. Even at the low current inflation rates of 1-3%, property prices will double every twenty to thirty years. For example, let's say I buy a rental house today which costs $150,000. By the time my niece, Lily, who is eleven-years-old, grows up and marries, this house will probably be worth $300,000.

The second reason I believe the real estate market will continue to appreciate is because of the population demographics of the United States. In 1970 the population of this country was 203,000,000. In 1980 and 1990, it increased to 227,000,000 and

249,000,000 respectively. According to the latest census it was over 281,000,000 in 2000. By the year 2010, the population is predicted to reach 310,000,000.

Where are all these people going to live? More houses and apartments and condominiums will be built, of course. But the locations of these new homes may not be as desirable as the locations of properties built before 2000. People will pay a premium to live in the better locations, meaning that these properties will appreciate at a rate that is greater than inflation.

Of course, not all areas of the country will benefit equally from this increase in population. The number of people living in some towns and cities will actually decrease. So pay attention to the projected growth rate for the area where you want to invest. The higher it is, and the tighter the supply of available land to build on, the better the appreciation rate should be long term.

Cash Flow

The second rate of return in real estate comes from cash flow. In many areas of the United States, if you have 20% equity in a property you can rent the property for enough money to cover the mortgage and expenses with some cash flow left over. Being paid each month for your property management duties makes being a landlord a lot more fun.

However due to rapid appreciation during the late nineties and the early part of this decade, 20% down in many area of the country will not produce a positive cash flow. If the properties you are considering for purchase fall into this category, you will have negative cash flow. Obviously this is a more challenging situation, but if appreciation is strong enough, it can compensate for the negative cash flow. Your overall rate of return can still be pretty good.

The danger of relying on appreciation is that it's not as predictable as cash flow. It tends to come in spurts with flat years tucked between periods of rapid price increases. If you decide to buy a property with negative cash flow, you must be prepared both financially and emotionally. It can be tough finding that extra money every month year after year.

Principal Paydown

The third rate of return you'll receive is principal paydown. Even if your properties never rise in value you will eventually pay off the mortgages. If your goal is to be a millionaire, you could buy properties worth $1,000,000 and pay them off. In the beginning years only a small portion of your payments would go toward principal, but the proportion of your payments that pay principal will increase as the years go by.

Principal paydown is an invisible rate of return. If you ask someone to tell you the four ways to make money in real estate, this is usually the last one they'll mention. In the past I've had students in my real estate investment classes tell me that principal paydown doesn't really count since you can't get to it without selling. After all, maybe the market will collapse and all your equity will disappear.

But principal paydown is real. When you go to the bank to get a loan, they will subtract your current mortgage balance from your property's current value when they calculate its contribution to your net worth. By paying down your loan balance, you are increasing your net worth. This makes you a stronger borrower in the bank's eyes. You can also borrow against your increased equity to pull out money to put down on another property. Banks obviously do not think your increased equity is imaginary if they are willing to use it as collateral.

At the end of your loan term, you will have paid off your mortgage. Eliminating the mortgage payment is a very real benefit! More than any other rate of return you can count on principal paydown to someday give you large monthly cash flows.

Depreciation

The last rate of return is the income tax savings you'll realize each year from owning real estate. Following the tax laws in this country, the Internal Revenue Service acts as if rental property is depreciating, that is losing value. Of course, if you purchase a desirable property and maintain it, the property most likely will increase in value over time. Despite this the Internal Revenue Service lets you shield some of your income through depreciation.

To calculate how much depreciation you can claim on each property, you must first determine what proportion of its value comes from the improvements and what proportion of its value is in the land. Why? Because although the Internal Revenue Service acts as if your properties are falling down over time, they realize that the land will still be there. Therefore land cannot be depreciated.

To depreciate a property, you need to determine its worth separate from the land beneath it. A simple way to do this is to use the tax assessor's valuation. Most assessors will give a value to the land, let's say $5,000. Then they'll assign a value to the improvements, let's say $20,000. According to the assessor, the total value is the combination of these two figures, $25,000.

When you divide the improvement value of $20,000 by the total value of $25,000, you find that the improvements equal 80% of the total property value. If you paid $170,000 for this house (ignoring some closing costs which can also be depreciated), you multiply the purchase price by 80% to get the value of the improvements. $170,000 multiplied by 80% is $136,000. This is the value you can claim for the improvements.

The Internal Revenue Service assigns a lifetime to all capital items. Houses, townhouses, condos and small multiplexes are currently supposed to last 27.5 years. In our example we divide the value of the improvements, $136,000, by 27.5 years. This produces an annual depreciation loss of $4,945. Since you are "losing" value in your investment, the Internal Revenue Service will let you deduct this loss against your income as long as you qualify as an active investor. (Per Internal Revenue Publication 527, you are an active investor if you make management decisions such as "approving new tenants, deciding on rental terms, approving expenditures and similar decisions.")

While depreciation is a wonderful way to reduce your current tax burden, there are restrictions. You'll need to check with the IRS or your accountant to stay current with the requirements.

Please realize that even if you don't like the idea of depreciating your properties, you still have to do it. Sometimes I'll meet people who say their accountant told them they don't have to depreciate their rental properties. But according to the tax experts I've consulted, and IRS Publication 527, when you sell your rental properties the Internal Revenue Service will calculate the taxes you owe as if you had depreciated the properties. If you didn't depreciate your properties, too bad!

By not depreciating you will lose the tax savings while you own the property and you will have to pay the taxes when you sell. Your only option if you haven't depreciated is to amend your tax returns for the last three years so you can depreciate your properties on those returns (three years is the limit for amending past returns). If you own rental properties and you haven't been depreciating them, you may want to ask your accountant if the numbers make it worthwhile for you to amend your most recent returns.

Depreciation is a wonderful tax shelter for the small investor. Whatever money you don't pay in taxes today can be invested to get you to your goal faster. While it's true that you will owe taxes on any gain you realize as an investor, these gains are only taxable when you sell. If you want to switch your investment in one or more properties into different ones, you can do 1031 tax deferred exchanges (see Chapter Eleven, 1031 Tax Deferred Exchanges) and defer paying taxes until you sell a property and don't reinvest the proceeds.

Or you can keep your properties until you die. The basis of your real estate becomes its value at the time of your death according to the Internal Revenue Service. Although normally your cost basis in a property is reduced each year by the amount of depreciation you take, when you die the basis jumps up to the current market value. If the total value of your estate is below federal estate limits, and your heirs sell your properties for the properties' values at the time of your death, your heirs won't owe any capital gains tax. By dying, you can do more than just defer taxes - you can eliminate them!

Of course, you should consult an estate attorney when you make your estate decisions. Avoiding taxes may not be your most important goal. You may not want to stay a landlord for the rest of your life! Plus tax laws change constantly. But this is one of the smoothest ways to avoid taxes that I've discovered.

Calculating Rates of Return

Rate of return calculations are done using five numbers. If you don't yet own the property, you'll have to make predictions. To see how well you've done on properties you already own, use your actual numbers. For any given year you will need to determine how much money you had invested in a property, the cash flow you received that year after subtracting expenses, how much your loan balance decreased (principal paydown), how much your property appreciated (or depreciated), and how much you saved on federal and state income taxes.

Almost all of this information has to be collected and put on your property tax return form, the Schedule E. Since you have to do the numbers for Uncle Sam, you may as well do one more step and calculate how fast your net worth is increasing.

To get an accurate number for your annual rate of return, you need to put the correct numbers into the formulas I'm about to give you. The definitions for each number will be explained.

Amount Invested

This number changes every year. The first year you need to add up the down payment, closing costs, and any expenditures during the year for improvements such as a deck or finished basement (do not include maintenance or advertising costs). This is the money out-of-pocket you had to pay for the property plus any capital improvements.

The second year you start with the first year's figure, but you add to it. Your loan balance is lower because you paid it down a bit the prior year, and that principal paydown has become part of the equity tied up in your property. The appreciation you received the previous year has also become part of your equity, and therefore part of your invested money.

You must take the first year's amount invested and increase it by adding last year's principal paydown amount and the appreciation amount. Each succeeding year, increase your total amount invested by adding the paydown and appreciation amounts for the previous year.

You should also add the cost of any improvements, not repairs, that you make to the property. An improvement is a large expenditure which cannot be written off in the year you pay for it, but instead has to be depreciated. An improvement would be something such as finishing a basement, adding a bath or deck, or getting a new furnace or roof.

If you refinance your property, you should reduce the amount invested by subtracting how much money you pull out of the property. For example, if you have $50,000 invested, and you refinance and take out $30,000 cash, you've reduced the amount of money you have invested in this property. Instead of $50,000 you now have $20,000 invested.

Don't get the amount invested confused with your equity. The amount invested is bigger than your equity because it includes money you'll never see again such as closing costs.

To keep your figures 100% accurate when you refinance, you will also need to allocate the cost of the refinancing to a particular property. You could add your closing costs from refinancing to the amount invested in the property you refinanced or if you refinanced to buy another property, you could add the refinancing cost to the amount invested for the new property. I prefer to put the refinancing costs toward the new property since I regard it as the price I had to pay to get the down payment.

Cash Flow

Add up your rent received for the year and then subtract all the nondepreciable expenses you claimed on your Schedule E such as maintenance costs, homeowner association fees, attorney or accounting fees, any eviction fees, interest, property taxes and insurance, plus the amount paid toward principal (principal is the only item affecting cash flow that isn't listed on your Schedule E - while it's not considered an expense because you owe less money on your loan, this forced savings does reduce your cash flow). If taxes or insurance are paid separately from the mortgage payments, subtract those costs as well.

Principal Paydown

This is an easy number because each January your mortgage company tells you how much you paid down your mortgage the previous year. The principal paid figure will include the principal you were required to pay each month plus any prepaid principal.

Appreciation

What is your house worth today compared to the same time last year? You may have a good feeling for the market value, or you can ask your real estate agent to run comps (comparison sales) for other properties which recently sold. (Instead of appreciation, you may experience depreciation some years if real estate values go down.)

There is no way to determine the exact amount of appreciation without selling the house and thereby establishing market value, so use your best guess. You probably keep an eye on sales of similar properties, and your real estate agent can provide comparables. When I calculate my rate of return I tend to err on the conservative side, that is I'll say my property appreciated $14,000 instead of $18,000. I can always adjust upward in future years if necessary.

Tax Savings

You will save on your taxes because of depreciation. If you own a house where the improvements excluding the land are worth $165,000, you are losing $6,000 per year according to the tax laws of this country. The value of this deduction depends on your tax bracket. What is your combined local, state and federal tax bracket? If your combined income tax rate is 20%, then multiply $6,000 by 20%. You will save $1,200 in the taxes you won't owe that year.

Calculating Your Total Rate of Return

Now that you have your five numbers, what do you do with them? You have two options. Take the numbers you calculated for cash flow, principal paydown, appreciation and depreciation, add them together, then divide them by the first number, your total amount invested. This is your total rate of return for the past year. If you want to see exactly how your rate of return is broken down by category, you should divide your cash flow, principal paydown, appreciation and depreciation each by the invested amount. Then add these four partial rates of return together to get your total rate of return for the year.

Realistic Rates of Return

What is a realistic rate of return to aim for when you buy rental properties? This varies depending on how much money you have invested in a property. How much you have invested usually depends on how long you've owned the property. Your leverage is higher during the first few years so this is when you'll probably see your highest rates of return. Since your rate of return will decrease over time due to your increasing equity and therefore decreasing leverage, you should aim for a first year return of at least 20% per year. If you can get 25% or 30%, that would be preferable.

If you've owned a property for a number of years, the annual rate of return on your invested money may go down to 15% or lower. If you've already purchased all the properties you need to achieve your goal, you may not care about a falling rate of return. All you want to do at this point is pay off your mortgages and retire.

But if you still need to acquire additional properties, you may want to pull some of your invested money out by getting a second mortgage or by selling and using a 1031 tax deferred exchange to switch your equity from one property into either a more expensive property or multiple properties. This will increase your leverage and help you increase your rates of return to above 20% again.

Rate of Return Examples

To show you two sample total rates of return you can expect as an average investor, we're going to look at the numbers for two houses I bought in Colorado, the first with positive cash flow and the second one with negative cash flow. A blank worksheet is provided in Appendix D for you to copy and use when you calculate the rate of return for a property you already own or to predict the rate of return for a property you may buy.

I bought the first house in the late fall of 1994, but the figures in this example are based on my first full year of ownership in 1995. The house was purchased for $124,500 with 20% down with closing costs of $2,155. In 1995 I experienced two weeks of vacancy and had expenses which equalled $7,506. My loan balance was reduced by $2,022 and I estimated my appreciation to be $2,000 for that year. I was able to write off $4,075 as a depreciation expense against my income. This house produced a positive cash flow from the beginning.

Purchase price	**$124,500**
New loan	**$99,600**
Down payment (purchase price - new loan)	**$24,900**
Closing costs	**$2,155**
Cash invested (closing costs + down payment)	**$27,055**
Income Received (11 1/2 months rent of $1,135)	**$13,052**

Expenses

Taxes		$983
Interest		$5,925
Insurance		$309
Misc:		
Sprinkler system maint.	$50	
Landscape plants	$60	
2 weeks electricity, new burner	$92	
Rental ad in The Denver Post	$60	
Gate repair - parts	$27	
Total miscellaneous expenses		$289

Total Expenses	**$7,506**
Principal Paydown	**$2,022**
Cash flow	
(Income - expenses - principal paydown)	**$3,524**
Appreciation	**$2,000**
Depreciation ($112,062 value of improvements divided by 27.5 years X 20% tax rate)	**$815**

The total rate of return is the combination of the four rates of return earned by real estate. In this example I've calculated the rates of return separately for cash flow, principal paydown, appreciation, and depreciation, and then added them together for the total rate of return.

The cash flow rate of return is the cash flow, $3,524, divided by the total amount invested, $27,055. The rate of return from cash flow in 1995 was 13%.

I followed the same process to determine the rates of return for principal paydown and appreciation. The rate of return from principal paydown was 7.47% ($2,022 divided by $27,055) and appreciation was 7.39% ($2,000 divided by $27,055).

The rate of return from tax savings varies for each investor depending on his or her federal tax bracket and state or local taxes. For this example I used a total tax rate of 20%. $4,075 multiplied by 20% gave me a tax savings of $815. Divided by the total amount invested, $27,055, the rate of return from depreciation was 3%.

Added together these four rates of return gave me a total rate of return of 30.86%. This meant that the property generated a 30.86% rate of return on the amount invested in it. In other words the $27,055 I had invested in this property increased by 30.86% in one year.

Cash flow	**13.00%**
Principal paydown	**7.47%**
Appreciation	**7.39%**
Depreciation	**3.00%**
Total Rate of Return	**30.86%**

After owning this property for eight years, my equity was close to 50%. My local real estate market was flat with little appreciation and falling rents. Because I had increased my retirement goal, I wanted to increase my rate of return. I could have refinanced the house to pull out a down payment for another property, but I didn't like this option. First, I didn't want to increase the number of properties I owned because that meant more work. Second, I wanted to invest in a neighborhood with the potential for dramatic appreciation. The neighborhood I selected was a infill project, and the only properties available in this neighborhood for sale to investors were expensive. Therefore the down payment would have to be substantial. So I decided to 1031 tax exchange all of my equity from the first example house into only one house.

Although I knew the new house would rent for less than the mortgage payment, producing negative cash flow, I predicted that the positive rate of return from appreciation would more than compensate.

I bought the house in the spring of 2003, but the figures in this example are based on my first full year of ownership in 2004. The house was purchased for $397,723 with a $117,223 down payment and closing costs of $3,685. In 2004 I experienced no vacancy and had expenses which equalled $20,325. My loan balance was reduced by $3,048, and I estimated my appreciation to be $40,000 for that year. I was able to write off $9,696 as a depreciation expense against my income.

When I calculated these rate of return numbers, I increased my cash invested amount by adding my selling costs, including the cost for vacancy while the first example property was for sale. One of the downsides to selling a property is that it does cost money! But I also calculated rate of return numbers as if this new house purchase hadn't been part of a 1031 tax deferred exchange.

Because my new property was literally brand new, I needed to immediately invest more money to buy blinds for the windows. I split the cost with my neighbors to install fences between our back yards. Other items such as the stove, microwave oven, and air conditioning unit that would have been cheaper to purchase after closing I chose to buy from the builder and include in the price of the house to reduce how much additional cash I had to invest.

My property taxes were temporarily low for this year because the assessor hadn't yet adjusted the value to reflect a completed house. General maintenance expenses were also low because it was a new house.

Purchase price	**$397,723**
New loan	**$280,500**
Down payment (purchase price - new loan)	**$117,223**
Closing costs	**$3,685**
Cash invested (closing costs + down payment	
+ blinds + fences)	**$124,482**
Additional cash invested	
(selling costs of exchanged property)	**$14,354**
Rent Income	**$20,111**
Expenses	
Taxes	**$1,470**
Interest	**$16,963**
Insurance	**$1,150**
Misc:	
Sprinkler system maint.	**$149**
Utilities	**$111**
Homeowners association fee	**$337**
Maintenance	**$145**
Total miscellaneous expenses	**$742**
Total Expenses	**$20,325**
Principal Paydown	**$3,048**
Cash flow	
(Income - expenses - principal paydown)	**< $3,262>**
Appreciation	**$40,000**
Depreciation ($266,640 value of improvements	
divided by 27.5 years X 20% tax rate)	**$1,939**

The cash flow was negative, <$3,262>, the loan balance was reduced by $3,048, the house appreciated $40,000, and the tax savings equalled $1,939. Because I actually incurred expenses equally $14,354 to sell the exchanged house, I added those expenses to my cash invested. So I divided $41,725 by $138,836 giving me a total rate of return for the first year I owned the property of 30.00%. If I had bought this property without doing an exchange, my cash invested would have been only $124,482. Dividing $41,725 by $124,482 equals a 33.52% rate of return.

Decreasing Rate of Return

Every year you own a property the total amount you have invested in it will usually increase because of the equity buildup from loan paydown plus accumulated appreciation. Each year when you calculate your rates of return, you'll be dividing your four rates of return by a bigger amount invested. When you divide by a bigger amount invested, you get a smaller rate of return. So your rate of return will decrease each year.

As an illustration let's look at the numbers from my first property example again. Let's say that all my numbers on this property stayed the same for 1996 as they were in 1995. Appreciation was $2,000 again. The principal paydown stayed at $2,022 (normally principal paydown goes up each year as you pay down a loan, but because I had an adjustable loan on this property anything could have happened). My cash flow was $3,524 again and I saved another $815 on taxes. Everything stayed the same except for the total amount invested.

The total amount invested MUST have changed because I had more equity tied up in the property. In 1995 the total amount invested was $27,055. To get the total amount invested for 1996 we add 1995's principal paydown, $2,022, and appreciation, $2,000, to the previous year's amount invested. The new total amount invested for 1996 was $31,077. If all the other numbers stayed constant, what would the total rate of return have been in 1996?

Principal paydown ($2,022/$31,077)	**6.50%**
Cash flow ($3,524/$31,077)	**11.34%**
Appreciation ($2,000/$31,077)	**6.44%**
Depreciation ($815/$31,077)	**2.62%**
Total Rate of Return	**26.90%**

Instead of a 30.6% combined rate of return, I would have received a 26.9% combined rate of return on my invested money. If these rate of return numbers stayed constant except for adjusting the total amount invested each year for another three years, my annual rate of return would have dropped to just under 20% by the end of year five.

There is one bright point to this tendency for rates of return to drop as the invested money in a property increases. The speed by which the rate of return decreases becomes slower each year. Between year one and year two the rate of return for this example drops by 3.08%. Between years four and five it drops by only 1.59%.

Though rates of return decrease as your leverage in a property decreases, there are some compensating factors. In the real world your principal paydown amount will probably increase every year instead of holding constant. Cash flow will hopefully rise faster than expenses. Even if appreciation stays at a constant percentage, say 3%, your appreciation amount will increase each year because 3% of $150,000 is more than 3% of $130,000. Only your tax savings which is based on depreciating your property at its original purchase price will stay constant assuming you remain in the same tax bracket.

Increasing Your Rate of Return

You can increase the rate of return on a property you have owned for a while by using one of two methods. First, you can refinance your property with a new first mortgage or add a second mortgage. Either way you are drawing money out to invest someplace else. Since you now have less money invested in the first property, you've increased your leverage and therefore your potential rate of return.

The second method is to sell your first property and 1031 tax defer exchange your equity into one or more properties with a combined value which is greater than the value of the property you've sold. For more information on 1031 tax deferred exchanges, see Chapter Eleven, 1031 Tax Deferred Exchanges.

No matter which method you decide to use to increase your rate of return, you'll lose some of your money in transaction costs. You'll either pay loan origination fees and title insurance for a new mortgage, or you'll have to pay real estate commissions, closing costs and exchange fees if you do a 1031 tax deferred exchange. Because of these costs, you shouldn't refinance or exchange until your current rate of return gets so low that it makes financial sense to restructure your investment.

When to Restructure Your Investments

When do you reach this restructuring point? There is no hard and fast rule, but keep this guideline in mind. Depending on how soon you want to have a certain net worth and how much money you have to start with, you should calculate a bottom limit rate of return that will allow you to retire within a time frame that's agreeable to you. If your rate of return falls beneath this bottom limit, you'll need to restructure your investments in order to retire when you want.

Let's say you have a goal of $627,485 in equity in ten years and you have $100,000 to start with now. To reach your goal you use your financial calculator and determine that you need to get a yearly return of 20.16%. Averaging out your rates of return for different years, you know you can do better than that in the early years of owning a property which will compensate for decreasing rates of return as the years go by. So you decide 15% is your bottom line, a rate of return you insist on getting. If you reach that, it's time to restructure.

Personally, I like to look at how much a five year certificate of deposit yields. I figure I should get paid at least 10% more if I have to manage properties instead of loaning my money to a bank. I want to be paid for my time spent showing houses, cleaning them up, and keeping track of the paperwork. So if certificates of deposit are paying 5%, then the bottom line rate of return I want to receive on my rentals is 15%.

If you abhor the idea of tracking your rates of return (too hard! you want to get rich, but you hate math), you can simply restructure whenever you can afford to do so. If investor loans require 20% down, wait until you have 40% equity in one property, then exchange your equity into two similarly priced properties (or refinance out the down payment for the second property), using additional savings to pay for the transaction costs.

Cash Flow Versus Appreciation

Ideally you would like to make money from all four possible rate of return areas. If you happen to buy in an area of the country with high rent-to-value ratios just before it experiences a surge in appreciation, this could happen to you. But generally areas with good cash flow due to high rent-to-value ratios haven't had much appreciation for years, and the prospects for it occurring any time in the near future are slim (for example Austin, Texas).

And expensive areas such as San Francisco or Boston with low rent-to-value ratios have terrible cash flow, yet good long term prospects for appreciation.

The reality is that usually you get good positive cash flow, or appreciation, but not both. Buying in an area with good cash flow will make you rich more slowly, but you'll earn money as you go to help you buy additional properties. Buying in an area with strong appreciation could make you rich much faster, but the negative cash flow can be very painful and you always face the risk that the appreciating market may instead stagnate for years.

For most people, investing close to home is the most important consideration. But if you live in a poor cash flow area and have ties to a community with better rent-to-value ratios, you may want to explore investing there instead. I discuss this option in more detail in Chapter Four, Selecting Properties.

Ignoring Rates of Return

Once you have acquired your target number of rental properties, you may no longer care much about your rates of return. If after you pay off the loans on your properties, they'll generate sufficient income after taxes for you to live on, you will no longer be at the accumulation stage. Growth rates will no longer concern you as you focus instead on eliminating your loan payments.

You'll be at the plateau stage where your biggest concern will be having your rents appreciate as fast as inflation so your buying power stays constant. Perhaps you'll exchange into newer properties to keep your time spent making house repairs to a minimum, but at a certain point, your properties will require very little attention from you beyond basic property management.

This is when you can turn your energies to other interests and no longer worry about making a living. If you want to travel or do volunteer work or spend years learning how to weave rugs, you'll have the freedom to do so. It may be hard to stop focusing on making your money grow, but you should remind yourself why you wanted that money in the first place. Don't let getting rich in a monetary sense blind you to all the other riches that life has to offer. Enjoy having an independent income!

Chapter Three

Down Payments

With the advent of loans that allow homeowners and investors to put down minimal amounts of money, down payments may not seem as important as they used to be. But sizeable down payments work well for the investor who wants to own properties for the long haul. Instead of trying to leverage your money to the maximum and hoping for appreciation, a decent downpayment allows you to lower your monthly payment. Larger down payments also allow you to avoid mortgage insurance payments or the higher interest rates charged on high loan-to-value mortgages. And it is easier to qualify for a loan if you have a healthy down payment.

Books have been written about how to buy real estate with no money down. It is possible, although it usually involves using somebody's money, even if it's not actually your money. The first time I bought a house was with a boyfriend in my early twenties. I borrowed $1,000 from my mother for my share of the down payment and closing costs. When I later bought a house by myself, she loaned me around $5,000. It wasn't a lot, but it made all the difference.

Milt, the small investor I mentioned in Chapter One, borrowed small amounts, ranging from $1,000 to $3,000, from many friends in order to accumulate 20% down payments and closing costs (he pledged the equity in his personal home as collateral). My sister and brother-in-law traded fix up labor in exchange for a fifty percent ownership in two properties with my husband and me making those nothing down deals for them.

One way to reduce the size of the down payment you need for an investment property is to buy with a partner. I've purchased most of my properties with someone else. Besides sharing the down payment expense, I like knowing someone else will help cover the costs of vacancy or maintenance expenses later on.

Building Up Equity

Many people obtain their down payments for future rental properties by buying their own homes first with minimum down payments. They prepay their mortgages and build additional equity through appreciation. Then they have the choice of buying a new personal residence and renting out their old house, or refinancing their home and using the proceeds as a down payment on a rental property.

The first house I kept as a rental property was one I purchased as an owner-occupant during the fall of 1992. I paid $97,000 and borrowed the $5,000 for the down payment and closing costs from my mother. To pay the mortgage, I found two roommates to share expenses. I lived in the house for a little over one year before I married and rented out my house. Voila! I had a rental property.

By the spring of 1998 my old home was worth $140,000 with a mortgage of $80,000, giving me $60,000 in equity. Yet I had put down no money of my own originally to buy this house. Borrowing against this equity gave me enough money to buy a half share in another house with my sister. My personal home became one and a half rental houses within five years. The increased rent on my old home (rental rates had risen along with property values) allowed me to easily pay both the old first mortgage payment and the new second mortgage payment.

You can see how this process of pulling money out of older rental properties can continue indefinitely. By the time I had purchased five houses, I discovered that each year another house had built up enough equity to allow me to finance out a down payment if I wanted to do that. Although it takes years, it's much easier to have more money to invest once the first few properties have had a chance to appreciate. The key is to acquire something in the first place to get the cycle started.

Saving Money

Saving is an old-fashioned method of acquiring enough capital to make investments. It works, but it can be slow in the beginning. As you buy properties each should eventually produce cash flow for you to save, reducing the time you need to wait while you save up enough money for the next down payment. But getting to this delightful point in your investment career takes time, patience, and a clear focus on your long term goal. You must save up enough money to buy your first property before its cash flow can help you buy the next house.

Saving is a difficult thing to do. Why? Suppose you have $5,000 in your savings account. This money is earning perhaps 2% per year, or $100. You will also have to pay taxes on this interest income, leaving you with very little gain as a reward for your frugality.

In contrast think of all the lovely things you could buy with that $5,000. You and your spouse could go on a cruise in the Caribbean. Wouldn't you have fun telling your co-workers where you spent your vacation? Or you could buy a new leather couch for the living room. After all your parents are coming to visit, or your boss, or your best friend from high school - you fill in the blank. A leather couch would show them you've done well. And there would still be money left over to buy new drapes, a matching lounger, and a new coffee table. And anyway, don't you deserve it?

Or you could fall prey to the lure of a new car. All families need a minivan, right? Only a few thousand dollars down, and you can own a depreciating asset that requires monthly payments. Not only can you spend your savings in one visit to the automobile dealer, you can prevent yourself from saving anything else for the next five years because you must make monthly car payments! Hard to resist a deal like that. Indeed, millions of new vehicles are sold each year on credit.

Saving today so you won't have to work tomorrow demands discipline. It requires the ability to see into the future. Saving can be fun if you believe that every dollar you save will help you buy your life. Just like the Greek slave who could earn and save money in order to buy his freedom, you can liberate yourself from the tyranny of earning a living. Thinking of your savings this way can make being frugal almost as much fun as spending.

It's Impossible to Save

Before you say it's impossible for you to save any money, I'd like you to look at your income. How much money have you earned over the last ten years? $200,000? $500,000? $700,000? And how much will you earn in the next ten years? Wouldn't it be nice if you kept some of that money?

If you lack the discipline to pay yourself every month, you could try this trick. Go to your bank or credit union and get a vacation loan, perhaps for $5,000. Then don't go on vacation. Put the money into a savings account in a different bank. Then pay back your monthly vacation loan. When you've paid off the loan, you'll still have the $5,000. Next, repeat the process until you have enough to make a down payment on a house.

Will you pay a higher interest rate on the borrowed money than you're earning on the money in the savings account? Yes, but it's better to save the money somehow than not at all. Maybe once you get into the habit of writing a $350 monthly check to the bank on your loan, you won't need to get another vacation loan. You can continue writing the monthly check, but to yourself. Then deposit it into your special savings account.

A technique I've often used is one deplored by financial experts; I withhold too much in taxes. Sure, I'm losing the minuscule amount of interest this money could be earning in a savings account for a few months. But instead of receiving an extra $50 a week that would be easily squandered, I get a refund check for $2,600. That's big enough to catch my attention.

My parents like to take cruises. One year they met a couple with an interesting story. This husband and wife agreed when they married that half of any raises he received would be spent, but the other half would be saved and invested in small apartment buildings. Though she stayed home with the kids, they still saved quite a bit of money. Eventually the cash flow from their apartment buildings was contributing substantially to their income.

They began to take three cruises a year. The husband's co-workers thought he must have gotten a big inheritance since they couldn't afford to travel as much as he did. But through the years his co-workers hadn't saved like he had. He had created his own financial windfall by making the decision to save and invest so many years ago.

Unexpected Money

Mini-windfalls appear in people's lives quite frequently. Since people don't have a plan for unexpected monies, it is spent ineffectively, usually on consumer items. But for someone who has a goal, these windfalls can speed up a retirement plan drastically.

I know someone who purchased his personal residence just before a burst of appreciation gave him a substantial amount of equity within a short three years. He then borrowed against this equity to buy rental properties. A woman with whom I worked told me how she was unexpectedly fired from her part-time position as a bank teller when the bank was purchased in a bank merger. She was paid $25,000 in severance pay! Another woman I know received a chunk of money as an insurance settlement for being the innocent victim in a car accident.

All of these people received amounts well below $100,000. This money wasn't enough for them to retire, but it was sufficient to give a real boost to their financial status.

Some of my students assure me they would never be the recipients of a lump sum of money, but none of the events I've just described could have been predicted. They could happen to you. You want to be ready with a plan in case they do.

When I met my husband, I owned my own home plus a half interest in a house in Austin, Texas, with my twin sister. My route to owning a small real estate empire looked like a long one. But I was only twenty-seven-years-old. I had time on my side. And I really didn't have a lot of other choices. If I didn't save then and get started, when would I ever do it?

I figured I would be able to buy another house when I turned thirty. I would leap frog into a new home using owner occupied loan terms and rent out my old house. It never occurred to me that within a short eight months after buying the house I planned to turn into my first rental I would meet the man of my dreams, five weeks later accept his proposal, and be married four months after that.

Although Steven made a limited income as a magazine writer, he did have a decent portfolio of stocks and bonds. This made lenders happier because they counted the stocks and bonds as liquid assets (meaning something the lenders thought we could liquidate easily to pay mortgage payments if necessary!) Plus Steven had money sitting in his savings account because of several recent bond redemptions he had been forced to accept. Instead of spending the money on fancy wedding rings or an elaborate honeymoon (my ring cost $140, Steven wore his dad's ring, and for a week we traveled on second class buses in Mexico and stayed in rustic hotels), we purchased two houses with low money down, non-qualifying loans in Texas with my sister and her husband.

So not only did my real estate investment plans unexpectedly benefit when I fell in love, so did my sister's plans. She located two houses in the suburbs of Austin that needed cosmetic work plus a bit of serious fix up work. My husband Steven provided the money for the down payments and supplies, and Shelley and Brandon did the work. For them it was a no money down deal they couldn't have predicted. How could they have known that a future, unknown brother-in-law would want to invest with them? The unexpected can happen to you as well.

Get a Partner

As the previous story illustrates, it's possible to find a partner who has the money to invest while you supply the know-how and handle the work. If you share your goals and talk about real estate throughout your day-to-day life, you will discover people who are interested in buying rental property with you. Depending on the current opportunities in your local market, you could buy fixer uppers like Shelley and Brandon did or you could buy premium condition houses in an appreciating market where you'll share the increase in equity with your partner. Your partner could supply the down payment while you handle the property management chores.

At some point you may find a house you want to own, but you don't have quite enough money to buy it by yourself. Once when my Realtor friend David Stein was showing houses to a former student of mine, they invited me to come with them. The first house we walked into was perfect. It was only four years old, priced a bit under market, and in great shape. The master bath had a separate tub and shower plus a walk-in closet, and several rooms in the house had vaulted ceilings. The deck in the backyard faced the mountains. I knew all these features would make the property very desirable to tenants.

I turned to my former student as we stood in the living room, and asked him if he wanted to make an offer. He said no. He wanted to buy a house in a less expensive price range. So I asked David if he wanted to buy the house with me. He was surprised. He knew I hadn't even been looking for a house. I didn't have enough money for a down payment. But I loved that house.

After making sure the client really didn't want to make an offer, David agreed that somebody should buy the house. We talked with our spouses and made an offer together for less than the already attractive asking price. Though the seller's agent told us that two full price offers had previously been rejected, the seller countered us at less than full price since we agreed to rent the house back to him for a few months until he could move into the new house he was having built.

A word of caution here: only take on partners whom you like and trust. In this case I had done short term business deals with David and was comfortable with the idea of trying a longer term partnership.

I also went into the deal knowing that people tend to feel that they are working harder than their partner. After all, if I spent two hours trimming the bushes in the front yard of our rental house, I'd be very aware of every minute. Yet if David spent time tracking down a plumber to fix a leak from the master bath, and then found a drywall guy to patch the family room ceiling where the water had come through, he could tell me about that in just two minutes. It would be easy for me to dismiss his time spent driving to the property to let in people to give us bids and then do the repair work.

Of course sometimes it's true, your partner isn't pulling his or her fair share of the load. My philosophy is to do the work myself, and either buy out my partner or get bought out as soon as it's feasible. Then I won't invest with that person again. In the meantime I'd still rather have half a loaf than none even if I'm the only one working in the kitchen.

Many real estate gurus warn against investing with partners because of potential disagreements. Yet in an appreciating markets buying with a partner allows you to avoid lost opportunity costs. Instead of losing the opportunity to make money while you wait to qualify for a loan by yourself, you can own a half interest in an appreciating property. If you have a history of getting along with people, having a partner may work for you. Pick a good partner and be prepared to be flexible and not quibble over who is working harder.

Borrowing Money

Any asset you own can be used as collateral for a loan. You can borrow against your personal home. You can borrow against one of your rental properties. Banks will set up lines of credit using your stock certificates as collateral, and 401(k) plans will let you borrow against your retirement fund. Friends and family may even give you personal loans secured only by their faith and trust in you.

You should only borrow money if you are confident you can earn a higher rate of return on it than you will have to pay in interest. If you have to pay your sister 8% on the money she loans to you, your anticipated rate of return on that money when you invest it in real estate should be at least two to three times that amount, or 16-24%. Otherwise the reward isn't worth the risk. And if the investment doesn't worked out as anticipated, you should know how you plan to repay her.

Borrowing money does involve a degree of risk. You are leveraging your assets which will allow you to earn a higher rate of return, but you are also incurring a debt which will have to be repaid. It is important to know how you will obtain the necessary dollars to make the debt payments as they come due.

When you borrow money to buy rental property it's best if the rental income will cover the payments on the borrowed money. If the income will not be enough to make the debt payments, you should have few other debts so you can easily handle the payments out of your regular income. For example, many people will casually sign up for a $450 a month new car payment. I'd rather see you keep your old car and make that monthly payment on a property.

You can borrow money by refinancing your personal residence in order to access some of your equity. As long as you resist the urge to finance out every cent, you'll still have equity in your home. Even though some lenders will lend up to the full value of your house, I suggest leaving at least 20% equity. This equity acts as an emergency cash reserve.

Some people have trouble with the idea of refinancing their homes or rental properties. After spending a couple of years watching the loan balances get smaller and smaller, they get bitten by the security bug. It can be quite reassuring to have a large equity position in your home and investment properties.

Unfortunately, your rate of return will get lower every year as your leverage decreases. It's much harder to reach your financial goal when you are earning 12% instead of 20% on your invested money. You need to acquire your target number of properties before you switch over to the "pay off all the loans stage." While you pay off one or two properties, the other properties you could have purchased may escalate dramatically in value. By the time you are ready to buy your next house, it may cost far more than it does today.

Remember that each property you buy is potentially a small money making machine. If your financial goal requires you to buy five properties, then the sooner you acquire them without taking undue financial risks, the better. Your tenants will help you pay them off, and you'll enjoy appreciation instead of worrying about how you'll be able to afford to buy your last house.

Taking a Breather

Keeping yourself leveraged can become more difficult over time. As you get closer to acquiring your last property, you may discover that you've become more conservative since you began your investment career. Even though you were happy with high loan-to-value ratios at the beginning, you may be reluctant to return to those same high ratios after you've paid down some of your loans. It's different than it was in the beginning - you've got a lot more to lose now.

This situation happened to a couple I know. They wanted five and one half rental properties in addition to owning their personal residence (they co-owned houses with partners which is how they owned half of a house). When they reached four and a half properties, they had the chance to buy another house at a below market price. But it would have required borrowing against the equity in one of their rental properties to get the down payment. That meant their cash flow from that property would have been drastically reduced. Even though the purchase of the new property would have brought their combined loan-to-value ratio for all their properties to only 70%, leaving a 30% equity position, they decided to wait to buy their last house.

Financially this wasn't the best decision. Houses in their target purchase area were appreciating rapidly, and they lost the chance to leverage their money more effectively. But everyone should take emotional comfort into account. Sometimes you will need to take a breather on your road to retirement.

This couple had just spent one and a half years building a duplex from the foundation up and doing the vast majority of the work themselves. They were tired of working hard and wanted to have a little fun to reward themselves. They wanted a chance to enjoy the cash flow they had built up, even if it meant delaying their retirement plans. They preferred to strengthen their financial situation by paying off two small construction loans before acquiring their final property.

You may have to make a decision like this where you evaluate financial benefits against emotional desires. Particularly when it comes to borrowing money to continue an investment plan, one spouse may be resistant. It's better to come to an agreement that makes both spouses happy rather than to fight about it. Decisions cannot be made solely on a financial basis. Unity in the home is crucial to a successful investment career. If that means you'll have to wait an extra year or two before you retire, so be it.

Moving

If you live where starter homes cost $400,000 and up, you may decide to move someplace where housing prices are more reasonable. Saving a down payment for a $150,000 house is much easier than it is for a $400,000 house.

To find a housing market you can afford may mean you have to move only a short distance. Even communities only twenty minutes apart may have housing prices which are dramatically different. Or you may decide to move to a different state.

If you decide to look for a community which offers you a better chance to invest in real estate, you should consider many factors. Comparing housing prices is just the start.

Everyone is familiar with the typical qualities you should look for in a new community. Quality of life is dependent on good schools, convenient shopping, a strong job market, and recreation opportunities. These are items I feel you can judge for yourself, so I won't go into them in great detail. But also research how landlord friendly a state is. Check with local apartment associations (many members own rental houses) and ask questions about state and local laws.

Potential for Appreciation

You may want to look for an area which you believe will experience appreciation. An area which is experiencing an inward migration of people is more likely to appreciate than an area which is losing population, but even areas with exploding job and population growth may not experience the appreciation you may expect. An example of this phenomena is the Austin area. Prices were stagnant for houses located in the suburbs north of Austin in the mid-nineties.

When I began to buy here in 1993 I thought Texas properties had more room to appreciate than Colorado properties did. Home prices in Austin were lower than the highs they had reached in the mid-eighties before sharply dropping oil prices damaged the Texas economy and caused housing values to plunge. In addition Austin had an unbelievable job growth rate, one of the top in the nation. Many high tech companies were building new facilities in Round Rock, a town on the northern edge of Austin.

What I didn't take into account was how many builders would leap at the chance to sell new homes to the new residents. Restrained by few growth limitations compared to the Denver metro area, houses sprang up like weeds. Prices on existing Austin homes remained stable while Denver suburban prices kept going up. Denver area residents, you see, were horrified at the idea of Denver becoming like Los Angeles, and so they passed many growth control measures. Fortunately, I owned houses in Denver as well as Austin.

Interestingly enough, houses in the center of Austin did appreciate quite a bit. Why? Because no more land for building was available near downtown. People had to compete for the existing houses, and prices rose.

What did this teach me? That if I could afford it, I should buy properties located close to something that limited future growth such as mountains, open space, locations close to a lake or ocean, neighborhoods in the center of an already developed area, or somewhere with strong growth control limits.

Many people confuse the rising cost of a median home in an area with appreciation. They read in newspaper articles that the median prices for homes in their city rose 6.7% in the last year. Hooray! they say. They think the value of their houses went up 6.7%. But the median price for houses sold in any given year may have no relation to the appreciation rate on existing houses.

A median price is the price at which half of all houses sold cost more and half of the houses sold cost less. The new houses being built in America are usually bigger than the older homes. At the very least they are constructed of brand new components which cost more than used components. So new houses cost more than the resale houses on the market. Whenever many new houses are being built, their higher sale prices will disproportionately increase the median sales price.

You need to look for the appreciation rate on existing home sales to find out what is happening to the values of your properties. The best way to do this is to request that your real estate agent run comps (sale prices for comparable homes) for the neighborhoods where you own properties. Or look on the internet for sites that provide sales information for properties in your area.

Local Regulations

Many cities regulate rental properties. Even if any additional costs these regulations create can be passed onto the tenants, the landlord still ends up spending valuable time documenting compliance. An example is the city of Boulder, Colorado.

Rental properties in Boulder must regularly have a rental inspection in order to get a rental license. You must pay for the license. The housing inspector has the authority to require you to "improve" your property in order to get or renew your license. Whether these improvements actually make the property safer is irrelevant. You will make any required changes and you will pay for them. Arguing about them may only result in the inspector going through all other properties you own in the city with a fine tooth comb. This happened to an investor I know. After that experience his advice to me was to grin and go along with any demand. Fighting a bureaucracy is a losing battle.

Other localities may have rent controls or are thinking about initiating them. To raise your rents may require the approval of some governmental body. If you don't like the idea of Big Brother supervising your investments, you should look for cities without housing departments.

Look in the phone book. Even if a housing department exists, you may still want to call them and discover exactly how big the department is. If it's small and has only a few rules which won't apply to you, you may decide to invest there. Just keep in mind that government has a way of growing.

Taxes and Insurance

Some states have much higher property taxes than do others. In addition some states such as Texas charge investors higher taxes than homeowners. I learned about this the hard way. My sister and I bought a house in 1993 and assumed the mortgage. The mortgage payment including the taxes and insurance was low enough to give us a positive cash flow. But the next year when the taxing authorities discovered that the house had become a rental property, they changed our tax status and increased our tax rate.

To add insult to injury, the previous owner had been over sixty-five, so the annual tax amount the real estate agent had given us for the house was even lower than the normal homeowner rate because Texas discounts property taxes for older people. A double whammy! Our taxes shot way up. This property became an alligator with a negative cash flow. It's one thing to plan for a negative cash flow, another to get stuck with it accidentally. You should check taxes for investors ahead of time.

Insurance costs also vary. Earthquake or flood insurance can add substantially to your monthly payment. Sometimes you will have to pay flood insurance if one corner of a property is in the flood plain, even if the structure itself is higher. Areas that have numerous wildfire claims may cause higher insurance rates for properties not located directly in the fire risk area. For example, even though the houses I owned in Jefferson County, Colorado, were located in the suburbs of Denver, a large fire that burned many houses in the foothills west of Denver, also in Jefferson County, caused my rates to go up dramatically when my policies renewed the next year.

However, higher taxes and insurance will usually not affect your comparative cash flow. Rents in Austin are much higher in relation to the value of the properties than they are in Denver, allowing landlords to pay for these higher expenses out of higher rent. A property worth $155,000 in 2005 in north Austin rented for $1,450. That's a 93.5% rent-to-value ratio which looks pretty fabulous until you adjust it to account for the higher landlord property taxes (even then it's still pretty good, but keep in mind that appreciation has been virtually non-existent in Austin for years).

Some states and communities charge a sales tax when you sell real estate. For example, Washington charges a 1% excise tax when a property is sold, and the counties in that state charge an additional .25 - .5% excise tax on top of the state tax. If you want to fix and flip properties here this will increase your selling costs. It's also a factor when you decide whether or not to 1031 tax exchange properties to improve your portfolio.

Many of the states with additional taxes are the ones that don't charge personal income tax. After all, the tax money is going to come from somewhere! Despite variations in taxes, any state can be a good place to invest. I just want you to be aware that expenses may differ from what you are used to depending where you invest in the United States.

Inheriting Money

The media has been telling us that Americans are about to witness the biggest inter-generational transfer of assets in our history. Some people, of course, will inherit a lot of money while others will inherit small amounts or none at all, but fifty thousand is enough for an investor's down payment on a nice single family home in many parts of this country. Half of that amount is enough if you can find a trustworthy partner to buy a house with you on a fifty-fifty basis. A fraction of that will help you into an owner-occupied home.

The main problem with inheriting money is its uncertainty. When will you inherit? How much will it be? It's not prudent to make your retirement plans around an anticipated inheritance. My father has warned me in jest since I was a child that he planned to spend my inheritance. That was fine with me since I wasn't willing to wait for him to die before I became financially independent.

Yet some people do sit around like vultures, ignoring their responsibility to take care of their own financial fortunes. They forgo sacrifice and planning in anticipation of a large inheritance. Besides the ghoulish nature of waiting for an inheritance, you can't count on receiving it.

My great-aunt and uncle were some of the first people to build on Malibu Beach. How much was their small apartment building worth when they eventually passed away? A bundle, but as far as my family is aware, only the Catholic church benefitted. While it would have been nice to have inherited something here, no one counted on it happening.

The moral of this story? It's best to plan as if you will receive no inheritance. Then if you do, wonderful. Depending on how large it is you will be brought closer to financial independence. You might even achieve it instantly. But on the other hand, if your relatives live into their nineties and spend all their money, you will still be okay. It is possible to take care of your own financial future. An inheritance is just a lovely bonus.

Life Insurance

Even if none of your relatives are rich, you may discover they had a life insurance policy and you are the beneficiary. While insurance money usually comes with an emotional loss, this money will at least help you to secure your financial situation.

My recommendation is not to make large investment decisions until you have had a chance to recover your emotional balance. Unless you are already an experienced real estate investor, it may be best to wait at least a year before making any big decisions about investing your insurance money. You may not get great returns by letting your money sit in a money market account, but at least it is safe until you are emotionally ready to deal with it.

Settlements

This is a litigation crazy country, yet some lawsuits are well founded. Unlike the huge settlements publicized by the media, most cases concern much smaller amounts of money. Minor accidents, sex or age discrimination at work, and product liability settlements may provide you with a small nest egg. When I was a real estate agent I met a number of people who had received modest settlements and used all or part of them to buy real estate.

Lease Options

Lease options are often hyped in the real estate investment community. Seminar leaders talk about how lease options will make you rich without having to buy any property. By tying up a property in a lease option you risk only a small option fee and your time spent managing the property until the time comes when you exercise your option, take control of the property, and perhaps even sell it mere moments later to an eager buyer who pays you much more than you paid for the property.

This sounds wonderful, but I still don't like the idea of lease options. I think many of the gentlemen traveling the country giving lease option seminars are making their money from being speakers, not by doing lease option deals.

I have two problems with lease options. First, it's similar to when you ask sellers to carry back notes on their properties. In bad markets they are forced to consider this option. But when interest rates are low and the economy is doing relatively well, only sellers with awful properties will carry back a loan or accept a lease option.

And when I say awful properties, I'm not talking about diamonds in the rough. I mean properties with incurable faults, or faults that would cost an exorbitant amount of money to correct. Items such as dreadful locations on busy streets or cracked foundations.

Secondly, even if your area of the country has a real estate market so weak that sellers with decent properties will agree to lease options, you are setting yourself up for an unpleasant experience in the future. If the property's value doesn't go up and you don't buy it, the sellers won't be happy. Reasonable or not, they may decide to try to harangue you into buying the property or threaten to sue you. Unhappy people will do amazing things.

Or else the property's value will rise just as you had hoped. Now you want to exercise your option, but the seller can see the equity he or she will be losing. Some sellers will go along quietly and sell to you anyway. Others will decide it's worth it to take you to court and fight the option contract.

Will they win? Maybe. You may be portrayed as the sharp real estate investor who took advantage of an ignorant person. Or your contract may not stand up in court for some nitpicky reason. In any case the battle over the lease option will absorb your time and energy.

If you are determined to do lease options, do get competent legal counsel to review your contracts and your risks. Make sure extended lease options are legal and enforceable in your state. Lease options that allow you to exercise your option several years in the future may or may not be binding. Find out the legality of your contract before you spend years managing a property, possibly for free.

Chapter Four

Selecting Properties

What is the best property to buy? The correct answer varies because the perfect property for one person may drive someone else crazy. Do you want to spend the time required to find properties priced right for fixing up? Prefer to buy new buildings so repairs won't be an issue for years to come? Insist on owning rental property within fifteen minutes drive of your home? Want to own whatever property will produce the highest total rate of return regardless of other factors? Don't care about cash flow as long as you get appreciation? Dream of buying a property for 30% less than its market value?

You need to evaluate potential purchases based on who you are, the amount of time you have to devote to real estate investing, and what opportunities are available where you live.

As a beginning investor it's hard to determine upfront what your niche in the real estate market will be. Over time you'll discover your preferences and what works best for you. Along the way you'll probably buy a property that you later decide you don't want to keep and you'll sell it. That's okay. Buying property is not the same as getting married. You can change your mind and trade your equity into something different without too much trouble.

Sometimes people freeze when they set out to buy their first rental property. Although it's true that at some point you just have to do it and buy something, you may be hesitating for a good reason. It took me six years from the time I started looking at houses with agents until I bought my first one. I'd look for awhile, get distracted by the rest of my life, look again, and so forth until the day came that I found a property that I could see would be profitable.

Sometimes people want to buy deals comparable to the ones promised by the marketers of real estate programs advertised on television or through seminars. Yes, great deals do show up, but they are a lot rarer than these promoters say. After all, if great deals are so readily available, why are the promoters selling programs instead of buying more property? The bottom line is, it takes time, knowledge, or connections to find the bargains. You can find them, but it will be easier after you get some experience as an investor.

If you want to make money in real estate on a part-time basis, I think your best approach is to buy a property in great shape for a bit below market price, and hold it for at least five years. Before you buy, you should be able to realistically predict that this property will generate a 20% or better annual rate of return the first year you own it. After buying this first property you will use it as your benchmark when you shop for your next property. You'll try to get a better deal each time by using what you've learned along the way.

Remember to only compare your success with your personal best. Don't worry about the great deals other people are supposedly getting. While great deals exist, real estate investors have a lot in common with fishermen - they tend to exaggerate. I remember several years ago when an investor told me about a property he had bought in Boulder, Colorado. The story went something like this. He bought a house for $175,000 and sold it after a little rehab for $235,000. I was dismayed. How come I couldn't find deals like that?

But my last name is Thomas for a reason, as in doubting Thomas. Because I was still a Realtor at that time, I had easy access to the public tax records and multiple listing service. In

Colorado you can find out what someone paid for a property by looking at the document tax. It turns out this man paid $185,000 instead of $175,000. And he didn't sell the house for $235,000, but for $225,000. Good-bye $20,000 in fictional profit. I didn't stop there.

According to the multiple listing page for his house, the rehab included a new roof, new windows, new kitchen and baths, and new flooring. Even if he did most of the work himself, that must have cost at least $20,000. Plus the agent's commission was probably at least 5%, or $10,000. And let's not forget carrying costs. Looking at the closing dates, I saw that he held the property for six months. Conservatively that must have cost $7,000 or so in interest. My conclusion? This guy was lucky if he made any money at all.

While I hope you do find one or more great deals during your investment career, it's okay to start out with a deal that's good enough. Realize that you are your only competition, and keep striving to beat your own numbers.

Single Family Homes

Single family homes are my favorite type of property. They are the best type of property for beginning investors. Why? Because they are plentiful, easy to purchase, and easy to sell. Lenders like single family homes, so it's relatively simple to obtain attractive loans to buy them. Most tenants prefer single family homes over other types of rental units. And if you get transferred or decide to liquidate your property investments, single family homes are readily marketable.

Single family homes also have disadvantages. If you own five different houses, each in a different area, it will take more time for you to handle routine maintenance chores than if you owned one small apartment complex. Apartments make it easier to hire a property manager, and may also produce an overall higher rate of return.

Despite these drawbacks I still recommend owning single family houses. A nice house with a reasonable rent will attract tenants who tend to be more desirable compared to tenants who rent smaller units. More affluent tenants tend to rent houses instead of apartments.

These tenants, in my experience, have a lower eviction rate. They have more financial options than do tenants in the lower financial brackets and they have more to lose if they let their credit records become marred. Therefore, they pay the rent more reliably. They are the tenants who, if carefully selected, will be low hassle and make it easier for you to be a landlord for many years.

Different Types of Single Family Homes

Not all single family homes are equal. The least expensive homes are older properties. These homes have higher rent-to-property value ratios than newer, more expensive, properties. This makes it seem as if you'll receive a higher monthly cash flow on your invested money, but this perceived advantage can, and usually is, canceled out by additional maintenance costs. Besides having to spend more money on repairs, you will have to invest more of your time either doing the repair work yourself or hiring and supervising someone else to do it.

After a number of years spent fixing up older properties I've switched to investing entirely in newer single family homes. These properties do have smaller rent-to-property value ratios, but they tend not to have any expensive maintenance problems for many years. Also tenants love to rent newer houses. They like master baths which have bathtubs as well as showers. They like vaulted ceilings in the living room, lots of big windows, and a spacious kitchen with lots of counter space. They also like double paned glass and modern insulation.

If it is possible in your area to buy newer houses in a lower price range, a price range where rent-to-property value ratios are the most profitable, great. Buy these houses as long as the area has strong long term rental demand. We'll talk more about evaluating that demand later this chapter in the section on location.

If newer houses in your area are in a price range too high to make good rentals, one alternative is to look for over-improved older houses. Some owners will upgrade their homes far above the level of the neighboring houses, ignoring the fact that they have the only house in the subdivision with hardwood floors and fancy French doors off the dining room. It is unlikely that they will ever recuperate the full cost of installing these extras when they sell their property. The lower values of the houses surrounding their house will limit its top dollar price.

Over-improved properties can be great buys. You may pay a small premium compared to the sale prices of comparable houses, but you'll get a lot more for your money. You'll have an easier time finding tenants if you can offer features not usually found in that price range. Someday when you decide to sell this house, your property will out-compete surrounding houses.

Brand New Houses

In the past I avoided buying brand new houses because of the hassle and expense of putting in the landscaping, buying window coverings, and getting the builder to fix problems covered by warranties. Not to mention that if I've already put down 20% or more to buy the house, why would I want to invest an additional 5% or so to pay for a deck, lawn, bushes, a tree, and blinds? This is especially a problem when I'm doing a 1031 tax deferred exchange. I can buy the property using the exchange money, but I'll need to come up with additional funds to cover these types of items that are purchased outside of the property closing. So I've preferred to purchase nearly new houses which are two to four years old at the time I buy them. These houses have already been landscaped and require little additional work. Yet there are exceptions to every rule of thumb.

Special Opportunities

One of the reasons investing in real estate is fun is because you can find myriad opportunities to make money. I always keep my eyes open, ready to spot a chance to acquire a property with potential. Even with my prejudice against buying new homes as investment properties, I put my first brand new house under contract in the spring of 1997.

Here's what happened. I was showing houses to a client in a new subdivision. Two builders were constructing different series of homes at varying price points. The least expensive homes would only be built in three areas of the subdivision. One area backed to a very large commercial building with noisy fans. Another area backed to a street. But the third area backed to some very large, awkwardly shaped housing lots.

The builder of these homes was asking the same prices for these houses regardless of where they were located in the subdivision. I knew that houses built in the third area which did not back to a noisy commercial building or onto a street would have a higher future resale value. Also, unlike a lot of Colorado houses, people living in the third area wouldn't look directly across their backyards straight into the windows of another house. The strangely shaped lots behind the third area would force any houses built there to be at an angle.

I told the students in one of my adult education real estate classes about this intriguing situation. The next week I mentioned this opportunity again, but still no one offered the builder a contract for a house in the third area. Finally, I showed the land and the model home to a good friend. He and his wife agreed to buy a house with my husband and myself.

How did it all turn out? The developer decided that the strangely shaped lots were unworkable and instead created a strip of open space. Lots in this development which backed to open space usually came with a lot premium of $5,000, but the builder had already signed contracts for all the houses along this newly created open space. So the location became even better than I had anticipated.

Getting the landscaping installed was a hassle, no doubt about it, but worth it in the long run. I had a half share in a brand new house, one of the least expensive in the entire development with one of the nicest locations. Besides backing to a small piece of open space, the house was only a block away from the community pool! I later sold my half share to my partner for a nice profit, and rolled the money tax-deferred into the office portion of the new personal home I bought.

Although it's much easier to buy a near-new house that's ready to rent, new homes do offer a compelling advantage in strongly appreciating markets. If you can lock in today's price, and not close for another nine to twelve months, you may make 8-10%, or more, in appreciation on the purchase price. Dividing that by the typically small earnest money deposit could give you an impressive rate of return before you even close on the property.

Model Homes

Most builders construct one or more model homes. These provide space for the sales office, usually in the garage, and are furnished to show the homes looking their best. Yet the builder's money is tied up in these model homes, making it harder for the builder to get the financing to build the houses to be sold to buyers.

Often the builder prefers to sell the model homes to investors and rent them back for the one to two years it takes for the builder to finish that subdivision. Some large builders have a network of investors that they contact. Other builders may be receptive to selling to someone they haven't worked with before. The only way to find out is to ask. Visit new subdivisions when the builders are still operating out of construction trailers and ask if they are looking for someone to buy the model home and lease it back to them. Or if these model houses are already under contract with a different investor, try to get on the builder's list of interested investors for future projects.

If a builder is interested in working with you, expect to receive a higher than market rent. After all, your carpet will have hundreds if not thousands of people walking across it, and the designer hired by the builder may install red wallpaper with contrasting black daisies in your downstairs bathroom. This may look fine with her decorative accents, but won't look as nice in an empty house being offered for rent to the average tenant. This means you may have to spend extra money when the builder's lease ends to take out some of the decoration. The builder may or may not agree as part of the lease to pay these expenses for you, but at the least the builder should be obligated to repair any damaged areas when the lease ends.

Another factor to consider when buying a model home is how many options the builder wants to showcase. To attract buyer traffic, most builders strip out every feature they can to create a low base price. Doing this also takes out most of their profit margin. In order to make money, they need to sell options to buyers. People buy what they can see, so builders tend to display as many upgrades as possible in their model homes. The net result is you could end up buying an over-improved house at a lofty price.

Because the builder has a hefty profit margin built into the price of the options, you may be able to get your purchase price reduced below what the builder would normally charge. The builder won't be losing hard money out-of-pocket by discounting the price of the options, and should be willing to negotiate here.

Some builders build one model house that is loaded with options, and a second model home that demonstrates the bare bones look. If you can't get a discount on the price of the fancy house, you may prefer to buy and lease back to the builder the plainer house. You can always upgrade some of the finishes later when you get the house ready for the regular rental market.

Obviously, one of the biggest frustrations of buying a model home is losing control over what options the house will feature and what colors and finishing materials the decorator chooses. But if the price and rent amount makes it worthwhile, you may be very happy with this type of purchase.

Justified Discrimination Against Investors

Some builders refuse to sell to investors, and for good reason. During times of fast appreciation, investors have figured out that they can control huge amounts of real estate by putting down minimal down payments, let the houses appreciate while they are being constructed, and then sell them for a nice profit as soon as they close on them.

Yet if the market slows, and the houses don't appreciate as expected, the investors shrug their shoulders and walk away from their contracts. They figure it's cheaper to let the builders keep the earnest money instead of buying houses that they will have to sell at a loss after paying closing and carrying costs.

This approach can leave builders stuck with a bunch of unsold houses. A builder may even go out of business because the houses cannot be sold quickly enough to other buyers. In a quickly appreciating, potentially even speculative, market, many builders decide not to sell to investors. Other builders limit their exposure by only selling a certain percentage of homes to investors. And some builders demand larger than normal earnest money deposits from investors.

Sometimes builders won't sell to investors because the master builder for a community won't allow it. The master builder may be concerned for many reasons, but generally investors are viewed as not being as committed to their properties as owners. And when communities are just being started, prices may be lower in order to entice the first buyers. These lower prices may attract more investors than the master builder wants, so a temporary moratorium on investors may be in place.

I suspect that this last situation was the problem when I decided to buy houses at Stapleton, the redevelopment of the old airport in Denver. The first few houses were just being framed when I went from one construction trailer to the next, asking if they sold to investors, and every builder but one said no. Notice that I kept asking despite the noes! And as the months and years passed I kept on asking. Eventually another builder said yes, and then another. Through persistence I was able to buy five houses from three different builders in a neighborhood I had identified as ripe for fast appreciation.

Another reason builders may refuse to sell to investors is purely financial. If a builder has reduced standard options to a minimum in order to have low base prices, the builder's profits may come from selling upgrades. Investors are notorious for foregoing expensive extras. If the market is reasonably strong and the builder can sell homes to homeowners who will splurge on options, why sell homes to investors and make less money on those sales? If you suspect this is the case with a builder, you may be able to buy a home if you agree to spend at least X amount on upgrades.

Overly Expensive Houses

You need to be careful not to buy houses which are too expensive. You've probably seen the pyramid that represents house buyers. There are lots of buyers for starter homes at the broad base of the pyramid. As the price increases, the number of qualifying buyers decreases. Multimillion dollar mansions located at the tiny tip are affordable for only a minute group of people.

This same pyramid exists for renters. There are many more renters at the bottom, less expensive, part of the pyramid. Because of the increased demand, these renters will pay a higher rent-to-property value ratio for an inexpensive rental. As you go up the pyramid the rent-to-value ratio will decrease until you will not be able to rent an expensive house for enough to give you a satisfactory rate of return on your investment.

How expensive is too expensive? Take a look at the median home prices for a given area. If you buy below those prices, you should be able to tap into a fairly sizeable rental pool of tenants. If you buy houses that exceed the median prices, you should be predicting some other financial benefit to make up for the low or negative cash flow.

For example, when I was a beginning investor, I made less than $20,000 per year. I wanted income to live on so I invested with an eye toward getting cash flow; the properties I purchased were inexpensive with good rent-to-value ratios. But as I started to earn more money from my job, I didn't need the extra money from my rentals to pay for day-to-day living costs. Then I became more interested in investing for long term appreciation rather than cash flow. Even negative cash flow became acceptable for the first time in my career as an investor. I considered the monthly payments contributions to my retirement fund.

With the tech crash in early 2001, the housing market in the Denver area started to soften. The rental market became downright soggy. The boom of the nineties had led to the construction of numerous luxury apartment complexes each with hundreds of units. With weak real estate prices and low interest rates, the best tenants were becoming home buyers. Although I had room to drop my rents on my suburban Denver houses and still have decent cash flow, I could see that my overall rate of return would be low for quite a few years.

One day while trying to chase down rent from a dead beat tenant, I drove past Stapleton. I'd been interested in this neighborhood's investment potential since the old airport closed, but that had been almost a decade ago. I hadn't been keeping track and didn't realize the project was finally getting off the ground. Thank God for that delinquent tenant, or I might have missed this particular opportunity. When I saw the signs and the framing for the first few houses going up, I turned in to investigate.

I discovered that the master developer had carefully selected builders who would construct housing in price range tiers, starting at the bottom end with condominiums and up through progressively larger single family homes. The only builder who would sell to investors offered houses at what was then the top price tier. I knew that buying a relatively expensive house would mean that my rents would fall short of my mortgage payments.

Despite the negative cash flow, I saw the potential for sizeable appreciation. Over the relative short term, I suspected the prices would bounce up after the nearest empty fields became filled with fancy new houses, swimming pools, parks and retail stores. Just as most home buyers can't visualize new carpet in an older home, they also can't envision a new development. Plus there exists the legitimate risk that a development will stall, leaving the pioneer buyers responsible for improvement bonds for sewers and roads meant to be paid for by hundreds of home owners instead of dozens. Therefore prices sometimes have to be lower than market value to get the first wave of houses sold.

In this case, I was able to confirm that the prices were indeed below market. The builder I was considering, the one who was willing to sell a limited number of homes to investors, was building the same floor plans in the redevelopment of Lowry Air Force Base, located just twenty or so blocks to the south of Stapleton. Both developments were infill Denver developments, meaning they offered new houses with modern amenities close to downtown. Yet Stapleton, in my opinion, had an even better location because of easy access to major roads and the new airport. Lowry's advantage was it was almost completely redeveloped. Would-be buyers saw green grass and finished houses instead of dirt and bare wood framing.

The difference in the base prices for the same houses in these two comparable developments ranged from $50,000 to $55,000. The builder explained that $15,000 of that cost difference was due to structurally more expensive basements required by the soil conditions in Lowry, but I knew that five years into the future, buyers comparing Lowry to Stapleton wouldn't care how much it cost the builder to build essentially the same houses. Current buyers were paying a premium for Lowry houses.

I predicted that in two to three years prices would equalize if Stapleton actually followed its development plan that called for constructing close to a thousand houses and lots of retail store space by 2005. I was willing to endure $5,000 in negative cash flow per house each year in exchange for a $50,000 jump in value. This would be in addition to any normal appreciation experienced by Denver homes. And I would also be paying down my mortgages and saving money on taxes.

Even though these houses wouldn't have been my first choice if I'd been looking for cash flow, they've been perfect investments as part of a long term retirement plan. The appreciation on these otherwise overly expensive houses will hopefully make up for the poor cash flow. And even the cash flow has improved as the construction dust and noise has moved miles away from the original home sites. I've been able to raise rents a little as the neighborhood gains a positive reputation as a convenient and beautiful place to live.

Location and Appreciation

As a beginning investor I bought what I could afford. This translated into houses on the outskirts of town in both the Austin and the Denver metro areas. Over the years I observed how these properties, as well as properties in other locations, appreciated. I learned the financial advantages to investing where growth limits exist, either because of the terrain, surrounding development, or anti-growth laws. These locations appreciated much faster.

In both cities I saw how the desirable downtown neighborhoods appreciated more than the suburbs. As cities grow larger, people place an increasing premium on living close to work instead of commuting for hours each day from the suburbs. Yet there is only so much land located in a downtown area. The surrounding city acts as a limit. Looking back I wish I had bought closer to downtown Austin. Because Austin has decent rent-to-value ratios, I could have afforded to do that and I would have made a lot more from appreciation than I did on the suburban properties. They didn't start to appreciate until six years later, not until the city sprawled past them and these properties were closer to the city center than the even newer suburbs.

In contrast, the Denver suburban properties I owned did appreciate even in the early 1990s. Why? Because of anti-growth laws. Coloradans are terrified that the Front Range will become one endless sprawling city like Los Angeles. To protect against that happening they have created legal growth limits.

Yet even in the Denver area I avoid buying properties in the most distant suburbs. For example, the new airport, Denver International Airport, is located to the northeast of Denver smack in the middle of empty plains. Housing developments keep springing up between it and the city. The prices of the houses are low, but any investor faces significant risk in this area.

Any appreciation will be held in check because builders can easily buy more land in this area. In a soft market buyers will be able to get great deals from national builders who can survive for years with very lean margins. Or because of weak prices, buyers may be able to afford to buy in more desirable areas with mature trees and real city centers. That means anybody, including regular homeowners, who needs to sell their homes out here will have trouble doing so. Some sellers will become what I become accidental landlords, and take whatever rent they can get to help cover the mortgage payments of the properties they can't sell.

So rents will go through unpleasant cycles of extreme softness, prices will appreciate slowly, and lots of other investors will be tempted by the low purchase prices so rents will likely never get very firm due to lots of competing rentals. A rising tide may lift all boats, but in real estate location matters. The tide rises faster and more permanently in some areas.

If you are investing for long term appreciation you should buy properties with the best locations you can afford. It usually is wise to buy properties located close to light rail stations, downtown, a water attraction such as a lake or beach, a classy park or open space. Pick locations that will only get more desirable as time goes by.

Negative Cash Flow

The advantages of buying a property that produces positive cash flow are clear; you get paid every month with spendable cash for your efforts as a landlord, repair costs don't come out of pocket, and you have money available to prepay on the mortgage.

A property with negative cash flow means you are paying cash every month in the hope that the other three rates of return, tax savings, principal paydown and appreciation, will cover the negative cash flow plus still generate a worthwhile total rate of return. This is a riskier investment decision, but it can be worth it depending on the real estate market and your personal finances.

While investors with a limited income or accumulated assets typically find it easier to start in real estate by investing in their own home and staying there until that home can be rented out for positive cash flow, then moving to another future rental as owner occupants, investors with a larger income may not mind a negative payment each month.

When I started investing in real estate to keep as rentals, I couldn't imagine buying a property with a negative cash flow. My income barely covered my expenses. My goal was to have my properties pay me an income. When I first bought them, they needed to pay for themselves. I saved money and increased my cash flow by doing a lot of the maintenance work myself. Considering how much I was making per hour at my job, it made economic sense for me to be the one to repaint my properties inside and out, to stain decks and pull weeds.

Fourteen years later my financial situation had improved. My annual earned income combined with my husband's income sometimes exceeded $65,000. Instead of needing cash flow from my rentals, I became more concerned about achieving long term retirement goals as well as minimizing how much time I spent managing my properties.

Whereas before I avoided expensive properties because of poor cash flow, their advantages started to appeal to me. More expensive properties tend to be those with a better location, and the demand for them is likely to be stronger than for other properties. Therefore they will appreciate faster and rent more easily even in soft rental markets. Higher end tenants also tend to cause less property damage.

By exchanging most of my properties into new ones that cost almost twice as much as the ones I sold, I was able to double the value of the real estate I owned while still having only a handful of tenants. So I was able to increase the total value of my properties to meet new and higher retirement goals without having to invest more time in management and maintenance. In exchange I had to accept worse rent-to-property value ratios on these pricier homes.

Fixer Uppers

I'm a fixer upper at heart. I adore the idea of taking a dump and turning it into a beautiful home. Unfortunately, very few shabby houses are worth the time and effort it will take to get them into tip-top shape.

Why are modest fixer uppers usually not worth buying? Because lots of people enjoy fixing houses. They dream about making money through sweat equity. So fix up properties are in demand, especially at the low end of the market. A property which will sell fixed up for $180,000 will sell quickly at $165,000 in shabby condition in a good real estate market.

But after you spend $2,500 for new carpet, $1,500 for new vinyl, $3,500 for new paint inside and out, $3,000 to update the bathroom, $2,200 for a new furnace to replace the old one which has a cracked heat exchanger, $1,000 to fix and stain the deck and $700 for new landscaping, your sweat equity will equal a measly $600. Maybe twice that much if you do all the painting and none of the siding or trim boards need to be replaced. That's not much of a return for all the hours you spent working on the house. And if you live in the property while you fix it up, you'll have the stress of living in an on-going project. It's hard to relax when you're surrounded by endless things to do.

The best properties to buy for fix up are those properties located further up the price pyramid. If starter homes are selling for $170,000, then you should be looking at houses which will sell for at least $350,000 after you've fixed them up. The people who buy houses in this middle price range are usually not interested in earning sweat equity. They already have high paying jobs. Or they've gone through the fix up routine on their first house and have no intention of doing that again. What they want are houses that look great from the moment they buy them. Actually, they often insist on it. They'll pay the necessary price to buy a property in perfect condition.

But if you fix up a property in a higher price range, it won't be in the ideal price range to keep as a rental if you need cash flow. Your best option may be to first rent it out for a year to establish it as an investment property, then fix it up and sell it as part of a 1031 tax defer exchange into one or two smaller houses which would be more profitable as long term rental properties. Of course, you could also fix up and sell the property immediately, but then you may incur a higher tax liability. The IRS tends to regard fast fixing and flipping profits as earned income rather than capital gains.

In some cases fixer uppers can be profitable and a great way to build your initial investment nest egg. Generally it's better to do fix-ups in more expensive neighborhoods. A 10% profit margin on a $400,000 house is substantial, whereas that same 10% margin on a $100,000 house may not be worth the time to earn it.

Older neighborhoods in desirable locations offer the broadest range in values. Some houses may be forty years out-of-date while others have been completely renovated. A neighborhood with this type of mix of values gives you the opportunity to buy something dated, improve it, and have comparables to justify the high sales price to the buyers and the appraiser. Then you could exchange your proceeds into properties that make more sense to hold as rental properties, meaning less expensive properties with better rent-to-value ratios.

Getting a Discount

I spent my first few years as a real estate investor buying dumps, fixing them up and selling them. When I realized that I had created a part-time job for myself but wasn't accumulating assets, I decided to keep my properties instead of selling them. I also figured out that at the prices I could afford to pay at that time, it was very difficult to make money on fixer-uppers. So I switched to buying houses in great shape that I could immediately rent to tenants.

Even if you buy properties that don't need a lot of work, you can still pay less than full market price. Here are three common and easy ways I've discovered to get a discount from some special sellers. Plus if you are willing to do a bit of fix-up, I've added my favorite type of problem property as a fourth suggestion.

Flexible Seller #1

The first type of flexible seller are homeowners who are building a new house. Let's say John and Patti Smith have a long time, maybe four to six months, to sell their current home before the new one will be ready. It seems as if they are in a good position to hold tight and get their full price.

In actuality these sellers have a big worry - what will they do if someone buys their old house before the new one is finished? No builder is dumb enough to set a final closing date until a new house is almost ready for delivery, yet how many buyers will purchase the sellers' old house without knowing when they will have possession?

Most people looking for a home want to move in as soon as they close, forcing John and Patti to make a double move complete with two kids, one cat, and a household of valuable furniture. This double move will cause havoc in their lives and cost them money. But if instead they wait for the builder to give them a final closing date, they may not have enough time to get their old house sold and then they'll lose the new house. These sellers are between a rock and a hard place.

You, the friendly investor, can be the perfect solution to their problem. You will close on the sale of their old house well before the estimated completion date for their new home. Until the new house is ready, the sellers can rent back their old home from you.

Although this is an ideal situation for the sellers, John and Patti will not want to pay you market rent for the property. Market rent is almost always far higher than the mortgage payment they are used to paying. They will balk at the idea of paying you $300 extra for two or three months. But oddly enough, while negotiating the contract they will agree to knock thousands of dollars off the price of their house. It can be profitable for you to offer a low rent in exchange for a good price.

For example, let's say the market rent is $1,300. The house is priced at $151,000, and you think it's worth $159,000. You offer to buy the house and rent it to the sellers for $1,000 per month for the three months until their new house is ready, but you want a $3,000 reduction on the already low price. Will they sell it to you for $148,000? Probably yes.

Mathematically this makes no sense. In exchange for $300 off the market rent for three months for a total savings of $900, why drop an already aggressive price by $3,000? Yet I've seen this type of offer accepted over and over again. Sellers understand monthly payments because they are used to paying their mortgages. They are very sensitive to their monthly budget. The equity tied up in their home, however, seems like funny money. They don't hold onto it as tightly.

It's easy to find out if sellers are having a new house built. The multiple listing ad may mention a delayed closing date or ask for a rent-back agreement. If you meet the sellers when you are looking at the house, they will be happy to tell you why they are moving because they are so excited about their new home.

If nothing is mentioned in the advertising material and you never get a chance to talk to the sellers, have your agent mention to the listing agent that you are thinking about making an offer. In order to make it as attractive to the sellers as possible, you want to know what closing date the sellers would prefer since you've got some flexibility. Listing agents will generally volunteer the uncertainty about the closing date in response to this question.

Making the Offer

When you make your offer, don't make your lease part of the negotiation. A long lease added to the contract may confuse the sellers. Instead, include a short clause that the purchase contract is contingent upon buyer and seller signing a lease back agreement within a short period of time. I usually give seven days to get a lease signed, or the purchase contract terminates (always remember to use time deadlines and consequences if something doesn't happen).

In your rental clause, state the modest rent the sellers will owe each month for the first two or three months of the lease, or however long they think it will take for the new house to be ready, and then include something that says the rent will go to market rent of X dollars after that point in time. After all, you don't want a permanent tenant at below market rates in case the new house deal falls through and the sellers are forced to stay in their old home for a while. Also, by specifying what the market rate is, you give the sellers the chance to appreciate what a great rent you are offering to them.

In the lease you should specify that the sellers must give you a certain amount of notice before they move, preferably at least thirty days since that's probably the notice the builder of their new home will give them. Your lease must give you the right to show the house to prospective tenants after the sellers have given you the thirty day notice. Specify exactly what days of the weeks and at what times you will have the right to show the property. Don't use some general phrase such as at mutually agreeable times; what if no time ends up being agreeable to them? Make sure the sellers are motivated to honor the terms of the lease by including the right for you to hold a security deposit. See Chapter Ten for ideas of what you may want to cover in the lease.

Flexible Seller #2

A new home builder's nightmare is to have a buyer's loan denied right before closing. The builder has a finished home with high monthly carrying costs sitting in inventory. If that builder knew someone who could close FAST, there is room to negotiate on the price, even in a hot real estate market.

Denver enjoyed a robust real estate market during the 1990s, but I was offered attractive prices when I let on-site salespeople for builders know that I was an investor who could get a loan quickly. Did they have any deals that were about to crash and burn? Would they like to keep my card in case of future emergencies? Most builders are happy to accept the original contract price or even less despite an appreciating market that has made a house more valuable by the time it's built. They want finished houses to be sold houses. A few questions when you're out looking at new homes may save you thousands of dollars.

If a particular development really interests you, visit it regularly during slow times such as weekdays. You'll become a familiar, friendly face to the on-site salespeople. Hopefully you'll be the first person they call if an opportunity comes up.

Flexible Seller #3

The people who own houses next door to your rentals may tell you they want to sell before they talk to an agent, offering to split with you the amount they save by not having to pay a commission. But why should you split the difference when otherwise they'll have to pay it all for another buyer who is brought to them by an agent? Feel free to compliment them on their lovely property, but make them an offer that is at least 5% below fair market value. Tell the sellers you know it's a low offer, and you wish them the best of luck in getting more. But if they should decide they need to sell fast, they should give you a call. And in the meantime, if they list with an agent they should write into the listing contract a provision that states that if they do decide to sell the house to you, they won't owe the agent a commission.

This approach works well for me. Once some neighbors wanted $139,900 for a house I valued at $138,000. I told the sellers I would be willing to pay them $132,000, but wished them luck in finding someone who would pay them more. A month later both of the sellers had lined up jobs in their home state of Minnesota, and they needed to sell fast. They called me, I showed my husband the house, and we bought it for $132,000. I only wish I had given them a lower offer in the first place!

This type of situation can occur with people other than the neighbors of your rentals. Anybody who knows you are an investor may ask you to consider buying their house. So let the world know you are in the market for rental houses. You can save thousands of dollars by broadcasting this tidbit of information far and wide.

Flexible Seller #4

Though I've warned you that many fix-up properties aren't profitable, a property with a certain kind of fixable problem can often be purchased at a worthwhile discount. The defect? Cat urine in the carpeting (and maybe the subfloor and walls, too!). It smells dreadful, and buyers legitimately wonder if they will ever be able to completely eliminate the odor. This problem also discourages the sweat equity folks who plan to improve a property over time. They don't want to live with that smell until they can afford to buy new carpeting, padding, and possibly new plywood subfloor.

Twice my sister purchased properties in Austin with a cat urine problem. The most recent one was shown to her in the fall of 2001. The 2,100 square foot house had five bedrooms, three full baths, a separate living room and family room plus a dining room, and a two car garage. Its amenities perfectly suited the group home tenants she had lined up to rent her next house.

The kitchen and bathrooms were dated, the family room was paneled in inexpensive dark wood, and the tiny backyard lacked landscaping, but these faults weren't major issues. Shelley knew her tenants wouldn't mind them. But the overwhelming scent of cat urine in the front hallway was too awful to ignore.

Shelley's agent told her the asking price started out at $147,000 before being reduced to $139,900. Fixed up, Shelley thought the house would be worth as much as $158,000. She would have to treat the subflooring and buy new carpet and pad to eliminate the smell.

She also planned to spruce the place up with new vinyl and new appliances. She and her husband could do most of the work themselves, but they wanted to get paid for their work by getting a good price. They figured their fix up expenses would total approximately $5,000.

Shelley really wanted the property and was willing to pay $135,00, but the agent and I persuaded her to offer $127,400. The sellers countered with $130,000. Shelley accepted the counter immediately. Even after including her fix up costs she believes she purchased the house at a 15% discount.

Condominiums and Townhouses

Condominium and townhouses are called attached housing. Homeowners associations usually handle most or all of the exterior maintenance, but sometimes the property owner is responsible for the roof maintenance and exterior painting. Always check the covenants before you buy so you aren't surprised by unexpected responsibilities and expenses. Also evaluate whether the association's reserves are adequate for the expenses they are supposed to cover.

Buying attached units may be your best choice if you have little spare time. Neither you nor your tenants will have to worry about shoveling walks, mowing grass, or doing exterior maintenance. But if you lose or quit your job, you will not have the option of handling your own maintenance in exchange for not paying your monthly fee. You also won't have much control over how the association is managed unless you are willing to join the board in charge of making the group spending decisions.

The biggest drawback to buying attached housing is its price volatility. In a weak real estate market the prices of attached units fall faster than do the prices of single family homes. On the other hand, these prices also appreciate faster when the market strengthens again.

What does this mean for you? You should be cautious about buying attached housing in an up market. Your downside risk is much greater than it would be if you owned single family homes. If your area is experiencing a down cycle, you may want to wait until prices appear to have bottomed out, then load up on as many attached units as you can prudently afford. When the market recovers, you'll get a higher rate of appreciation on your money invested in attached housing than you would on single family houses.

In the late eighties oil prices dropped sharply. People who worked in oil dependent states such as Texas, Oklahoma and Colorado lost their jobs. Some moved away to take new jobs. Others couldn't afford to make their house payments. Foreclosure rates skyrocketed as housing units were dumped on the market. Real estate prices weakened, then sank.

I was in college at this time. With a limited income and no savings I couldn't take advantage of the situation. I knew a successful businessman, however, who decided to visit a brand new condominium complex near his office. Units which had been selling for $65,000 were available for only $45,000. He eagerly bought four units.

But prices continued to drop. Soon units with two bedrooms were selling for $22,000 and one bedroom units were selling for $17,000. Due to the monthly homeowners association fee, it was hard to rent the properties for a positive cash flow even at prices this low. Why? Because potential renters were either buying properties at bargain prices, or they were negotiating hard with property owners.

Instead of panicking because his first four units had dropped in value by more than 50%, Jerry bought another thirteen units in this same complex. Unwilling to manage the units himself, he hired a property manager. The management fees on top of the other costs produced a negative cash flow every month. Fortunately, he could afford the small monthly alligator produced by the combination of high expenses and low rents.

After a few years the market turned around. Prices and rents both went up. Soon the properties were producing a cash flow of over $50,000 per year. When Jerry retired, this extra income allowed him to enjoy a comfortable lifestyle. In the fall of 1997, and again in the winter of 2005, he and his wife treated all five of their children and their children's spouses, plus the grandchildren, to a cruise in the Caribbean. Jerry's patience and the courage he displayed by investing in condominiums in a down market paid off handsomely.

If your area is experiencing an up real estate market, but you don't have the time to take care of single family homes, attached housing may still be your best option. Look for units which are as nice as houses. Units with garages are best. Luxurious master baths will always be in demand. Basements offer valuable storage. People also prefer end units because they have neighbors on only one side.

A desirable location for an attached unit is more critical than it is for a house. While townhomes or condominiums in the suburbs are often second-best to houses, purchased or rented only because they are more affordable, attached housing in an urban environment can be part of the desired city lifestyle. The occupants of these properties don't want to take care of a yard. Instead they want to enjoy the cultural amenities of living close to nightclubs, museums, and theaters. Even if the real estate market softened, they would not prefer to move into a house.

You should probably avoid converted apartments in most smaller cities. If these units feel like boxy apartments rather than more upscale condominiums, they will be the least desirable of all attached housing. Their prices are the first to suffer in a down market and are the last to recover. In addition some lenders will refuse to provide financing for converted units. In general, you should buy converted apartments only if they are highly desirable in your area.

Duplexes, Triplexes and Four-plexes

The biggest advantage of these small multi-unit properties is their financing. Unlike large complexes which require commercial financing, you can buy these properties using owner occupant or investor residential financing.

The biggest drawback is trying to find small multi-unit properties in good locations. Zoning tends to cluster these types of properties in unappealing settings. I've seen many side streets filled with tacky looking four-plexes. The front yards are nonexistent, sacrificed to make room for parking spaces. The tenants' cars look like they've seen much better days and everything feels dirty. Who would want to live in an area like this? Not you nor anyone else who is likely to keep a rental unit in good condition.

You may find an exception to the situation I've just described, a nice small multi-unit located in a pleasant residential neighborhood. That property would most likely be a good one to own. Do, however, avoid other properties which are surrounded by an entire trashy block. You could fix up your building to look nice, but it won't help if all your neighbors don't care about their properties.

Many people I talk with are convinced they can make a ton of money by owning a duplex or four-plex. They assume multi-units are always profitable so they don't bother to look at the rate of return numbers. They often end up paying far more for a property than its rents will justify. I'm not sure where this idea that multi-plexes are always incredibly profitable comes from, but it isn't necessarily true.

If you want to buy a multi-plex, do the numbers. You're investing to make money. What would your projected total rate of return be if you buy a multi-unit? What would it be if you bought a house instead? Learn about your market so you can make educated decisions.

If you do buy a multi-unit, your units will be inexpensive compared to single family housing. This may mean you will get tenants who are not as financially stable. Even if you carefully select tenants who have finances like the Rock of Gibraltar, you will still probably have to spend more time managing the property. After all, if a four-plex costs $300,000 in your area, and two single family homes cost $150,000 apiece, then you're going to have twice as many tenants for the same total investment. Your rate of return must be higher than you could get buying single family homes to make it worth your while.

Apartment Houses

Buying apartment houses is not the focus of this book though much of the information provided will still apply. Rates of return can be attractive, but managing many small units is a full-time job. Eventually, if your property is large enough, you'll be able to afford to hire a resident manager, but that may be years away.

Just as with small multi-unit buildings, the supply of small apartment houses is limited. You will have to look in a larger market area, perhaps buying a building that is not located close to your own home.

The best opportunities for profit occur if you are willing to take on a problem building. One of my students told me about a building with approximately thirty units he bought on the opposite side of Denver from where he lived. One tenant was using a ground floor unit as a drive-up drugstore for illegal drugs. Other tenants were equally shady.

The seller wanted out and was flexible on the financing terms and purchase price. Though my student would have preferred a building that was closer to his home, he wanted a property he felt he could improve for profit.

For the next two years he drove to the apartment house almost daily to handle evictions, repairs, and to show the property to new tenants. Over time he eliminated the bad tenants and replaced them with good tenants. Though this man does not intend to keep the building forever because of the large amount of time it requires, he should do very well when he decides to sell. His building is a far more attractive and valuable investment property now than when he bought it.

Functional Obsolescence

Whatever properties you buy, keep in mind the concept of functional obsolescence. Forty years ago it was okay in the Denver area for a house to have only a carport. Thirty-five years ago new houses featured one car garages or even two car garages. Now two car garages are standard and three is considered luxurious.

The same situation has happened with bathrooms. My grandmother's house had a bath which was accessible only through the bedrooms with no direct access from a hallway. As time went by, houses started to be built with half baths located on the main floor. Then master bedrooms appeared with private three quarter baths. Now many new houses are being built with five piece master baths. These bathrooms have a separate oval tub and shower plus two sinks and a walk-in closet.

In either of these examples the older houses are less desirable not only because of their age, but because they lack features expected in a modern property. This same problem occurs in apartment units without room to install microwave ovens or enough counter space for the numerous modern appliances Americans own today. These problems are built-in and can be costly or impossible to fix.

Always try to buy properties which are as close to the current standards as possible. In any given price range some houses have more desirable features than do others. It's hard to predict future trends, but I think people will continue to want multi-car garages, nice master baths, and kitchens with plenty of space. Personally I've noticed a sharp upswing in the demand for air conditioning over the past few years.

Watch for articles in your newspaper or visit model homes to learn what people want. Current home buyers, and presumably tenants as well, are looking for kitchens with islands, space for multiple cooks, large pantries, some sort of visual connection with the family or great room, plus a window above the sink.

Also popular are main level master bedrooms, media rooms for a home theater system, separate studies on the main level, and higher ceilings for a feeling of spaciousness. In terms of neighborhood amenities parks and bike paths are replacing preferences for tennis courts or swimming pools. The more features that modern buyers/tenants want that are present in or around your properties, the longer it will take before the properties become functionally obsolescent and less desirable to tenants or future buyers.

Falling in Love

Most real estate investment books will tell you to look only at the numbers on a property. Whether you personally like the property is supposed to be beside the point.

But as a small investor looking to purchase five or so properties, you can and should really like your rental units. Feel free to buy houses with views of the mountains or the lake. Admire the five piece master bath. Marvel at the feeling of spaciousness created by the vaulted ceiling. You'll be proud of your properties and tenants will be eager to live in them.

All houses are NOT created equal. Some have very small backyards while others have yards which are difficult to reach because there is no back door. Some lots back up to a four lane street or a highway. These types of backyards aren't positive features. Home buyers want private backyards with easy access and so do tenants.

I've seen the dumbest things. Narrow, twisting staircases in houses less than five years old, floor plans that make no sense, houses with windows only on the north side, and houses located next to busy streets or commercial buildings. On paper these houses look fine because the agent writing the description neglects to mention the problems. When your agent shows you the properties, you discover that they aren't nearly as nice as you anticipated.

It's okay to look at fifty houses to find the one that sings, though it usually takes me no more than twenty before I find one

I want to buy. I listen for the music when I step into a house. Maybe the house is smaller than what I would want to live in, but that's okay. Would it be ideal for some potential tenants? Would this darling two bedroom, two bath house be perfect for a single person, two roommates, or a single parent? Is this four bedroom house located in a popular school district so families with children would want to live in it? And most of all, would tenants who take pride in their homes want to live there?

Comparing Properties

If you want to compare two properties you like, project the rates of return for each of them. You want to know what your projected annual rate of return would be on your invested money if you bought property A versus property B. If you think you can earn 25% the first year on property A or 28% on property B, all other things being equal you should buy property B.

How do you project your anticipated rate of return? Use the worksheets provided in the Appendices. The maintenance cost worksheet in Appendix B will help you to predict the expenses you would have for each property averaged over ten years. This figure is your anticipated average annual maintenance expense. It can vary quite a bit. For example, a brick house with a new furnace and roof will likely have less anticipated maintenance costs than a twenty-year-old frame house with its original furnace and roof. Yet the higher price for the brick house may end up canceling some or all of your savings, especially if rents are comparable. So we need to look at the rest of the numbers.

Next complete the rate of return worksheet in Appendix D. Call the tax assessor for tax rates and the percentage of the purchase price attributed to the improvements so you can calculate your depreciation amount. Call your insurance agent for a rough quote on each property. Ask your lender or real estate agent to help you with the loan payments for principal, interest and any mortgage insurance premiums. The lender can also tell you the down payment and closing costs you will need to get a loan. The real estate agent should be able to help you project what appreciation, if any, you can expect in the near future.

Finally you need to do some research to come up with the rents you think you can charge. Look for "For Rent" signs in the neighborhoods of your properties. Call on ads in the newspaper to find comparable properties. Ask your real estate agent, or check with an appraiser (appraisers do rent surveys as part of their appraisals when people buy houses or attached units for rental properties). Talk to other investors. Or check the tax records to learn the names of non-occupant owners who own similar properties, find their phone numbers, and ask them what rents they are getting (this is what the appraisers do if necessary).

When you've completed the rate of return worksheet for both properties you'll be able to compare the projected rates of return you would receive. True, your projections are based on a lot of educated guesses about maintenance costs, future appreciation, the stability of interest rates if you are getting an adjustable rate loan, plus how much rent you'll receive. But if you are consistent in your approach, you should be able to at least compare these two properties against each other to determine which one would be the better purchase.

If the difference in the projected rates of return is dramatic, you might want to recheck your numbers and the assumptions you made. Did you make a mistake either for or against one of the properties? If your numbers stand up to review, you should buy the property with the higher projected rate of return if the properties are otherwise comparable. Of course, you may be willing to accept a lower rate of return for a property located conveniently close to your home or work, or if it is in some other way particularly desirable to you.

Deciding Between Two Available Properties - The Shortcut Method

If you don't want to take the time to analyze the projected rate of return numbers for two properties, you can use a more intuitive method instead to decide which one to buy. Let's say you are looking at two houses. One house has two bedrooms and a loft, a two car garage, and one and a half bathrooms. You like the layout, though the yard really needs a deck to make it attractive to either tenants or future buyers. The asking price is $135,000.

The other house has three bedrooms, a full bath, a three quarter master bath, and a three quarter bath in the basement. The layout is attractive, the yard has a deck, and the garage is a double. This house is the same age as the first one, seven years old. The price is $148,000. Which of these two houses would be the best one for you to buy?

First, ask your real estate agent or lender to tell you what the difference in the monthly payments would be. Let's say that including principal, interest, taxes and insurance, the second house will cost you $100 more per month.

Now ask yourself: If you were a renter who had $100 flexibility in how much rent you could afford to pay, how much more would you be willing to pay for the second house compared to the first? If the difference is more than $100, you should buy the second house. If it's less than $100, you should buy the first house.

Magic Price Point

When you shop for houses in the lower price ranges you'll notice that a ten or fifteen thousand dollar difference in price will equal a huge difference in the type of house you can buy. This is why home buyers (and renters) in the lower price ranges stretch themselves to their financial limits when they look for a home.

The example I just used of a two bedroom house asking $135,000 and a three bedroom house asking $148,000 is based on two houses I showed to a buyer on February 1, 1998. The thirteen thousand dollars difference in price equaled a third bedroom, a master bathroom instead of a shared one, plus an extra bathroom in the basement for guests.

When the buyer and I looked at houses which cost an additional thirteen thousand, that is $161,000 instead of $148,000, we didn't find such a contrast in features. The individual rooms became bigger or the architecture had expensive details, but the actual number of bedrooms and bathrooms and garage spaces stayed the same. Since a larger room size or stained trim is not as important as a private master bath or a third bedroom, this price increase didn't add key features.

The magic price point where a house became noticeably more desirable was somewhere between $135,000 and $148,000 for that neighborhood at that time. You should be able to find this same type of price point in your neighborhood, adjusting for the different prices in your area. If you can afford to buy just above this price point, that's the best single family home to buy.

Why? Because neither renters nor future buyers will have to compromise on basic desirable features when they look at your house. Someone who currently can't afford to rent a house without a master bathroom will eventually want to rent a house which has that private bath. A renter who already has all the minimum features expected in a modern American house, however, will not bother with moving until he or she is ready to buy.

If a potential tenant or buyer can afford to go to the other side of the magic price point, they will. This means that the second house in my example will always be easier to rent or to sell, saving you time and money. And the tenants you get will be more likely to stay for a couple of years. Therefore if you can afford it, buy a house above the magic price point.

Properties with Two Bathrooms

I look for properties with two bathrooms, meaning at least two toilets and preferably two showers. The cutest little house in the world won't interest me for long if there is only one bathroom. Why? Because if the only bathroom develops a problem, the tenants are correct if they think that this is an emergency. Since tenants notice problems when they are home, which is usually during the weekends and in the evenings when plumbers charge higher rates, a one bathroom house emergency can get expensive to fix. If your property has a second bathroom which is functional, then the plumber can be scheduled for regular business hours.

If you are buying smaller units such as one bedroom condominiums or apartment buildings with many small apartments, you will have units with only one bathroom. This is unavoidable. Up your budget for plumbing repairs accordingly.

Speculative Markets

Sometimes real estate values fall. In a normal market, they may just get soft for a few years. In a speculative market, overinflated prices can burst like an iridescent soap bubble. Values can drop significantly and take a decade to recover. Recent buyers take the biggest hit. All of their equity plus more can evaporate in a few months. Rates of return can be negative on their investments for years as they wait for prices to climb back to previous highs.

It's impossible to predict exactly when a real estate bubble will burst. Some call it too early and miss out on a lot of money, others call it too late and take a hit, while a lucky few sell at the optimum moment.

Generally houses should appreciate at least as quickly as the overall rate of inflation. Plus, even though new houses are built to accommodate rising populations, in some areas the land to build new housing is limited. So prices in these areas can appreciate faster that the rate of inflation and these increases can be sustainable. Locations that are limited by either physical constraints such as the ocean or by human constraints such as zoning laws and open space have the strong potential to appreciate faster.

But sometimes appreciation rates are fueled not by long term demand, but by speculators. These people see the strong appreciation rates and bid up prices. Others see prices appreciating even more and jump into the market. People who would normally sell their old homes when they move instead keep them as investments. This makes the supply of houses for sale even tighter and encourages even higher prices. People start to make tens of thousands of dollars every year or sometimes every few months. People engage in frantic bidding wars for every available property. Prices go up, up, up!

Until they don't. And when prices stop rising, a seller's market can disappear in no time at all. After all, these homes weren't being bought at high prices because that's what homeowners were willing to pay to live in them. Investors and homeowners alike were counting on appreciation to justify large monthly mortgage payments. Without the prospect of continuing outsized appreciation, the investors want out. Some regular homeowners will need to sell because of routine changes in their lives. Supply outpaces demand, and prices can plummet.

At what point in this cycle did it become speculative? How can you tell if an area where you may want to buy is entering a bubble? You'd hate to miss out on all this fabulous appreciation, but you don't want to be the last sucker to buy in either.

Here are some numbers to look at. First, has your market appreciated strongly, 10% or more annually, for five or more years? The bubble may or may not be about to burst, but it's already inflated. Prices tend to go through cycles. After five years of rapid appreciation, it's going to be harder for it to continue.

Second, take a look at interest rates. As interest rates drop, prices rise. People buy based on their monthly payment, not on the size of the principal balance of their loan. As rates rise, many buyers can't afford a higher payment. The maximum loan size they can qualify for restricts how much they can offer for a house. Buyers at the low end drop out of the market (good for increasing the supply of tenants, but not good for the demand for houses). Other buyers can still buy, but they are forced to be tougher negotiators. They can only afford to pay X, take it or leave it.

If you think interest rates are going to rise, you should reduce your anticipated appreciation on your investments. With lower appreciation, your projected rates-of-return may not be attractive. You will have to find ways to create value, or invest elsewhere.

Third, what are the rent-to-cost-to-own ratios for the area where you are considering investing? In expensive areas of the United States it can cost far less per month to pay rent than to own and have to pay mortgage costs plus maintenance expenses. In 2004 this ratio was as low as 40% in San Diego, 45% in San Francisco, 55% in Los Angeles, 59% in Washington D.C., and 64% in Miami. This compares to rates in the mid eighties for the Denver metropolitan area and over 100% in Austin.

Even though many East and West Coast cities have historically had higher appreciation rates and lower ratios of rent to ownership costs, super low rent ratios mean substantial negative cash flow. Do you really believe the appreciation rate will be high enough to make up for the negative rate of return on cash flow? Enough to give you a great rate of return to make up for the risk you're taking? Because if appreciation disappears for a few years, you would have been better off investing in mutual funds. Or at least investing in real estate somewhere else.

Moving to a Different City or State

It's possible in many areas of this country to buy property which will produce cash flow with 20% down or break even with only 10% down. You, though, may live somewhere with extremely high prices and low rent-to-property value ratios. Even with current low interest rates, starter homes in your area would produce no monthly cash flow or a negative cash flow even if you put down 30%. In addition, you're scared to buy in a housing market where the prices seem "frothy." You don't want to buy right before the local real estate market crashes.

If you are serious about investing in real estate, you may decide to move somewhere else. Maybe it would be worth it to take a job for less pay if you could move somewhere with a lower cost of living. Have you been dreaming about moving someplace far away from the rat race once you've made it financially? Maybe you should advance the time table for your moving plans.

If you've been offered a transfer, don't just tour around with an agent looking at homes you could buy. Also look at homes for rent and do some projected rate of return calculations. Ask your agent about state and local laws regarding rental properties. Is this state a property owner friendly state? Can you evict someone in less than a month, or can it take half a year? Once you add in the benefits of moving someplace where rentals are profitable, an only okay job offer could become really tempting.

If you're not willing to move, perhaps you should broaden the area where you are looking for potential rental properties. Sometimes you don't have to go very far. The city limits of Boulder and Westminster in Colorado are only twelve miles apart, yet the rent-to-property value ratios are quite different. Even if you chose to live in an expensive area, you could own properties in a nearby, less expensive, community.

Buying in a Different State

Sometimes people fall prey to the grass is greener somewhere else syndrome. They aren't willing to move to this other place, but they want to invest there. They, or more usually a developer who specializes in selling to investors, project rates of return that are so attractive it won't matter that they have to pay someone else to manage their properties for them.

Perhaps this other place really is a much better place to invest than where you live, but I have strong reservations about this idea. It's too easy to be overly optimistic about an area you don't know. Since you don't live there, you haven't learned about the problems. Instead you'll have to rely on someone else, probably someone who will make money if you decide to buy, to help you evaluate the investment possibilities.

It helps to invest with a local partner whom you trust explicitly as I did with my twin sister in Texas. Because your local partner lives in the area, he or she will hear all the news about problem areas and new development. Is the university expanding its enrollment without adding dormitories? Has hazardous waste seeped into the ground water to the west of town? Is a major corporation moving its headquarters to the north side? Whether bad or good, all this information is valuable.

Sometimes you don't have an investing partner, but you have either lived in an area in the past or you visit it often. Or maybe it's where you plan to move someday, so you want your rentals there. Or maybe it's where you grew up, and someday you want to move home. You may even have a family member or friend who can keep an eye on things for you (just don't expect too much if they aren't financially involved - an occasional drive-by to report on the exterior maintenance is probably going to be the limit of their help). In any case, subscribe to the local newspaper so you know what's happening there.

Plan on hiring a property manager unless you have a very flexible job. Renting out a property can take a few weeks, sometimes more. Routine maintenance is a major problem if it requires flying to town to fix something. Owning a property long distance means you'll have to pay someone else to do a lot of the work. Of course, that may be fine with you - you don't want to do that kind of work in the first place! As long as the property produces enough cash flow to cover costs, or you have excess income to cover a negative cash flow, owning long distance can work.

Looking with an Agent

Finding a good agent can be difficult. When my sister moved to Texas she told many agents that she planned to buy six rental properties in twelve months. At the start, perhaps because she hadn't yet bought any properties, we understood when none of the agents seemed excited. But when she told them she had purchased three houses in the past six months, and she wanted to buy three or four more, we were surprised when the agents failed to follow up.

Why did this happen? Because most agents look for the best buyer they can find, defined as someone who needs to buy within two months because their lease ends or their old house is being sold or the company paid housing allowance is about to expire. In contrast, investors don't have to buy unless they are in the middle of 1031 tax deferred exchanges. Agents also worry that many investors are looking for the impossible-to-find fabulous deals. If all an investor does is look without buying, the real estate agent will have wasted time and energy showing property. Unless the market is slow, many agents prefer to work with home buyers, not investors.

What can you do? You can ask people you know to refer you to agents. Agents like getting referrals so they take more care with referred clients. They know that if they don't, the flow of referrals might stop. So even if they aren't sure how serious you are, they may still be willing to invest some time with you in order to keep the referring person happy.

You can also find agents by calling on ads in the paper or by going to open houses. Look for a good click between you and the agent. Do you trust this person? Do they seem to know what they are talking about? Does the agent own rental properties? An agent who is a property owner can tell you what the market rents are based on experience and can better help you project your rates of return.

In my opinion the best agent of all is one who is also an investor in the type of properties you want to buy. Some investors don't want to work with agents who are also investors. They believe the agents will keep all the good deals for themselves. This is partially true. The agents will buy any super deals if they can afford to do so. If you want a super deal, you'll have to find it yourself. But if you want a good value, successful investor agents can be a great source of leads.

Agents who are investors are more familiar with investor loans, tenant-landlord laws, and going rent rates. Agents like the one I work with often have a policy of offering their investor clients first dibs on most properties. David has sometimes quickly put a good house under contract so no one else could buy it, and then offered to assign his contract to his clients, figuring if none were interested he would keep the property for himself.

I also like agents who are loan brokers (yes, my agent is a loan broker, and that's worked out great for me). Just as an agent will frequently reduce his or her usual commission on a listing if the seller buys a replacement house with that agent, an agent who is a mortgage broker can offer cheaper loans if you buy a property using that agent. But do shop their rates to make sure you are actually getting a discount.

Helping Your Agent

You can make your agent's job easier if you are willing to take a list of houses she or he gives you and drive by the houses without the agent in tow. As long as your local market isn't hot, you can receive a faxed list of new properties two or three times a week and have time to do a drive-by preview before scheduling a showing with the agent.

You can also tour the open houses each weekend. This will help you discover the neighborhoods you like. Agents don't want to hear that you are willing to look at anything. They want a specific target. If you can tell them where you would like to buy, that's a great help.

Remember, do not get so excited at an open house that you write an offer with the agent who is sitting there. If another agent has been working with you, and you think she or he is competent, call that agent to write up the offer. If your agent isn't available, and you're worried that someone else might make a competing offer that same day, ask another agent in your agent's office to help you. Explain to them that you are working with someone else at their office, but you need help today. The agents can work out how to share the commission later.

Buyer's Agent

Hiring a buyer's agent is generally a good idea. If an agent knows that you will buy through him or her, then it makes sense for that agent to invest time in you. In the beginning you may want to sign a short term contract, perhaps for one to three months. If you decide you like the agent you can always extend the agreement.

What If Your Agent Doesn't Do a Good Job?

Sometimes agents will insist on long term buyer agency agreements. What happens if you sign a buyer agency contract and later decide that the agent isn't giving you enough attention? Or that the agent isn't competent?

In most states it is very easy for the consumer to break a buyer's agency agreement. If you feel you aren't getting good service, write a letter to the real estate company's managing broker and tell him or her that you want to break the agreement based on the agent's failure to do his or her part as an agent. Specify exactly what you want that you aren't receiving.

The managing broker may tell your agent to get with it or may ask you to work with a different agent. If the agent you signed up with is also the broker, you can write a letter to him or her directly. If service doesn't improve, insist on the agent agreeing to terminate the contract. If the agent refuses, call your state's real estate commission. The people there can tell you exactly what your rights are and how to assert them.

Only in the worst case situation would you have to consult a lawyer. Most agents want happy customers and will respond quickly to clearly presented complaints. If your agent is not a good agent, merely mentioning that you will be calling the real estate commissioner may be enough to get him or her to cooperate in releasing you from your contract.

Feeling Nervous

When I started in the real estate investment business I was in my twenties. I set a goal, found houses I could afford, made offers and bought properties. I never felt nervous.

To my surprise, that changed in my thirties. Despite my years of success and experience, buying houses began to make me nervous. What was the difference? Perhaps in my twenties I had nothing to lose. Or maybe it's because many properties in Colorado don't produce a positive cash flow anymore. Who wants to sign up for a monthly payment that requires management work, too?

Yet when I look for alternatives, all I see are variations on the stock market. I can buy stocks myself or invest in a mutual fund. Or I could invest in a business (actually, I did try that and lost roughly $90,000 - ouch!). In the end, real estate still looks like the best investment to me. I've certainly done well owning houses so far.

Feeling nervous can be an advantage. It may motivate you to negotiate harder, take a closer look at your projections, and keep your overall debt obligations to a minimum. These are good things. Yet nerves can stop you from ever getting into the game. That would be a shame.

If you are feeling nervous, here are a few suggestions. Become more educated about your market so you trust your predictions about the future of real estate in your area. Get a partner to share the risk. Put down more money so your loan payments are smaller. Track your family finances so you can see where the money will come from to cover a negative cash flow. Set aside an emergency fund to deal with unexpected costs or an extended vacancy. Postpone buying your first investment property for one or two years while you save money or increase your income. Space out your purchases to make sure you can handle what you have before you rush out to get something else.

But please, don't become one of the people I meet so often who tell me they would have made so much money if only they had followed their hunch to buy real estate twenty or thirty years ago. Taking a risk is scary sometimes, but isn't it even scarier to think about yourself in the future bemoaning the properties you didn't buy? If you want to reach your financial goals, at some point you must get into the game.

Making an Offer

I love making offers. The thrill of the hunt, the strategy of the negotiation, the satisfaction of getting a good property under contract! Yet you must remember that you are an investor. Fall in love with properties, but don't lose your good sense. In most cases, you can find another property equally as good as the one you want today if you and the seller don't come to agreement. Often you'll find a property you like even more. There are LOTS more properties out there, so don't get stuck on any particular one. If you are willing to walk away from any deal, you'll be in a strong negotiating position.

It's almost always worth it to make a lower offer than what you're willing to pay. One exception would be the property that's already underpriced by the seller - go ahead, snap it up! Another exception is if you are involved in a 1031 tax deferred exchange and you're running out of time to identify your replacement property (which is a good reason to start looking well ahead of your exchange deadlines - don't wait until the last week).

Remember, too, that it's okay to change your mind about a potential purchase, even if originally the deal looked great. During the inspection period, or when you apply for a loan, you may discover issues that make you uncomfortable. Maybe there is more damage than you originally noticed, or a loan for this type of property is very expensive or difficult for you to afford.

It's hard to let go of a cheap property, but sometimes it isn't worth it no matter how low the price. Enjoy the excitement of the hunt, but don't let your emotions cloud your judgement. Remember, if you're a beginner your best deals probably won't be your first ones. You will find better bargains later after you've learned more about real estate and can confidently recognize the truly great deals.

Chapter Five

Loans

Most people have gone through the loan application process at least once, but they don't understand how the lender qualified them. They know it had something to do with their income and their debts, but how this information was transformed into a maximum loan amount is unclear.

This chapter will show you how lenders qualify borrowers and how you can find lenders with more generous qualifying standards. We'll also discuss the different kinds of loans which are available. Discussing loans means talking about numbers, but don't worry. If you don't like math, you can let the lenders tell you how much you can borrow without doing the numbers yourself. But you should understand this important fact: different types of lenders qualify borrowers using different criteria. So if one lender won't give you a loan, others may be willing to let you borrow from them.

Before you start going from one lender to the next, you need to learn how to tell if two lenders are the same type of lender or different. Otherwise you'll waste your time. You may think that by asking five lenders for a loan and being turned down by all of them that you've explored five lending opportunities. But if these five lenders all use the same qualifying requirements, you may as well have talked to only one.

Even if the first lender you talk with tells you they will give you a loan, you should still investigate other possibilities. Why?

Because the first lender may not have the best loan for you. Another lender may be offering a different loan you would prefer if only you knew it existed. You can't rely solely on your real estate agent to direct you to the best or most flexible lenders in town. Many agents are not familiar with the more unusual loans which are available.

Loans can be divided into three broad categories: government backed FHA and VA loans, conforming and non-conforming conventional loans which are frequently referred to as Fannie Mae loans, and portfolio loans. Different lenders or mortgage brokers will offer loans in one or more of these categories. For clarity's sake, I will discuss the lenders/mortgage brokers as if each offers loans in only one category.

FHA (Federal Housing Authority) and VA (Veterans Administration) loans offer very low to zero down payments. Mortgage insurance premiums or funding fees are charged to the borrowers to insure these loans since the down payments are so small. These loans are generally offered only to owner occupants though FHA does offer some special loans designed for investors which require larger down payments than for owner occupant loans.

Most real estate agents can help you with questions you have about FHA or VA loans. The qualifying ratios for these loans are handled similarly to the conventional loans (ratios are discussed in more depth later in this chapter). Because the government programs come with large funding fees or upfront mortgage insurance costs, you should try to get a conventional loan instead whenever possible. However, these loans can be good for people with spotty job histories as they are more forgiving about problems like that.

Conventional lenders typically require minimum down payments of 3-5% for owner occupants and 10-20% for investors. Some conventional lenders strictly follow Fannie Mae guidelines when they originate conventional loans. These loans are frequently called conforming conventional loans. If you as a borrower can meet the guidelines, you will be approved for the loan you want.

And if you don't meet these guidelines, you probably won't get the loan because this lender can't bend the qualifying rules very much.

A second type of conventional lender requires the same down payment percentages, but is more flexible about bending the Fannie Mae guidelines. This lender will allow you to have higher ratios than is normally allowed. You may also be able to put down only 10% on investor loans. These conventional loans are sometimes called non-conforming conventional loans.

Portfolio lenders also originate loans, but unlike conventional lenders who plan to eventually sell most or all of their loans, portfolio lenders tend to keep their mortgages. This means they don't have to follow Fannie Mae guidelines. They set their own rules, and they can break them if they think you are a good credit risk. In other words, they have the flexibility to practice "make sense" underwriting when they evaluate loan applicants.

Conventional Loan Lenders

Most homeowners in America get a conventional loan if they don't get a FHA or VA loan. As an owner occupant you can get 100% financing (you'll have to pay mortgage insurance premium (MIP) unless you put down at least 20%, or do a combination first mortgage/second mortgage). Conventional fixed interest rate loans are available to investors with a minimum of 20% down. If you can qualify for a conventional investor loan, these loans are some of the most desirable ones because they usually offer the best fixed rates available.

Sometimes the conventional lenders will also offer community home loans to first time buyers or to households with limited incomes. These community home loans usually have very attractive interest rates and low origination costs.

Most lenders who originate conforming conventional loans do not keep them. Having your loan sold may be a minor inconvenience to you when you keep getting notices to send your mortgage payments to different lenders, but it also has a more serious consequence for you as an investor.

Since these lenders plan to immediately sell the loans they originate, they need to make sure these loans will be salable on the secondary market. This means they must follow the Fannie Mae guidelines exactly. These guidelines tend to disqualify many small investors who do not have large incomes.

Secondary Loan Market

Overall, the existence of the secondary market for mortgages is advantageous because it allows for a free flow of money across the United States as well as between nations. If more money is available to loan in California than there are people who want to borrow it, the large institutional investors who have this extra money can buy mortgages originated someplace else. The institutional investors in other countries may also choose to purchase U.S. mortgage backed securities if the U.S. economy is perceived as safer or more profitable than their home economies.

This vast secondary market for loans makes it easy for local lenders to sell the mortgages they originate. The lenders can then originate more mortgages in their local markets. These lenders make their money from the origination fees they charge, not from holding the mortgages and receiving the interest payments.

The big investors who buy mortgages on the secondary market do not want to lose their money by buying non-performing mortgages. They want to buy loans which will have a low default rate. This means they want to buy mortgages which are as standardized as possible. A mortgage which conforms to Fannie Mae guidelines can be originated anywhere in the United States, and then be packaged with other Fannie Mae mortgages. An investor who buys a package of these mortgages knows exactly what is being bought.

If lenders don't follow the Fannie Mae guidelines, they may have trouble selling their loans immediately. Before the lender can sell non-conforming loans, the loans sometimes must be held for a period of time to season them. If the loans are current in their payments after one to two years, these loans can be sold on the secondary market just like conforming Fannie Mae conventional loans. If your lender doesn't want to hold loans to season them, then you may have to qualify using strict Fannie Mae guidelines. If you don't fit neatly into the Fannie Mae "box" your loan may not be approved.

If a conventional lender rejects your loan application because you don't meet the strict Fannie Mae guidelines, you can still approach a lender who offers non-conforming conventional loans. This lender can be more flexible because it's willing to hold the loans it originates for a short time to season them or else the lender has found an "investor" who will provide funds for loans with standards which are more flexible than Fannie Mae's. This is where a mortgage broker who works with a number of these investors can be very useful to you as a borrower because the mortgage broker will know about these loans.

Fannie Mae Limit on Number of Loans

Even if your income is sufficient to allow you to qualify for a conforming conventional loan, you will eventually reach your limit of allowable Fannie Mae loans. This limit changes and currently is ten loans, including the one on your personal residence. If you co-own houses with partners, you may consider that a half share. But if everybody signed the mortgage agreement, the loan counts as one for each partner.

Some investors want to purchase more than ten homes. Maybe you live in a part of the country where houses are inexpensive so you need to own quite a few properties to reach your income goals. Or you have fairly high income goals that require you to acquire numerous houses. Or maybe you're buying houses with a partner. If together you own six houses on a fifty-fifty basis, each of you effectively only has three houses. If together you want to buy five more houses because you like to share down payments and management responsibilities, then you will have to explore non-conforming loan options for your last house.

Fannie Mae Limits on Loan Amounts

To reduce risk, Fannie Mae doesn't want to back loans that are too large. Therefore Fannie Mae issues loan limits. Because home prices increase over time due to inflation, these limits are raised on an annual basis. As of 2005, the limit was $359,650. Loans over the limit are considered jumbo loans by most lenders, and have higher interest rates.

If you live in a part of the country with high home prices, you may not be able to get conventional Fannie Mae backed loans without putting down a substantial down payment. Fortunately, you can usually get non-conventional mortgages instead.

Portfolio Lenders

Portfolio lenders include a broad spectrum of money sources, but I'm referring to the ones commonly used to obtain first mortgages. The national biggies I'm familiar with are World Savings and Washington Mutual (these two lenders also do loans other than portfolio loans). Portfolio lenders get their name because they keep many or all of the loans they originate in their own investment portfolio of loans and/or do their own loan servicing.

These lenders are not worried about selling your loan on the secondary market. Because they keep their loans, they can make their own loan qualification requirements. If they think you are a good loan risk according to their qualifications, they will approve your loan application. They set their own definitions of what is or isn't a jumbo sized loan, and are more flexible and generous in how they qualify borrowers, particularly small investors. This type of lender also offers the more unusual loans.

Portfolio lenders are great for anyone who doesn't fit into a neat set of qualification rules. Self-employed people, limited income people (based on family income and the number of people in the family), and investors will find loans designed for their particular circumstances. Even parents who don't want to co-sign on conventional loans with their children, but who want to help their children buy homes, are offered an alternative.

World Savings doesn't limit the number of loans any individual can have with them, although they will make your loan application pass through a second level of approval once the total of all the loans you have with them exceeds $1,000,000.

Washington Mutual also has no arbitrary limits on the number of loans per investor. If your credit score is high they are willing to loan an individual many millions, especially on full documentation loans instead of stated income loans.

Washington Mutual also offers option adjustable rate mortgages for loans bigger than the Fannie Mae limit with an interest rate than is only 1/8% higher than loans that are under the limit. However, once your loan amount exceeds $1,500,000 the interest rate premium increases to 1/2%.

Qualifying Ratios

Both conventional and portfolio lenders use what are called front end and back end ratios to determine how much they will loan to a borrower. The front end ratio, also called the housing ratio, determines the maximum mortgage payment amount they think you can handle. The back end ratio limits your total monthly debt obligations including the proposed mortgage payment.

A conventional rule of thumb is to use 28% as a housing ratio. If you earn $5,000 per month gross income before taxes are taken out, the lender will multiply $5,000 by 28%. The result, $1,400, is the largest monthly mortgage payment the lender thinks you can handle. This amount must include principal, interest, taxes, hazard insurance, plus any mortgage insurance premiums and homeowner association dues. If the borrower intends to get a second loan in addition to the first loan, the payment for the second loan will be included as well.

You must also qualify for the loan using the back end ratio. The conventional lender will multiply your income by 36%. Using $5,000 as your gross monthly income, your back end ratio number would be $1,800. This is the largest amount of total monthly debt the lender thinks you can handle. It must include all of your long term monthly debt obligations in addition to the mortgage payment on your new loan. The lender will look at such things as car payments, leases, student loans, alimony or child support and minimum monthly credit card payments, and any other revolving installment debt obligations you have.

In our example if you have a $350 car payment and a $150 student loan payment, the lender will subtract $500 from your back ratio number of $1,800 to get $1,300. Then the lender will compare your back end ratio number with your housing ratio number, in this example $1,400. Your approved loan amount is limited by the smaller of these two numbers. Since $1,300 is less than $1,400 you would qualify for a loan with a total payment of $1,300 per month.

With lenders now using automatic underwriting, a computer program will weigh a number of factors that can influence these two ratios. For a strong borrower, defined as someone with an extremely high credit score and/or lots of liquid assets, these ratios can be very flexible. Back end ratios can sometimes be pushed into the forties or even the low fifties.

Portfolio Lender Ratios

Portfolio lenders set their own ratios. Based on their lending experiences, they may loosen or tighten their requirements. For this next example, we will use the ratios that are similar to those in effect at World Savings and Washington Mutual as of 2005.

Remember that these ratios, especially the back end ratio, can be stretched for strong borrowers at the lenders' discretion.

Using a 33% housing ratio and a 45% back end ratio in our example of a $5,000 gross monthly income, the housing ratio amount is $1,650 and the back end ratio amount is $2,250. Subtracting the same $500 in car and student loan payments from $2,250 gives us $1,750. Since $1,750 is larger than $1,650, the maximum monthly loan payment you would qualify for is the smaller amount, or $1,650. This is significantly higher than the $1,300 a strict conventional lender would establish as your maximum payment based on the same income and debts.

NOTE: Remember, just because you qualify for a loan based on these ratios does not mean a lender will give you a loan. Besides the ever present requirement of good credit, each lender has additional qualification requirements for the loan products they offer. Ratios are only the starting point for lenders when they qualify borrowers for a loan.

Minimizing Monthly Debt

As these ratio examples show, it's important for an investor to minimize monthly debt obligations. If you want to qualify for real estate loans, don't buy furniture on a monthly payment plan, purchase a new car as soon as the old one is paid for, run up half a dozen charge cards and carry balances on them all, or co-sign on your brother's motorcycle. The most difficult consumer loan to qualify for is a mortgage. Make it easy for a lender to say yes to the big loan you want (as well as to a prosperous future with plenty of money to pay for consumer items) by avoiding the temptation to incur numerous small debts.

Rental Income

Most investors assume lenders will look at the anticipated rent for a rental property and then at the mortgage payment, and as long as there is a positive monthly cash flow, everything will be fine. It's true that when you buy an investment property the lenders will be looking at your mortgage payment for the property and the rent you will receive. But they usually will not credit you for the full amount of rent and they will also be looking at your personal debt situation. Even with a projected positive cash flow, the lender may not give you a loan.

Conventional Lenders & Investment Loans

Conventional lenders will not count your full rent as income against your debt obligations. Instead they will discount your rents. Let's say you want to buy a property, 354 Primrose Drive, which will rent for $1,000 per month. Conventional lenders will give you credit for 75% of the rent, or in this example, $750. They assume that the other 25% of your rent will be spent on maintenance, advertising, and vacancy expenses.

Let's assume that your loan payment on 354 Primrose Drive will be $800. This includes principal, interest, insurance, taxes plus any homeowners association fees. Since the payment, $800, is larger than the discounted rent, $750, the lender will consider the difference, $50, as a debt which must be subtracted from your back ratio just like a car or student loan payment.

The conventional lender will look at your personal debt situation using their normal ratios. In our earlier example with a $5,000 gross monthly income, the housing ratio of 28% gave us $1,400 as the maximum amount for personal housing expenses and the back end ratio gave us $1,800 before being adjusted. The adjustments meant we subtracted $500 for the car and student loan payments from the back end ratio number, and now we must also subtract the negative $50 cash flow produced by the lender's discounting of the rent for your new rental property. This produces a maximum back end ratio number of $1,250.

Since $1,250 is smaller than $1,400, $1,250 is the maximum amount we can have for a total loan payment on our personal house and still qualify for the $800 payment on 354 Primrose Drive. If the total mortgage or rent payment for our personal residence exceeds $1,250, we may not qualify for the investment loan unless we put down additional money (a smaller loan equals a smaller loan payment) or unless we pay off some of our personal debts (to increase our back end ratio number by eliminating the car or student loan payment).

Portfolio Lenders & Investment Loans

Portfolio lenders are more lenient when they decide how much to loan on a rental property. In addition to using higher ratios, they generally do not discount rents on the property you are buying (an exception would be if the property had more than one unit). This makes it much easier to qualify for an investment loan because it's much more likely that the difference between the rent amount and the mortgage payment will be positive instead of negative. Any positive difference will be added to your income to help you qualify for your personal debts.

Since 354 Primrose would rent for $1,000 per month, or $250 more than the mortgage payment of $750, these lenders would add that $250 to your monthly income of $5,000 to produce a new monthly gross income of $5,250.

NOTE: When you buy an investment property and already have investment properties, these portfolio lenders will look at the rents from your current properties differently than the projected rent for the new property. If you get your new loan on a low documentation basis (in other words you don't provide copies of your tax returns) then the rents on your current properties will be discounted by 25%. If you get a full documentation loan, these lenders will subtract your actual costs from actual rents received as reported on your tax return. If the result is a positive number, it will help you to qualify. If it is a negative number, it will be considered part of your monthly debt obligations.

Using the portfolio lender ratios, the housing ratio of 33% would be multiplied against $5,250 instead of $5,000 since the difference between the expected rent and the mortgage payment is added to your income. This produces a housing ratio number of $1,732.50. Multiplying the back end ratio of 45% against $5,250 gives us $2,362.50, but then we must subtract the $500 for the car and student loan payments to produce a final back end ratio number of $1,862.50. Since $1,732.50 is smaller than $1,862.50, $1,732.50 is the maximum monthly payment we can pay for our personal housing expenses in order to qualify for the $800 payment on 354 Primrose Drive.

NOTE: Lenders can, and do, change their qualifying procedures at their own discretion. You must always check with local loan representatives to find out exactly how much you can qualify to borrow. Currently, neither World Savings nor Washington Mutual charges an application fee when borrowers apply for pre-approval on a loan. Some lenders do charge an application fee. Before you start looking for a rental property, you should get pre-approved, or at least pre-qualified, by a lender. Then you will know exactly how much you can spend.

Comparing the conventional lender against these portfolio lenders, we see a $482.50 difference in the allowable size of our personal housing costs, $1,732.50 versus $1,250. The portfolio lenders would allow a personal housing expense which is 39% higher than what a conforming conventional lender would allow.

So even though a fixed rate conventional loan may be attractive, it is easier to qualify for an adjustable rate portfolio loan. When you buy your first investment property, you may be able to qualify for a conforming conventional investor loan. For safety's sake, I'd prefer to see you start off with a fixed rate loan if the property is one you plan to keep for over five years. This is especially true if interest rates are relatively low.

But if you are trying to buy your third or fourth rental house or condominium, it will become increasingly more difficult to qualify for each subsequent loan.

Why? Because each new property, assuming they are the same as our example, would count as a $50 monthly expense according to a conventional lender. Unless you have a very high income or minimal debts, your back end ratio number will quickly decrease. Eventually your back end ratio number will become too small for you to qualify for another conventional loan. At this point in time you can switch to a portfolio lender. Since the portfolio lender uses higher ratios and because the rent on the new property you are buying won't be discounted, you should still be able to get loan approvals.

Credit Scores

Lenders increasingly rely on credit scores. This score may be called a FICO, Beacon, or Empirica score. Scores are based on your past credit history. The companies use statistical analysis of your payment history, how much money you owe, what kind of debt you have, how much new credit you've asked for, and the length of your credit history.

Lenders use these scores to determine whether or not to loan you money. Lenders will also loan a borrower with a high credit score more money than someone who has a similar financial situation in terms of income and liquid assets but a lower score. This is because a borrower with a great credit score will be allowed to have a higher back end ratio. That is, the borrower's total monthly debt obligations can equal a lot more than the standard 36%.

Borrowers with high credit scores also get better loan terms. They can qualify for the lowest interest rates and closing fees. So although a credit score of 620 or higher may be enough to get you a loan, it's best to maximize your credit score so you can save money on interest and fees.

Having no debt at all won't result in the highest possible credit score. You need to demonstrate that when you have been given credit, you've handled it responsibly. The companies that calculate credit scores also want to see how well you've handled credit over many years.

Here are a few tips for maximizing your credit score. First, if you don't have any credit history, get a credit card. Use it and pay off the balance on time, or early, every month.

Limit how many credit cards you get to three to five plus perhaps a few department store cards. Make sure your balance isn't more than 50% of your limit on any of the cards. In terms of your score it's better to pay a higher interest rate on a second card rather than to exceed half your credit limit on your favorite, low interest rate card. Reapportioning your debt on your cards can be a fast way to pump up your score a bit.

Keep your cards for a long time. Switching to new cards to take advantage of introductory offers can hurt your credit. Adding a new card tends to reduce your score. Keeping your cards for years, even if you don't use them, can help your score. If you've had a card for many years, but don't use it anymore, you may reduce your score if you cancel that card. It may be better to keep it in a drawer somewhere.

Be careful about shopping for a car. I've run a tenant's credit and received a red flag warning because the previous summer she shopped at five different dealers before buying a car. Each dealer had run a quick credit report on her and it had a negative effect on her score. If you hand over your driver's license so you can test drive a car, the dealer usually has the necessary information to run a report even if you don't know it's being done. Ask. Find out alternatives such as taking the salesperson with you on the test drive.

Develop a system to make sure your bills are paid on time, or to at least pay them before the lender reports you. Most lenders won't file a late report unless you are at least thirty days late. Pay by phone or over the internet if you get close to the deadline. Occasional late payments can easily pull your score down. If your payment is late to a creditor, but you've had an otherwise pristine payment history, call and ask to have the late fee removed. I've done this a couple of times when I misplaced credit card bills, and the companies have always agreed to do it.

Avoid getting judgements against you. If you have to appear in small claims court, bring your checkbook in case you lose. If you pay as soon as a case is decided against you, your credit shouldn't be harmed. But if you say you need to pay later, the court will order a judgement against you and that will ding your credit. Don't let a dispute with a tenant, perhaps over withholding part of a security deposit, damage your credit score.

And of course, avoid bankruptcy and foreclosure. Before you say duh, remember to keep this in mind when you decide whether you can afford to buy a property. If things go wrong - you lose your job, can't get the rent you wanted, the property doesn't appreciate - will you be able to make it through the hard patch? Are you stretching yourself too thin, or leaving yourself too few liquid assets for emergencies? New investors often want to jump in as fast as they can, but it's generally better to pace yourself. Tuck away some reserves as part of your investment plan. Make sure you can stay in the game.

Owner Occupant Versus Investor Loans

You can count on three things when you get an investor loan instead of an owner occupant loan: your closing costs will be higher, your interest rate will be higher, and your required down payment will be higher.

Why? Because lenders perceive investors to be riskier borrowers. When a house goes into foreclosure, both owner occupants and investors face the loss of their good credit rating and their equity. The owner occupant, however, will also lose his or her home. Lenders think homeowners will work harder to keep their homes than an investor will work to keep a rental property.

Leapfrogging from Home to Home

If you want to get the best terms on your rental loans, you may want to acquire your rental properties by leapfrogging. Leapfrogging means you buy a personal home using owner occupant financing, stay there long enough to satisfy the lender's occupancy requirement for an owner occupant, then rent that house and buy a new personal residence. You repeat this process until you've accumulated the number of rental properties you need to achieve your financial goal. Then you concentrate on paying off your mortgages to the point where you can semi or fully retire.

Leapfrogging does have its disadvantages. You may have a spouse who will invest in real estate, but won't move repeatedly. Since my husband made it very clear that he won't move, I have been forced to use only investor financing to purchase houses since marrying Steven. The additional costs have been worth it to maintain my husband's enthusiasm for me buying rental houses.

Leapfrogging also requires time. If you have enough money to buy more than one house, you will only be able to get an owner occupant loan on one of them. The other house or houses will either have to be purchased using investor financing or you will have to wait to buy them. You are supposed to live in the first house long enough to satisfy your lender's occupancy requirements before you move into a new house using owner occupant financing again.

Lenders do realize that borrowers are sometimes forced to move and rent out a home before the occupancy time period is up. If you are transferred, the lender is most likely not going to foreclose on you or increase your interest rate, assuming that the lender notices you've moved. As long you don't tell the lender to send the payment coupons to a new address, how will the lender know? Most lenders don't pay attention until there is a problem with a loan such as late payments.

Some investors count on the lender not to pay attention. They get owner occupant financing and then immediately buy another house using owner occupant financing through a different lender. I personally do not recommend this approach, but it is done. If you are caught, you won't be sent to jail; however, the lender could call the loan due and payable. If you don't pay off your loan, the lender could then foreclose. Since a foreclosure would ruin your credit history and make future loans very hard to get, you should play by the rules or know how to get a lot of cash fast if necessary.

World Savings includes a requirement in the deed of trust for you to live in the property for at least one year if you get owner occupied financing. Washington Mutual wants owner occupants to have the intent to live in a home for a year. Yet while you wait a year to become eligible for owner occupant financing again, housing prices may go up more than what you can save by avoiding the additional cost of investor financing.

If you have enough money to buy more than one house at a time, you have to look at what's happening in your local real estate market. If the market is appreciating, it may be best to get your money invested at today's prices, even if it means paying extra for an investor loan.

Of course, if you have to save up a down payment before you can buy another house, you can console yourself with the fact that leap frogging is custom tailored to your situation. You will qualify for some unusual and useful loans available only to owner occupants, and it will be easier to get a fixed rate loan if you want one. Plus you will be prevented from buying multiple properties at a price peak for your market. By having to buy houses across a span of time, you will be forced to dollar cost average.

Loan Terms

Should you get a standard thirty year mortgage? Or would a fifteen year mortgage be better? Maybe you should get a loan with a bi-weekly payment schedule instead of a monthly schedule. How do you decide which one is best? Sometimes you can get a better rate on a mortgage if you get a fifteen year mortgage instead of a thirty year mortgage. But the difference is usually not much, and the payments are much higher because the loan is being paid off so much faster.

These big payments are why I don't like short term loans. Sure, you can make the bigger payment today, but what happens if you have financial troubles sometime in the future? You've thrown away your safety margin. I prefer longer loan terms.

You can still prepay on the mortgage despite the lower required payment amount. Most prepayment penalties won't kick in unless you prepay a substantial portion of your mortgage. As long as you stay below your loan's prepayment limit, you won't owe any penalties. Check your loan documents to be sure - don't accept a loan if you aren't allowed to prepay at least some of the principal.

If your loan has an adjustable interest rate, prepaying helps to protect you against rising interest rates as well as creating additional cash flow if interest rates stay stable. Prepaying on a fixed rate mortgage builds equity faster and shortens the term of the loan. Because prepaying is optional, if you get in a tight spot financially you can always stop making prepayments for a while. When you get back on your feet you can start prepaying again. This flexibility in how much you pay on your thirty year mortgages will make it easier to be a long term investor.

Forty Year Mortgages

Some lenders such as World Savings will give owner occupants a forty year mortgage instead of a thirty year mortgage. Washington Mutual will also do forty year mortgages for investors who get an option adjustable rate mortgage. A loan for $100,000 at 7.5% interest over thirty years would have a principal and interest payment of $699.21 per month. If you lengthened the loan term from thirty years to forty years, the principal and interest payment would drop to $658.07.

The payment difference is only $41.14 per month, or $493.68 per year, but if you leap frog from one property to the next, you could get this extra leeway on several loans. Multiplying $493.68 by five properties would be $2,468.40 per year.

Personally, I've never gotten a forty year mortgage, but it's another technique you can use to lower your risk as an investor by reducing your required monthly payment amounts. It also may make the difference between qualifying for the next loan or not because it reduces your monthly debt payments.

Bi-Weekly Mortgage Payments

When you compare bi-weekly payment mortgages against monthly payment mortgages, you should realize that the only net difference is you will make one additional principal and interest payment per year with the bi-weekly payment mortgage. Assuming that your loan doesn't have a prepayment penalty, or if it does that the penalty only kicks in for very large prepayments, there is nothing to stop you from making this extra payment with a typical monthly mortgage. You can either make an extra principal and interest payment each year, or you can divide that payment by twelve and add that amount to your monthly payments. The effect is the same as the bi-weekly mortgage except that if you run into financial tough times, you can stop making the extra payments on the monthly mortgage.

For someone who has the discipline to prepay, I believe a bi-weekly mortgage is not a good choice. You will be sacrificing financial flexibility in exchange for a twenty-three year mortgage. Instead of signing up for a bi-weekly mortgage, I believe you should retain the ability to decide whether or not to prepay based on your year-to-year financial situation. You can still reduce your mortgage term by prepaying, but you will have room to maneuver financially just in case.

Prepayment Penalties

Prepayment penalties can come in many different forms. Sometimes you are limited as to what percentage of your loan balance you are allowed to pay off in any one year. Sometimes you will owe a penalty if you pay off your entire loan too fast. For example, if your loan has a three year prepayment penalty, and you sell the house after owning it only two years, you will owe a penalty which may equal thousands of dollars.

Always ask about prepayment penalties when you are shopping for a loan. Sometimes lenders will waive any prepayment penalties if you pay an additional amount in closing costs. If you are buying a fixer upper that you plan to improve and then sell quickly, you may be willing to pay an extra point in order to get a loan without a prepayment penalty.

If, on the other hand, you plan to own the house for at least as long as the prepayment penalty period, you will probably want to get the cheaper loan. Sometimes lenders will offer you ways to avoid paying the prepayment penalty even if you do sell the house within the penalty period.

World Savings, for example, does have prepayment penalties, but they will waive or refund the prepayment penalty if you get another loan through them within six months of paying off the old loan. They will also waive the penalty if the buyer of your house gets a loan through them or assumes the old loan

Keep in mind that a three year prepayment penalty may be in force slightly past the three year anniversary of your loan origination. Depending on how the lender calculates it, you may have to wait a couple of extra months. Always check with your lender before you sell or refinance a property close to the end of your prepayment penalty period. You don't want to be hit with a $8,000 penalty because you paid off your loan thirty days too soon!

Chapter Six
Adjustable Rate Mortgages

Adjustable rate mortgages used to scare people. These loans originally were offered without rate or payments caps, and when interest rates rose sharply so did people's mortgage payments. Some people lost their properties to foreclosure because they couldn't make their payments.

Now many borrowers don't think twice about getting an adjustable rate mortgage. Part of this is due to the introduction of caps that prevent sudden increases in required payments. But borrowers have also gotten used to historically low interest rates and rapid appreciation in home values; they no longer see much risk with adjustable rates. Yet with lenders offering so called option loans that start off with payments that don't even cover the interest due on a loan, some people are going to end up in trouble.

Overall, though, I love adjustable rate mortgages. They have allowed me to buy properties I couldn't have purchased otherwise, and the way they calculated payments when I prepaid principal allowed me to increase my cash flow without the expense of refinancing. The better you understand how adjustable rate mortgages work, the more easily you can use them without getting in over your head. In this chapter you'll learn what a teaser rate is, the meaning of the words index and margin, and how different types of caps on your loan's interest rate and payment function. When you know how and when to use them, adjustable rate mortgages have a valuable place in an investor's strategy.

Adjustable Interest Rates

When you shop for loans you'll discover that adjustable interest rates are generally lower than fixed interest rates. This difference in rates is insurance for the lender. On a fixed rate loan, the lender is concerned about interest rates rising. Since the lender won't be able to raise the rate on the fixed rate loan, the lender has the potential to lose money in the future. To compensate for this risk, the lender charges a higher fixed rate. If rates do rise, the lender will have been collecting a higher amount of interest ahead of time. If rates don't rise, the lender will make additional money.

With an adjustable rate mortgage the lender is protected if interest rates go up; therefore the lender will generally offer a lower starting interest rate on an adjustable rate mortgage. If interest rates rise, the borrower will have to make bigger payments to the lender. If you prepay on an adjustable rate mortgage, you'll decrease the principal balance of your loan. As your loan balance becomes smaller, an increase in interest rates will be less painful.

Teaser Rates & Teaser Payments

Many lenders offer adjustable rate mortgages with teaser rates. The interest rates are abnormally low in the beginning and then adjust upward. If you didn't expect and plan for these adjustments, you could find yourself in a bad position. You always need to find out the current fully indexed rate when you shop for an adjustable rate mortgage. The fully indexed rate is the interest rate you would be paying if you had been holding the mortgage long enough to be past the limited time period that the teaser rate is in effect.

The loan officer may not understand what you mean when you ask for the fully indexed rate. He or she may keep telling you about the teaser rate, explaining that the fully indexed rate can't be determined until you've had the loan long enough for the rate to adjust to future market conditions. Since no one can foretell the future, they can't tell you the fully indexed rate.

Fine. Tell the loan officer you realize you won't have to pay the fully indexed rate right away. You know it's impossible to predict the future, so of course they can't tell you what the fully indexed rate will be in two years. But they can tell you what the fully indexed rate would be today assuming you had this loan for the past five years. If the loan officer still doesn't know what you're asking for, you can figure it out yourself.

Another, newer, twist lenders use to make initial loan payments low is to offer teaser payments. Your required minimum payment, called an option payment, in the first years of the mortgage may not cover all of the interest due much less include any money to pay down the principal balance of the loan. This payment is called an option payment because the lender will also tell you what payment would pay your interest, what payment would pay the interest and principal based on the remaining term of your loan, and often what the payment would have to be to pay off your loan in fifteen years from its origination date. It's up to you, at your option, to select which payment to make. Again, find out what the fully indexed rate is for the option loan. This is the rate you will be paying even if your option payment doesn't cover it. The unpaid interest will be added to your loan balance.

Index and Margin

A fully indexed rate is the index plus the margin. The index changes over time and it causes your interest rate to change along with it. Many conventional loans use the treasury bill rate as their index. This index responds very quickly to changes in interest rates. This is a good thing if rates are falling, but not so good when they are rising.

Portfolio lenders frequently use an index such as the COFI, the cost of funds, index, the COSI, the cost of savings index, or the CODI, certificate of deposit index. Each of these indexes is based on interest rates paid by banks on various financial products such as savings accounts, certificates of deposit, and money market accounts. These indexes have interest rates that generally rise and fall more slowly. This is good if interest rates rise because your interest rate will rise more slowly than it would if it were tied to a more responsive index such as the twelve month MTA, monthly treasury average, index, which is based on the average rate paid on treasury notes and securities for each of the preceding twelve monthly periods. On the downside, a loan tied to a slower moving index means your interest rate will drop more slowly when interest rates are falling. Ask lenders to tell you what indexes are used for the loans you are considering, and how fast these indexes adjust compared to other indexes.

I personally like adjustable rate loans based on an index that is tied at least partially to certificate of deposit rates. Most people who have certificates of deposit want to avoid early withdrawal penalties. Even when interest rates are rising they tend to wait until their certificates of deposits mature before they pull out their money to reinvest. So when interest rates increase these indexes lag behind while people wait to roll over their certificates of deposit. Adjustable rate mortgages that use these indexes will have interest rates will increase and decrease more gradually than will mortgages whose interest rates are determined by more volatile indexes. The more slowly my loan interest rates change, the easier it is for me to adjust my investment plans accordingly.

You will also need to know what the margin is for the loan you are considering. The margin represents the lender's gross profit margin before subtracting expenses. If the index is at 4.651

and the lender's margin for an owner occupant loan is 2.5, your fully indexed loan rate will equal these two numbers added together, or 7.151%. The margin for an investor will be higher, perhaps 2.8 instead of 2.5, making the investor interest rate 7.451%.

Your margin will remain constant for your loan unless otherwise specified in your deed of trust. However, lenders do change the margins they charge for new loans depending upon market conditions. You may get a COFI loan with a margin of 2.6% this year, but next year when you buy another house using a COFI loan, the bank may have increased or reduced its margin. The index will be the same for the two loans since they are both tied to the COFI index, but if the margin is different, your loans will have two different interest rates.

At one point I had four adjustable rate mortgages linked to the COFI index. Despite sharing the COFI as their index, only two of my loans had the same interest rate. Depending on when I bought my houses, the lenders were offering different margins. Because the interest rates for my loans were calculated by adding the margins onto the COFI index, the varying margins attached to each loan resulted in different interest rates.

Comparing Adjustable Rate Mortgages

Teaser rates make it hard to compare different adjustable rate mortgages. A teaser rate may be only 4% the first six months of the loan, but then the terms of your loan agreement may allow it to increase a maximum of two points every six months until you reach the fully indexed rate. Assuming the fully indexed homeowner rate is 7.151, you'll pay the 4% teaser rate for the first six months, 6% for the next six months, and then 7.151%, assuming that the index rate hasn't changed between now and then. How do you compare this against a loan that starts out fully indexed at 6.955%?

Option loans may start with a rate as low as 1% to calculate your required payment and have caps on how fast the required payment can rise. But the lender usually charges you the fully indexed interest rate, and adds the unpaid interest to your loan balance. It's very important to understand whether your teaser rate is your full payment, or simply a portion of it. Otherwise you can't accurately compare different adjustable rate mortgages. To compare them, look at how much each loan will cost you in interest over a set period such as the first year. Assuming interest rates stay the same, and counting interest that is added to your loan balance, which loan charges less?

Also look beyond the first year. Compare the fully indexed rates. It is possible that one loan may have a great teaser rate without unpaid interest being added to your loan balance, but this loan's fully indexed rate is much higher than the loan with no teaser rate. If you plan to own the property you are buying for a significant length of time you would be better off choosing the loan with the lower fully indexed rate.

If you hope to fix up a property and sell it quickly for a profit, you may want the loan with the lowest teaser rate, even if its fully indexed rate is higher than for other adjustable rate mortgages or interest is added to the loan balance. Getting the lowest interest rate may not be as important as getting the lowest payment while you hold the property.

Some lenders offer two loans with identical fully indexed rates. In order to get the loan with the teaser rate you must pay higher closing costs. The money you'll save while the teaser rate equals the higher origination fees. Usually when you compare the total costs for either loan, they are equal. However, by starting off with a lower interest rate and therefore a lower required payment, it will take longer for your required payment to rise if you choose the loan with the teaser rate.

Interest Rate Caps

Comparing the fully indexed rates of two different loans is important, but you should also look at the caps for each loan. A cap is a maximum interest rate. Most adjustable rate mortgages have two caps, an annual interest or payment cap and a lifetime cap.

The annual cap comes in many versions. The most common cap is an interest cap which allows the lender to raise the interest rate on your loan on an annual or sometimes bi-annual basis. The cap is the maximum amount your interest rate can increase or decrease in a given time period (yes, there is a limit on how fast your payment can drop as well as increase). Many loans have caps which allow your interest rate to increase by only one or two percent with each adjustment, for example from 6% to 7%.

Other loans have payment caps instead of interest rate caps. This type of loan can raise your principal and interest payment by a certain percentage of the payment itself, for example 7.5%. As an example let's say your principal and interest payment is $1,000. The lender could increase your required payment by 7.5% of $1,000, or up to $1,075.

Sometimes caps are true caps and sometimes they are not. What I call a true cap works as follows. When your rate adjusts, you owe a certain interest rate on your loan balance and that's all you must pay. No unpaid interest is added to your loan balance. Other caps may limit your required payment, but not the interest rate you are charged. If the required payment isn't large enough to cover the increased interest, the lender adds this difference to your loan balance. These types of loans are called negative amortization loans.

For example, let's say that your loan payment was $1,000. The index rate your loan is tied to has gone up and therefore so has the interest rate on your loan. If your loan has a 7.5% payment cap, the lender can only increase your required payment to

$1,075. But let's say this is not enough of an increase to pay for the higher interest charges. Since the lender can't increase your required payment again until the next adjustment time, the lender takes whatever interest charges are not covered by the new payment and adds this amount to your loan balance.

This doesn't necessarily mean that your loan balance will increase. Some of your required payment may be paying off principal. Let's say that $200 of your $1,075 payment is going to principal, and your unpaid interest each month is $35. If your loan balance was $120,000, then the lender would subtract the principal payment and add the unpaid interest.

Principal portion of mortgage payment = $200
Unpaid interest = $35
Loan balance = $120,000
New loan balance after receiving payment = $120,000 - $200 + $35 = $119,835

You won't be paying off your loan as quickly because some of your monthly principal payments will be canceled out by the unpaid interest. In worst case scenarios it could mean your loan amount actually starts to increase because your payments toward principal are less than the unpaid interest.

This type of loan may sound awful, but don't panic and swear you would never get a negative amortization loan. You always have the option to pay the unpaid interest. The lender will tell you the required payment you must make, and also tell you how much extra to pay if you want to keep your loan on a regular thirty year amortization basis.

When you have a choice it is best to get a loan where the lender swallows the negative amounts when interest rates are rising. These loans are usually the conventional loans. Most portfolio loans are negative amortization loans.

Remember that the lenders don't want to foreclose on their loans. By limiting how much you have to pay when interest rates rise and adding the unpaid interest to your loan balance, they are in effect giving you a mini-loan without you having to apply for it. You may not worry about your loan balance increasing as long as your property is appreciating in value at a faster rate. Plus the limitation on your required payment increase gives you time to possibly raise your rents to cover your new, higher payment amounts.

Lifetime Caps

The lifetime caps are the maximum and minimum your interest rate can ever be. This cap is almost always a true cap. That means that if interest rates exceed your lifetime cap, you don't have to pay the difference even on portfolio loans. No unpaid interest will be added to your principal balance. No matter how high rates go, the lifetime cap interest rate is the worst case scenario for you even if you have a negative amortization loan. Of course, the reverse is also true. If interest rates drop below your minimum cap, you will still be charged that minimum interest rate. I think you should only get loans which have true lifetime maximum interest caps. Otherwise the risk is too great. It's been a while, but I've seen interest rates climb astonishing quickly, and I know people who lost property because of it. With so many loans offering true rate caps, you should make sure to get one.

Worst Case Scenario

You can use the worst case interest scenario when you look at loans. This scenario assumes that rates shoot up to your maximum cap rate as soon as possible. Ask the lender to tell you what your principal and interest payment would be based on the lifetime cap rate and the full balance of your loan. (Yes, your loan balance may be less if your payments include principal, but it could also be more if your loan starts off with negative amortization. The difference either way won't significantly change your worst case, fastest, payment amount.) Also ask the lender how fast you could reach your maximum payment based on the loan's payment caps. Would it take two years? Five years? This worst case payment with monthly prorated taxes and insurance added will almost always exceed the anticipated rent. Do you think you could handle this worst case scenario? For how long?

If you're looking at an adjustable rate mortgage which is tied to the Treasury bill rate as its index, ask yourself how high and how fast you think the Federal Reserve will let rates increase. Or if it's tied to the COFI index, ask yourself how fast you think the interest rates paid on savings and checking accounts are going to rise. If your margin is 2.5 and your lifetime interest rate cap is 12.5%, that means the COFI index would have to be 10 before you hit the maximum interest rate.

How soon do you think savings accounts will be paying 8%, or certificates of deposit will be paying 12%? These are the types of interest rates you would probably see before the COFI index became 10 or higher. It happened in the eighties. Do you think it will happen again? How fast do you think it could happen?

Five Year Payment Adjustments

Most lenders offering adjustable rate mortgages reserve the right to readjust your payments every five years to an amount that will keep you on a thirty year payment schedule. This could be a problem if interest rates rise sharply for many years in a row or if you made option payments that didn't cover all the interest due much less any principal. Although your annual cap will normally limit any increase to your required payment, every fifth anniversary of your loan the lender may be able to raise your required payment to whatever amount is necessary to get you back on a thirty year payment schedule.

If you've been making minimum required payments that are significantly smaller than the fully amortized payments, you could get hit with an increase that is larger than you can handle. If you are approaching a five year anniversary for one of your loans, make sure you can afford the new minimum payment if the lender is allowed to make this kind of payment adjustment. If your new payment will be more than you can afford, you could refinance to stretch your loan period out to thirty years again. That may reduce your payment enough for you to manage.

In a worst case scenario with fast rising interest rates and personal financial trouble, you might have to sell the property. It's better to anticipate this type of situation so you have time to market the property for the best price. So pay attention. And if at all possible, pay more than the minimum required payment!

Loan Modification

What if interest rates fall drastically? Because payment caps also prevent the lender from reducing your required payment more than the annual limit, you'll end up prepaying on your mortgage. Let's say your payment has a 7.5% annual cap, and your payment this past year was $1,000. The most your principal and interest payment can decrease is $75. Yet interest rates have dropped enough that your payment should only be $900. The extra $25 will be credited against your loan balance.

Even if interest rates stay the same, your required payment could still temporarily be higher than the payment necessary to pay off your mortgage in thirty years. This can happen if you've been prepaying on your mortgage. You'll owe less interest because the balance of your loan is lower than it normally would have been, and your payment toward principal will also decrease. Together these two reductions in how much you owe each month may be more than the annual payment change cap.

So if you've been prepaying while interest rates drop, your required payment could end up hundreds of dollars more than it has to be. This may be fine with you because your goal is to get your loans paid off, the sooner the better. But if you want more cash flow to live on or want to improve your debt ratios by decreasing your required monthly payments, you may want to modify your loan.

Contact your lender and tell them you want to get your loan payments reduced to the thirty year payoff schedule. Most lenders are thrilled to do this because they don't want their loans to be prepaid when interest rates are falling. Usually the fee they charge is modest, typically $200-$300.

Sometimes your lender will contact you and offer to do a loan modification for free. World Savings did this on my two loans with them in the spring of 2002. I was happy to accept their offer. One payment dropped from $989 to $833. The other went from $1,091 to $1,003. This equalled a $244 increase to my monthly cash flow if I chose to make the lower payments. In the meantime, by reducing my required minimum payments, it was easier for me to qualify for loans on other properties.

Incidentally, modifying these loans also slowed down how fast rising interest rates could lift my required payments. My annual payment caps were now applied to my new, lower, payments.

Why I'm Not Afraid of Adjustable Rate Mortgages

I figure that if interest rates go up, it will be harder for home buyers to qualify for loans. That means there will be more renters competing for rental properties. High interest rates will also stop many investors from purchasing properties because their caps will be set at 15% or higher on new loans. So with more demand for rentals and a limited supply available, I think I'll be able to raise my rents enough so I won't have a negative cash flow.

Also, because I prepay on my adjustable mortgages if I have positive cash flow, this helps to offset rising rates. Hopefully my cash flows will be large enough to accommodate the maximum allowed payment increases even if I can't raise my rents.

So do I only have adjustable rate mortgages? During the 1990s, the answer was yes. Interest rates were stable or dropping, and I got better rates by getting adjustable rate mortgages. Also, I couldn't qualify for fixed rate mortgages at good rates because I was self-employed.

Yet it's important to adjust when the real estate world changes. With interest rates dropping in the new century to lows not seen since the 1960s, I've switched mostly to fixed rate loans for properties I intend to keep for many years. Interest rates are highly unlikely to go much lower, which means they'll probably rise instead. The idea of having many loans with interest rates between six and seven percent while interest rates for new loans rise higher than that is very attractive to me.

Always carefully evaluate your situation, what you think is going to happen to interest rates, and how long you intend to own a property before selecting your preferred loan. Don't automatically favor fixed over adjustable rate mortgages or vice versa. Both types of mortgages have their advantages and disadvantages depending on the circumstances.

Prepay Your Adjustable Rate Mortgages

If you get an adjustable rate mortgage, do protect yourself by prepaying at least a little every month if you can. Yes, it's tempting to take your cash flow and save it all toward the down payment on your next house. And as long as interest rates don't rise substantially, you'll be okay and you'll get rich faster than the person who is more cautious. Why? Because you'll own more houses sooner since your money is going toward down payments instead of to prepayments.

But the downside is what happens if interest rates do rise. Will you be able to make your mortgage payments if your payment amounts rise and you haven't been prepaying? Deciding how much risk you are willing to tolerate is up to you, but I'd rather strengthen my ability to keep what I have than gamble it all on having even more. I strongly recommend prepaying your loans even if it means slowing down your acquisition program.

The best part about prepaying your loans is that if interest rates don't rise, your payments will start to decrease and your available cash flow will increase. Although normally you would continue to pay that extra cash flow toward your mortgage balance, if you hit tight financial times you'll have the option of using that cash flow for living expenses instead.

Of course, someone who has fixed rate mortgages could refinance in order to reduce their payments, but this poses a couple of problems. It costs money in the form of the closing costs for a new loan on each property that you refinance. And interest rates may not be favorable.

Plus if your need for money is due to financial trouble in your life, you may discover that lenders aren't willing to let you refinance your fixed rate mortgages. You may be forced to sell a property to get the money you need for living expenses while you reorganize your life.

So keep an open mind about adjustable rate mortgages. They can be wonderfully flexible and useful for an investor.

Chapter Seven

A Selection of Loans

A wonderful smorgasbord of loan products is available in the United States. The majority of lenders and real estate agents are very familiar with FHA loans, VA loans, and conventional loans. Since information on these loans is widely available, this chapter concentrates instead on a sampling of the loans offered by the portfolio lenders.

These loans are not familiar to most people, even real estate professionals. Some of the loans I'm about to describe are offered to investors, but others are only available to owner occupants. Keep in mind that most of these loans are adjustable rate mortgages unless I indicate otherwise.

Even if some of these loans won't work for you, they may work for someone you know, or one of them may be perfect for you in the future. The variety of loans available makes it possible for almost anyone with good credit, or even not-so-good credit, to borrow money. After reading this chapter, you'll know about more types of loans than do many real estate agents.

While any bank can be a portfolio lender if its loan officers decide to lend money to someone and keep the loan in the bank's portfolio, these loans are uncommon and are awarded on a case-by-case basis. If you have a strong relationship with your bank, you may be able to obtain one of these individualized portfolio loans. Usually, though, portfolio loans will come from one of the big national savings and loans who specialize in this type of loan, or through a mortgage broker.

Two of the biggest national lenders who do portfolio loans are World Savings and Washington Mutual. These two companies offer many similar loans, but with some differences. Margins and caps rates on their adjustable loan products change frequently, and so do down payment requirements. These lenders also have different restrictions on what types of properties they consider acceptable as collateral.

World Savings, for example, doesn't do loans for units in mixed use properties. So if you decide to buy a condominium in a building that also has office spaces, World Savings may not be able to help you. However, Washington Mutual may be interested in taking a look at your application. The unit must be 100% residential, not a combination residential/commercial space. And this type of residential unit in a mixed use building must be readily marketable in the local area.

Since lenders change, add or eliminate loan programs at their discretion, the loans described in this chapter may change. But most of these loans have been available for years and will continue to be offered for the foreseeable future. Check with your local loan representatives for the latest information on loan availability and requirements.

Keep in mind, too, that not all loan officers who work for the same company are equally helpful. Some of my readers and I have learned that although we may love the loans offered by a particular lender, we had to search to find the right loan officer to help us. If you don't form a good rapport with someone at one branch, try talking with someone at a different location.

The 100% Loan (Or How Not to Co-sign)

This loan is offered by both Washington Mutual and World Savings. It can be a fabulous loan for two types of people - those who want to help a friend or relative to buy a personal residence, and those who need that help. You may find yourself in either of these positions.

The most familiar way to assist a weak borrower to obtain a loan is for someone to co-sign on the loan, but this ties up the co-signer's credit since she or he also becomes liable for the full monthly payment. This makes it more difficult for the co-signor to qualify for other loans. And if the borrower doesn't pay the mortgage payments, the co-signor's good credit may be ruined.

If the potential co-signer doesn't want to tie up his or her credit or risk it being damaged, he or she could still help the weak borrower by giving the borrower a large sum of money to use as a down payment. Loans called low documentation loans are available which will look at a borrower's credit but not at the borrower's income if the down payment is large enough.

The problem here is obvious. It's one thing to help a borrower, but another matter entirely to give the borrower twenty or forty thousand dollars. Also some lenders don't want the down payment to be a gift instead of the borrower's own funds. The lender will check bank statements to make sure the borrower has had the down payment funds for several months.

The 100% loan solves these problems. World Savings or Washington Mutual will lend 100% of the purchase price of a home to a borrower. Instead of a down payment they will expect a sponsor to put 20% of the purchase price into a certificate of deposit to be held by the lender as collateral in addition to the house itself.

The sponsor does not co-sign the loan with the borrower and the sponsor retains ownership of the certificate of deposit. The sponsor can choose to invest his or her money in any type of certificate of deposit offered by the lender, from a three month certificate to a six year certificate. The sponsor will receive the monthly interest earned on the certificates of deposit.

The risk for the sponsor is that the borrower will not make the loan payments. The lender will notify the sponsor if payments become delinquent. If the payments are not brought current the lender may foreclose and the sponsor will lose some or all of the money held as collateral. But even if this happens, because the sponsor did not co-sign on the loan, the sponsor's credit will not be affected.

This type of loan also provides the sponsor with several other advantages. The sponsor's ability to borrow is not reduced by the new mortgage because he or she is not co-signing the loan. This makes it easier for the sponsor to qualify for other loans. Also, since the money in the secured certificate of deposit is not given to the borrower, it still belongs to the sponsor. As such, it remains in the sponsor's estate in the case of death to be divided in whatever manner the sponsor wants among his or her heirs (though it will remain pledged as collateral until released). This can be very advantageous when a parent wants to help one child without causing resentment in the other children.

It is not even necessary for the sponsor to risk the full 20% of the purchase price required for the collateral. If the borrower puts down some money, then the sponsor only needs to put the difference into the secured certificate of deposit. For example, if the borrower puts down 5%, then the sponsor will need to put 15% into the secured certificate of deposit.

The funds in the certificate of deposit are not tied up forever. As soon as the equity in the property reaches 20%, then either the borrower or the sponsor can pay for an appraisal to prove this. If the appraisal shows that the loan balance equals 80% or less of the property value, the secured certificate of deposit is released. This reduction of the loan-to-value ratio to 80% is accomplished through a combination of principal paydown on the loan balance and appreciation of the property.

At this time, this loan product is offered only to owner occupants, but it can be great for the younger investor who has a parent or grandparent who would like to help him or her buy a personal residence. And it can be just as advantageous for the parent who hates the idea of co-signing. You can help your kid buy a house without hurting your ability to qualify for investment loans!

Low Documentation Loans

Low documentation loans, commonly called low doc loans, stated income, or no income verification loans, are offered both to investors and to owner occupants, although an investor loan will have a higher margin and a larger required down payment. Both the margins and down payment amounts may change depending on market conditions. As of summer, 2005, the down payment for a Washington Mutual or World Savings low doc owner occupant loan was 20%. For investors Washington Mutual wanted a 20% down payment on single family homes and 25% for 2-4 unit properties. World Savings required more, 30% for single family properties and 2-4 unit buildings.

Low documentation loans are some of the easiest loans to get. They are ideally suited for self-employed people who have successfully utilized the tax system to reduce their reported income to next to nothing. It's also a great loan for people who have an erratic employment history. With this type of loan, however, you must have sparkling credit. If you have a small ding on your credit history you may still qualify for a low documentation loan, but the required down payment may be increased.

An example of someone who used this loan to his advantage was a student I knew who wanted to sell his townhouse and buy a house closer to the school he attended. As a student working part-time evenings and weekends, his income was just over $10,000 per year. The house he wanted to buy cost $122,000. Normally he would never have been able to qualify for the loan until after he had graduated and found a full-time job.

But this student had quite a bit of equity in his townhouse, enough that when he sold it, he had the required down payment on the house. Since low documentation loans don't require the lender to verify a borrower's income, he told them he made the amount necessary to qualify for the loan. The lender did not ask to see his income tax returns because lenders don't verify income for low documentation loans. This student's loan was approved with a minimum of fuss.

Most low doc lenders will want to know where a borrower is getting the down payment. It's okay to borrow against your stocks, get a second mortgage from a friend against a rental property you own, or pull the money out of savings. World Savings will also allow it to be a gift for both owner occupied and investor loans, while Washington Mutual will allow a portion of it to be a gift for owner occupants.

In addition you will need to provide proof of your employment. If you say you are an author, you may need to produce a copy of your book or a portfolio of your published magazine articles. If you are a real estate agent or professional masseuse, you'll need to provide a copy of your license. The lender will help you determine what will serve as adequate proof.

Limited Income Loans

Another loan that works well for the self-employed who are masters at reducing their taxable income is the limited income loan offered at World Savings. This loan also works for those borrowers who have large families because the maximum income allowed for borrowers is increased when the borrower has additional dependents. Elderly people who want to reduce their monthly mortgage payment can also be ideal candidates to refinance with this program.

This loan can be used as purchase money when you first buy a property, or as refinancing money. The closing costs charged by the lender total only $500, though additional closing costs may be charged by other parties such as the title company who handles the closing. It can be used to purchase an owner occupied single family home or duplex.

This loan is unusual even among portfolio loans because it has a fixed rate with very low closing costs. If you can qualify for it, it may well be the best loan available for owner occupants. Unfortunately, this fabulous loan is not available to investors, though an owner occupant may use it to purchase a duplex.

You'll have to check with World Savings to see if your income falls under the maximum allowed for your geographical area. Your maximum allowed income will also vary depending on the number of people in your household. World Savings can be very broad in its interpretation of household members, but everybody's income will have to be counted, including social security payments. Keep this loan in mind for older folks. Since this loan is also available for refinancing, this could be a perfect loan for retired people who would like to refinance to lower their mortgage payment.

Typical Investor Loans

In order to get the best interest rates, whether for fixed or adjustable rate loans, typical investor loans require full documentation of your income and debts. You must put at least 20% down. You should be a strong borrower (defined as good credit, adequate income, with some liquid assets such as cash, stocks, or a retirement plan you could access in an emergency), and the property must be one considered desirable by the lender. Properties with odd floor plans or locations outside of predominantly residential neighborhoods may cause the lender to demand a larger down payment.

Other investor loans require down payments as low as 10%. The interest rates on these loans are higher because the lenders correctly perceive the risk of default to be higher. After all, with less money down the cash flow will be that much less. If the cash flow is negative, the additional capital influx required to make your mortgage payment each month will be bigger. In addition to paying a higher interest rate, the borrower will also have to pay for mortgage insurance.

With the creation of MIP (mortgage insurance premium), lenders were able to approve loans with less than 20% down without taking undue risk. If a borrower defaulted on the loan, the mortgage insurance company would either buy the property from the lender at the lender's cost, or else pay the lender money to defray any or some losses when the lender obtained control of the property and sold it.

This mortgage insurance is not the same as the type sold to homeowners which guarantees to pay off your mortgage if you die. MIP insurance is entirely for the lender's benefit, but you are the one who will pay for it. You shouldn't complain, though, because otherwise you would have to put down much more money in order to qualify for a loan. However, there is a way to avoid mortgage insurance while still putting down less than 20%.

80-10-10, 80-15-5, or 75-20-5 Loans

If you don't like the idea of paying mortgage insurance payments, you have two options. You can put down 20% of the purchase price. Or you can get a first mortgage and second mortgage combination. Lenders offer these loans in various ratios. You could have an 80% first mortgage and a second for either 10% or 15% of the purchase price with the final 10% or 5% as your down payment. Or you could get a 75% first with a 20% second and 5% as your down payment.

The interest rate on the second mortgage will be higher than on your first mortgage. In addition the loan term will generally be shorter for the second, perhaps fifteen or twenty years instead of thirty years. The combination of these two factors can make the total of your two mortgage payments fairly high. But unlike the mortgage insurance payments, the interest on the second will be tax deductible when you are buying a house as your personal home. The key question is whether it will cost less for you to get a 90% loan and pay the MIP, or to get an 80% first mortgage plus a second mortgage at a higher interest rate. Also keep in mind, if this will be an owner occupied home before you turn it into a rental, MIP is not a tax deductible expense, but the interest on a second mortgage is.

To determine whether to go with the 90% loan or the combination of loans, you have to do the numbers and compare your monthly payments. More precisely, you can ask your lender on the first mortgage to do the numbers for you. Loan officers can tell you who offers these second purchase money loans, what the terms are, and what your payment will be. This is another good time to shop around, comparing the terms for the second mortgage.

If the first mortgage lender you select directs you elsewhere for your second mortgage because they don't do them in-house, look for a lender who offers a thirty year amortization on the second mortgage. This will make your monthly payment much lower than having a second mortgage amortized over ten or fifteen years. Verify that you are allowed to prepay on the second mortgage. It makes sense to concentrate all of your prepaying into the second mortgage because it will be such a small note. In a few years you may be able to pay it off and have your total monthly payments drop in a very satisfactory way.

Foreign Nationals

Sometimes it can be difficult for foreign nationals to get loans. Washington Mutual offers adjustable rate mortgages to owner occupant foreign nationals with 30% down while World Savings requires 30-35% down.

Fixed Rate Investor Portfolio Loan

Both Washington Mutual and World Savings offer fixed loan products for investors though the interest rate may be higher than for conventional fixed loans. If you can't qualify for a fixed rate conventional mortgage, but you hate the idea of an adjustable rate mortgage, this loan may be your best choice. The portfolio ratios may make the difference in getting your loan approved or not.

Construction/Permanent Financing

Washington Mutual offers a construction loan which becomes permanent financing after the building is completed. The minimum down payment can be as little as 10% for owner occupants. Washington Mutual also offers this loan to builders who are constructing a number of homes.

Stacked Units

Both World Savings and Washington Mutual will loan on townhouses and condominiums, but they have a few restrictions. First, World Savings requires at least a 50% owner occupancy ratio. For example, if there are 100 units, a minimum of 50 need to be owned by owner occupants. (This information can be obtained from the homeowners association.) Washington Mutual requires a 70% owner occupancy ratio if an investor buys a unit, though if an owner occupant is buying using a full documentation loan the owner occupancy ratio can be as low as 10%.

Convertible Loans

World Savings offers loans which start out as adjustable rate mortgages, but later can be converted to fixed rate mortgages between months thirteen and eighty-four. The fixed rates are not as attractive as those offered by conventional lenders, but this loan may be your best choice if at this point in time you can only qualify for an adjustable rate mortgage, but you really want a fixed rate.

After waiting a year you can convert your mortgage without requalifying and get that fixed rate. By starting with an adjustable rate mortgage you will pay smaller closing costs than if you had started with a fixed rate portfolio loan. The convertible loan is only offered to owner occupants.

Fixer Upper Refinance

Imagine this scenario: You buy a house for a great price, fix it up so it's worth a lot more, and then want to refinance out some of your new equity so you can buy another house. In the past lenders would refuse to give you a new loan based on the improved value until you had owned the property for at least a year. In the meantime your equity was trapped in the property if you didn't want to sell it.

World Savings will make an exception to this common requirement if you can show them receipts of money spent improving the property. They may then agree to refinance the property based on the current appraised value. The receipts don't need to equal the difference between the purchase price and the new appraised value, but they should be a substantial percentage of the change in value. If you haven't done any fix-up work, try Washington Mutual. They will let you refinance based on a new appraisal without a waiting period.

Second Loans on Investment Properties

When you buy a property you use what is called a purchase money loan. Later when you decide to refinance the property you use a refinancing loan. What is the difference between these two types of loans? The most important difference is the loan-to-value ratio. If a lender will loan up to 80% of the purchase price of a property to an investor, that same investor may only be able to get a loan with up to 70% of the appraised value when doing a refinance. Plus the interest rate on a refinance loan for an investor will probably be higher than for an investor purchase loan.

This makes it difficult to get equity out of an investment property without selling it. The solution can be a second loan. Though many lenders will only lend up to a total of 70% loan-to-value including the second, a reasonable number of lenders will lend up to an 80% loan-to-value. Another advantage to getting a second instead of a new first mortgage is lower closing costs. Instead of paying an origination fee for a large loan, you pay an origination fee on the much smaller second.

Finding a lender who offers good terms on investment property second mortgages requires making a number of phone calls. Not a lot of lenders like to do this type of loan. Your best bets will be the small local banks instead of the large regional or national banks. The last time I wanted a second mortgage on one of my investment properties, I was quoted an amazing variety of terms, from great to financially prohibitive.

When you make your calls you'll want to ask the following questions. What is the interest rate? Is it fixed or adjustable? Or is it fixed for a number of years and then it becomes adjustable? Over how many years is it amortized? What are the closing costs? Besides origination fees, make sure to ask about loan processing fees and any title insurance requirements. Will you have to pay for an appraisal on the property or will the lender accept documentation on comparable sales in the neighborhood?

Some lenders I talked with made their loans economically unattractive by their demands for appraisals and title insurance. I thought paying $300 for an appraisal and $700 for brand new title insurance plus other closing costs on a $28,000 second mortgage was too expensive.

But other lenders were more reasonable. One bank's total closing costs were less than $250. Combining the new $28,000 second with the existing first mortgage brought my total combined loan-to-value ratio to 80%. This beat out a number of other lenders whose second loans would bring up the combined value of my first and second mortgages to only 70% or 75%.

Since I was quoted such widely varying terms, my advice is to call at least five banks. Even if the first couple of lenders act like you are unreasonable to expect a combined loan-to-value ratio of up to 80% or closing costs which are less than $500, don't give up. I got lucky with my second call (later banks I called couldn't compete with this bank's good terms), but you may have to search a little harder. If the first five banks offer terms you don't like, go on to the next five. Focus on new banks in your area or banks that are advertising - they usually want new business and will be flexible in order to acquire you as a customer.

The number of small local banks have recently exploded in this country. One of them would really like to have your business, especially if you mention that you reward banks that work with you by giving them additional business. After all, why should you keep your checking and saving accounts with a bank which won't help you as an investor?

Even if you find a bank that's great for one product area such as second mortgages, it's valuable to establish relationships with additional banks. I personally work with three banks. One is great for my rental checking account because it has branches close to my rental properties. This makes it convenient for my tenants to make direct rent deposits. Another bank offers great terms on second mortgages. And the third bank provides a competitive interest rate and low annual fees on two lines of credit I keep handy to buy great deals that require fast cash.

Bankruptcy, Foreclosure and Other Credit Problems

Portfolio lenders are much more flexible about credit problems such as a bankruptcy or foreclosure than are conventional lenders. After two years, both World Savings and Washington Mutual will look at a loan applicant who experienced either of these problems. As long as the applicant has been financially responsible during the intervening two year period the chances are good that she or he can get a loan.

Sometimes credit problems are more general, resulting from such things as late payments and bounced checks. This means that an applicant can no longer qualify for "A" rates, but some conventional lenders and Washington Mutual offer "B" and "C" rates. These rates are higher, sometimes much higher, than "A" rates, but at least it is possible to get a loan. If the borrower later improves his or her credit, it may be possible to refinance and get a better interest rate at that time. World Savings offers the same loan rates to everyone who qualifies for a loan, but someone with less than stellar credit may be required to put down a larger down payment.

Chapter Eight

Qualifying Potential Tenants

Good tenants make being a landlord a pleasure. Bad tenants, however, can chase you right out of the real estate business. This chapter will share with you what I've learned in over a decade of being a landlady. While it's impossible to shield yourself from every bad tenant, you can eliminate most of them upfront. This requires establishing qualification requirements and sticking to them. This may sound simple enough, but it becomes difficult when you try to say "no" to a flesh-and-blood person.

Many tenants are a pleasure to know. If you would like to have tenants like these, you can tilt the odds in your favor. The first step is to choose the right properties. Property selection and tenants are inextricably intertwined. Good properties almost always attract good tenants.

The type of tenants you want are people who will insist on renting a nice property. They want it to be clean and in a well-kept neighborhood. Since they are good money managers, they can afford to rent a nicer property.

The not-so-good tenants will settle for whatever they can get. They may be slovenly or they may have bad credit. They have to rent from people who won't insist on a credit check. They don't have much money so they want inexpensive rental units and nonexistent or extremely low security deposits.

If something goes wrong in their financial lives, they have no reserves and few options. Unlike a person renting a property for $1,500 per month who could move into a smaller unit for $850 per month if times got tough, there is no place cheaper for low end tenants to go. Their best option may be to live in your property for free until they get evicted.

Property Location Is Important

Many investment guides focus almost solely on the rate of return a property can generate and ignore the type of tenants that property will attract. And it is true that a four-plex located on the corner of two busy streets can produce an amazing cash flow, one far superior to what a nice suburban house can produce.

But you will work hard to earn that higher rate of return. You will spend a lot more of your time handling tenants. After all, who wants to rent a unit in a building with a poor location? Any good tenant who has fallen on hard times will move as soon as she or he can afford to do so. The bad tenants won't have other options. They'll stay until they stop paying the rent at which point you'll have to evict them.

I'm not saying you must buy only single family houses if you want to avoid having tenant problems. Smaller units which are kept in spotless condition will also attract tenants with pride in their home environments if these units are located in a quiet residential area. However, you'll have to sort through a greater quantity of "bad" tenants before you find someone acceptable.

Who Are Your Prospective Tenants?

Tenants come from a broad spectrum of people. The most obvious group are students. Any area near a college campus will have a huge tenant market. However, students are not my ideal tenants. They are young and careless. They don't know how to maintain properties, and they are liable to leave before their leases are up.

If you live in a college town, you may or may not be allowed to discriminate against students. They are not protected by any federal laws, but your state or city may have passed local laws prohibiting discrimination against students. In this situation, if you don't want to rent to students, you should buy properties as far away from campus as possible. Avoid properties next to bus routes as well. This will make your properties less desirable to the type of tenants you want to avoid. You'll still sometimes have students as tenants, but not as often.

Even though I live close to Boulder, a city with a large student population, I've purchased rental houses in the city of Denver instead. The higher rents students pay are not high enough for me to endure the additional property damage and management duties. My target tenants are responsible adults who for some reason prefer not to own their homes.

It may be hard for you to imagine someone who wants to rent instead of own. After all, you are the type of person who understands the benefits of being a property owner or you wouldn't be reading this book. You believe that real estate is the best way for people to acquire wealth. For most families their home is their most valuable asset. Why would intelligent, responsible people choose to rent?

I've encountered a number of reasons. Sometimes tenants are in the process of a divorce. Until it is final they will not be able to qualify for a loan. Since divorcing spouses rarely continue to share their old home, one of them must rent a place. If he or she can afford it a divorcing parent will want a house for the kids instead of an apartment.

Young adults who are not sure where they want to settle down will prefer to rent for a while. I've rented to groups of singles and to newly married couples. These tenants will eventually buy their own homes, but they may rent from you for a couple of years before they move on.

Some tenants have owned houses in areas which recently experienced a market downturn. Several of my Colorado tenants came from California in the mid 1990s. In contrast to the red hot market of the early 2000s, California real estate was not doing well at that time. These tenants' experiences in a down market made these people real estate shy. They were reluctant to buy a house even in an appreciating market.

Some tenants are new to an area. Before they buy a house, they want a chance to investigate the various neighborhoods. Although these tenants tend to move as soon as their lease runs out, they are excellent tenants in the meantime. They are very motivated to keep their credit clean so they can qualify for a loan when they are ready to purchase.

Other tenants are corporate employees who know they will be transferred again. Rather than go through the hassle of buying and selling a house, they find it easier to rent. They know they will never stay in one place long enough to benefit from appreciation, not after they subtract selling costs. They plan to make their money through a great job and its benefits, not through owning real estate.

Some excellent tenants are couples who haven't married, and are reluctant to buy a house together. Perhaps one of them has been divorced before and hesitates to tie the knot with the new partner. I've had excellent tenants who fell into this category.

Other people have experienced some trauma in their lives, perhaps the death of someone dear, a serious medical problem, or they lost a job and went through their savings before being hired by another company. They don't want or can't afford to own a home at this point in their lives.

All of these people can be great tenants. They are out there looking for a wonderful place to live. If you take the trouble to buy and maintain special rental properties, you will be able to select from the best tenants available. You'll be able to take pride in providing a valuable service to the community while furthering your financial goals.

Eviction Rates

I've taught hundreds of people about rental real estate. During my classes I've surveyed my students to find out how many leases they've signed while they've been in the rental business. Then I've asked them how many tenants they've had to evict. Some of my students have been property owners since the 1970s or 1980s, and have weathered bad times as well as good. The average eviction rate has been 3%.

Out of the fifty or so leases I've had, I've never had to do an eviction, though my sister once posted an eviction notice on one of our joint properties (the tenant paid in full the next day). My father owns seventeen condominiums in a suburb of Denver. Out of almost one hundred leases, he's only had to do four evictions.

A few of my students, though, have experienced eviction rates as high as 50%. When I questioned them, I discovered the following common factors: these students had properties at the low end of the market, the properties were not kept in tip-top condition, and the properties were almost always located in areas which were considered undesirable.

Good tenants want what anybody wants; a nice place to live. You should buy properties where you could imagine living. Maybe you need a fairly large personal residence because you have several children. But when you look at a one bedroom condominium as a potential rental unit, it should make you think, "I would have liked to live here when I was young and single." When you look at a starter home, you should think, "This would have been perfect when I was first married." Besides attracting good tenants, desirable properties will give you more liquidity in your real estate investment. If you want or need to sell, you will be able to do it more easily and faster when you have attractive properties.

The second thing you need to do to keep your eviction rate low is to choose good tenants. Even though good tenants won't rent bad properties, bad tenants will still want to rent good properties. Your goal is to eliminate these prospective tenants.

Setting Your Asking Rent

Setting a rent rate can be a hit or miss endeavor when you first invest in a new neighborhood or type of property. Even before you buy a property you should have done some research on competing rental units. How much are they asking for rent? For the security deposit? Are the landlords paying for some or all utilities? Offering flexible lease terms? Accepting pets, and if so, how many and what kinds? Do they charge extra rent for pets or ask for a larger deposit? Is part of the deposit non-refundable?

How much competition is there? If "For Rent" signs are rare, the rental market is probably strong. If you see "For Rent" signs everywhere, and apartment buildings have banners saying "First Month Free!" the rental market is soft and your rents will have to be very competitive in order to avoid vacancy.

Experience with a neighborhood, of course, helps. When I first invested in the Stapleton neighborhood in Denver, it was a very different market than the suburbs where I'd been investing for years. But at least I could use those suburban houses and their rents as a starting point. If a $230,000 twenty-year-old house in the suburbs rented for $1,400, then a $398,000 brand new house near downtown would rent for more. But how much more?

Here are some of the factors I considered while setting the rent for the first house I bought that was located in a different subset of the Denver rental market than I was familiar with. I knew the rental market was weakening because the tech crash in the spring of 2001 hit Colorado hard. Banners were popping up on apartment building saying "$99 Moves You In!" My new house was mostly surrounded by dirt, and every time the wind blew it created a dust storm. Construction trucks rumbled through the neighborhood early in the morning. And because Colorado was experiencing a drought, no one was allowed to install new sod.

Because so few houses had been built yet in Stapleton I couldn't find any competing rentals. So I did research to find other neighborhoods that were similar in terms of features and location. Then I called on properties offered for rent in those neighborhoods. Letting them know I was a landlord, I asked them about their experiences and opinions. One lady in particular was very helpful. Her house was comparable to mine, and although she had at one point rented it for $2,100, she was now asking hundreds less, $1,795, because of the soft rental market.

Even though my new mortgage was $2,000, I decided to ask $1,650 in rent. Although I thought I could get more in a couple of years if the Colorado economy improved, I didn't want to experience months of vacancy by starting off with too high of an asking rent. The neighborhood was too raw and unfinished to ask for more rent, even though the house itself was gorgeous.

As I bought more houses at Stapleton, I used the first house as my reference point. If another house was larger, I knew I could get more than $1,650. If it were smaller, I would take less, but not a lot less. Why? Because through research I'd discovered that the three bedroom, two and a half bedroom townhomes with attached two car garages in Stapleton were renting for $1,300. So even a small house would likely rent for at least $200 more.

Now each time a property becomes available, I try to push up the rent a bit. As long as I have no trouble finding a tenant, I know I can keep pushing on the next property. When I discover a point of resistance, I keep my rents stable for awhile. It's always a balancing act between maximizing my rents and keeping my vacancy as close to zero as I can get it.

Dropping Your Asking Rent

If you are doing a good job letting the world know that your property is available for rent, but you aren't receiving at least four calls on it per week, then you need to drop the rent. It's rarely worth it financially to wait for the tenant who will pay top dollar.

For example, it's better to have one month's vacancy and rent a place for eleven months for $1,200 for a total of $13,200 than to have two months vacancy and rent a property for ten months at $1,300 for a total of $13,000. Besides earning an extra $200 in rent, you'll have someone living in the property. That reduces the chance of vandalism and provides someone else to maintain the yard and pay the utilities. Plus you won't have to worry for that extra month about whether or not you're going to find a tenant to pay the $1,300.

Sometimes a property won't rent for the same amount as the previous tenant paid. In the spring of 2002 I tried to re-rent a suburban property which I had previously rented for $1,550. Potential tenants called and drove by, but few wanted to see inside. I dropped the asking rent to $1,495. No difference in response. Two weeks later I went to $1,445. Still no applications. Another two weeks passed and I changed the ad to $1,395. Boom! Lots of interest, and the property rented quickly.

Was I thrilled about dropping the rent? No. Was I upset? Also, no. Rents sometimes go down as well as up. I focus on the long term trend, not the short term gyrations. My goal is to keep my properties rented to good tenants. If the market has dipped, or I overestimated the potential rent for a new property, I adjust my asking rents quickly.

It's important to have a plan as to how you will handle dropping your asking rent. Otherwise the decision can be very emotional and confusing. After double-checking my advertising - is the ad in the correct section of the newspaper? is the sign still in the yard and upright so people can see it? - I automatically go into my standard rent reduction process. Every two weeks the rent goes down $50, or $75, or $100, depending on how expensive the asking rent is. After all, $50 isn't much of a decrease if I'm asking $2,100, but it's substantial if I started off at $1,095.

I also take a look at the season. Spring and summer months I'll be more aggressive on the initial asking rent and more conservative on the rent decreases. In the fall and holiday season the pattern reverses. I'm conservative about the rent I'm asking, and aggressive about cutting it if I'm not finding a tenant.

How much time I have to find a tenant is an important factor, too. If the current tenants have given me two months notice, it's safer to try for a higher rent. Even so, I still drop the asking rent if I'm not getting very many phone calls. Vacancy is very expensive, so I do what it takes to keep my properties occupied. That generally means being very responsive to the rental market demand. I know my rents are where they need to be when properties gets good applicants inside of two to three weeks.

Following a plan to drop your rents is much better than having no plan and then panicking. I remember another landlord who bought a rental house in Stapleton when I was first investing there. He didn't seem to be aware that the rental market was soft. Although $1,975 would have been a fair rent for his house a year before, it was now too much. And his house was surrounded by construction. That also made the house less desirable, and therefore reduced the market rent.

He stuck at $1,975 for more than six weeks, then hired a property management company and dropped the rent to $1,475. Based on my research, I thought he could have easily rented the house at $1,595. Granted that wasn't a lot more than what he eventually got, but it was $1,200 more per year. He also had two months vacancy at a cost of lost rent equal to $3,200, plus now he was probably paying 10%, or about $1,800 per year, to a management firm. That's $6,000 he could have saved if he had had a plan to drop his rents at a measured pace until he hit the fair market rent. Not to mention that he should have done better research from the start so his initial starting rent wasn't so unrealistic.

This example may sound scary, but it's really not that difficult to determine current rent rates. You have lots of practice shopping for good buys all the time, whether it be for clothing, cars, or food. That's what your prospective tenants are doing. They quickly find out what they can get for their money by calling on "For Rent" signs and ads. Do they have to pay more if they have pets? Do they really want to pay extra to live near a park or open space? Pretend you are a tenant and investigate your local rental market like the expert shopper that you are.

Keep in mind that you can ask prospective tenants for feedback. Are the other properties they've seen as nice or nicer than yours? Does your rent seem out of line? Is your deposit a lot higher than your competitors? When I show a property, and the would-be tenant says no, I ask them these questions. While I take what they say with a grain of salt, any consistent pattern in their comments can be very useful.

Finding Tenants Through Ads & Signs

While you may come up with your own creative ways to get tenants, I consider the best sources to be classified ads, "For Rent" signs, and referrals from tenants or other investors.

Classified ads are the tried-and-true way to get numerous leads. Unfortunately, running an ad continuously for several weeks straight can add up to a big bill. It's best to keep your ad length short. State the basics such as the number of bedrooms, baths and garage spaces, the rent and deposit amounts, and whether or not pets or smokers are welcome.

Besides the basics, your ad should have a teaser at the very beginning. This is where you mention a special feature of the property. Don't get carried away and list every feature; pick one or two. "Brand New House" is appealing to potential tenants. So is "Luxury Master Suite." If it's a big deal in your area, brag about views of mountains or water. If your rental is located in a popular school district, you could say "Eisenhower school district, nearly new three bedroom, two bath house."

Don't put the address of your property in the ad. If you do, it will be difficult to track how many people are interested in your rental. Make them call you to get the address. Even if you leave this information on your voice mail, you'll get the click of a hang-up to tell you that someone called.

If your lease stops at the end of a month, I've found it's best to advertise either six to five weekends ahead of the vacancy or during the two weekends before the property will be available. Advertising three to four weekends ahead generates far fewer calls and wastes advertising money.

Why does this happen? Because tenants who must give one month's notice will look well ahead of the date they hope to move. Tenants who don't pre-plan or who are transferring from out of the area look when they are about to move. It may be different in your area, but my advice is not to panic if you get few calls during weeks three and four.

Internet ads on free sites such as Craigslist haven't yet produced a tenant for me. But it's free to post, so why not? I've had better luck paying to have a newspaper ad also show up on the internet. Doing that with *The Denver Post* produced a fine tenant who rented a property based on pictures I sent him.

Before you pay good money to place your ad in a publication, look at what type of properties are being advertised there. You should see plenty of ads that offer properties similar to the one you have. In *The Denver Post* I saw lots of ads for houses renting between $1,200 and $1,400 in the suburban cities where I owned properties for many years. This paper always generated plenty of calls from my ads.

But after 1031 tax exchanging all of my suburban Denver houses into Stapleton, the newspaper ads stopped working. The neighborhood surrounding what used to be the airport consisted of lower end, older homes and duplexes. The newspaper ads generated calls from people who wanted to know if I accepted Section 8. I did not receive calls from the high income tenants I wanted for these expensive homes. Stapleton was new with hardly any houses and it was the only upper end neighborhood in this quadrant of the city. My newspaper ad was put in a section with ads for a completely different kind of rental property.

In the past I hadn't been impressed with the calls I'd received from "For Rent" signs. Most calls came from people hoping that my rents would be way below market. But because ads didn't work in Stapleton, I had to try something else. I had a sign company make a large professional "For Rent" two-sided sign and put it into a metal frame like real estate agents use. Although the sign cost around $200, I thought it was cheap compared to a newspaper ad because the sign would last for years.

In Stapleton, the sign ended up working very well. Many of the people who were checking out the new homes were also interested in renting. I expect that as Stapleton becomes an established and recognized community, newspaper ads will again become effective. And as the new builder traffic fades, the sign will become less useful in attracting tenants. The point is to be flexible. Just because one method has proven to be effective in the past doesn't guarantee that it will always be the best one.

When you advertise a property using a sign you could put a rider on top with the rent amount. That way people who can't afford to pay that much won't bother to call. However, I don't do this because it would cost too much to get riders made for the different rent amounts I charge. I own a handful of houses at Stapleton, all at different rent rates. The rents I ask change with the season and by how long I've been trying to rent a property. Plus sometimes I have more than one property becoming available. When I get sign calls, the first thing I tell the prospective tenant is the asking rent, then ask if that's in the price range they had in mind. This is a delicate way to ask if they can afford it, and it seems to make people comfortable. If it's too high, and I have another, less expensive, property coming up for rent, I tell them about that property instead.

Sometimes a prospective tenant will ask if I have any flexibility in the rent. I tell them that if the property doesn't rent, I will drop the rent. If they are hoping to pay something close to my asking rent, I request their names and phone numbers so I can call them if I have trouble renting the property. If they are hoping for a drop of many hundreds of dollars, I tell them to watch the sign. If it's still there after a month, they should call me again.

Referrals

Getting tenants referred to you is the least expensive way to find them. If one of your good tenants gives notice, ask them if they know someone else who may want to rent the property. Also let the rest of your good tenants know about this upcoming vacancy. Especially if you own more than one house in the same neighborhood, one of your tenants may know a friend or relative who would like to live close by.

If your property is located near new homes currently being built, give the on-site sales people copies of your flyer. Many new home buyers need rental units until their houses are completed. Even though these tenants tend to be short term, people who can qualify for a loan to buy a new house should easily pass your credit check.

Other investors can be a great source of referrals. If you belong to an investor association, you can let other landlords know about your vacancy during the monthly meeting. Or you may become friends with a few other investors you meet over time. Besides sharing tips on good painters and the best places to buy carpet, you can share tenant leads.

For example, I once ran an ad to rent a house available in May and ended up with two good applicants. A friend had told me he had a vacancy coming up in the middle of June in the same neighborhood. One of my applicants had to give thirty days notice and preferred a later move date so I told them about the other house. That worked better for them, and they ended up renting it. That was the easiest to fill vacancy that my friend ever had.

Screening Phone Calls

Depending on how hot your local rental market is, you may get a deluge of calls or just a slow trickle. The Denver area experienced a fairly tight rental market in the summer of 1998. When I placed an ad for a property at the end of June, I received between two and three calls per day. In the spring of 2002 the market had slowed down considerably. It took a week to receive that many calls.

You should have a list of questions you want to ask when a potential tenant calls. You should also include on your list additional information you want to tell callers, information you didn't include in the ad itself. If you know that your property has a drawback such as no basement, mention it up front. Ask the tenant if that will be a problem for them. It's better to find this out immediately rather than after you've talked to someone for five minutes.

If you allow pets on a negotiable basis, find out what pets they have. Most pet owners will volunteer this information immediately. If you won't accept their pet, the phone call is probably over.

Remember to ask when the tenants need to move in because it won't necessarily be the same date your rental will go vacant. If someone calls me about a property available the first of this month, but they want it for the first of next month, I volunteer to split the month with them. I remind them that the extra two weeks will give them plenty of time to move. Almost everyone will agree to this compromise. If not, I prefer to take my chances on finding another tenant who will move in more quickly.

Do inform callers about the amenities you didn't mention in the ad. Tell them your property is located only two blocks away from the elementary school or the city recreation center. Tell them about the public swimming pools, parks, and bicycle trails.

Short Term and Long Term Tenants

A tenant who plans to rent from you for two years is generally more desirable than someone who wants a place for a year or less. Be careful about accepting short term leases. Too soon you'll be facing the hassle of renting your property again. Your property will also suffer the additional damage caused by more people moving in and out of the house. Short term tenants will rarely be willing to pay you a rent premium large enough to compensate you for these problems.

Tell people interested in short term leases that you might consider taking them if you don't find a long term tenant in the next two weeks. Write down their names and phone numbers so you can call them back if the property is still available. Maybe you will be happy to take a short term tenant at that time, but unless it's Thanksgiving or your rental market is very soft, you should give yourself a chance to find a long term tenant instead.

Showing Your Properties

When you start to receive calls on your properties, don't rush right out to show them. You can waste a lot of time this way. If prospective tenants called on an ad instead of a sign in the front yard, they may drive by the property after you give them the address, decide they don't like the exterior or the neighborhood, then not bother to show up for their appointment.

You can avoid this problem by advising them to drive by the property first, then call you back if they are interested in seeing the interior. Be sure to remind them not to peer in the windows or wander into the backyard if someone still lives there. On the other hand, if it's vacant, you may want to intentionally leave a few blinds half-pulled so people can see the lovely hardwood floors or beautiful kitchen.

When you schedule a time to show a property, try to cluster another showing close to it. If a prospective tenant wants to see the property at two in the afternoon, tell the next caller you could show it to them at one forty-five or two-fifteen. Since some of your prospective tenants won't show up for their appointments, you'll increase your chances of a productive trip by scheduling more than one showing.

The ultimate in scheduling all prospective tenants at the same time is to hold a rental open house. Advertise your property in the rental section as usual, but include open house hours. Make sure the newspaper doesn't stick your ad under houses for sale like they did to me once (that produced zero response!). Hold the open house on a Saturday. Many tenants set aside one weekend to find a rental house. If they can find something they like on Saturday, they won't wait to see other houses on Sunday.

Avoiding Dangerous People

You should realize that not all callers are looking for a house to rent. They may not be tenants at all. While rare, you may find yourself showing an empty house to someone who is dangerous. When I schedule a showing, I get that person's name and phone number and tell them I'll have to check if I can show the property at the time we've agreed on. Then I call them back. That way I know I have a phone number where they can be reached. Then I give this information to my husband or business partner.

When you show the property, it's best if you have someone with you. I tell my current tenants to feel free to stay in the house during showings. Sometimes I take my husband or sister with me when I show the property. If I'm doing a rental open house, I always have someone with me.

Sometimes you will decide to show properties alone. Tell the tenant that you told other people you would be at the property showing it, and that you invited them to drop by at the same time. I leave this invitation on my answering machine in case other potential tenants call so somebody else could indeed be showing up unexpectedly.

I don't want to scare you unduly with this advice, but you should be careful. Each year a few real estate agents, both male and female, are killed showing properties to buyers they don't know. Property owners face many of the same risks as agents. Though it's unlikely you'll encounter someone dangerous, it's best to be cautious.

Bad and Good Tenants

Who is a bad tenant? Your definition must comply with all federal, state, and local laws. If your definition of an undesirable tenant includes someone with children, I sympathize. Children do tend to cause damage. However, it's illegal to select your tenants based on family status. I'll tell you more about these protected classes later in this chapter in the Fair Housing Section.

You do have the right to discriminate based on other criteria which are perfectly legal. I use a number of criteria to qualify prospective tenants as either desirable or undesirable. First, will they make the monthly rent payments? This involves more than having an adequate income to pay the rent. I once had some female tenants who danced at a strip club. They made a lot of money, but paying the rent wasn't always their number one priority.

You may decide not to rent to people with certain professions. This is usually legal if you are consistent. Some local governments, though, may prohibit restrictions against certain types of employment such as military personnel.

Another group of tenants I've learned to avoid based on other property owners' experiences are those people who rely on someone else to help them pay the rent. These people range from trust fund babies to people receiving financial help from their parents to Section 8 recipients.

Regarding Section 8, I will say I've met landlords who love this government sponsored program. The government pays part of the rent payments, and it's easy to find new Section 8 tenants. You may be willing to participate in this program, but realize that you could be required to allow Section 8 tenants in all of your properties if you decide to accept a Section 8 tenant in even one of your properties. Since leases will not end all at the same time because of the occasional broken lease (the tenant leaves early), you may not be able to exit the program once you start.

You will also have Big Brother supervising you. If you and Big Brother disagree, Big Brother employs bureaucrats to harass you. And just to drive you crazy, not every bureaucrat will interpret the rules the same way. It's the nature of working with the government. Personally, I'm not interested in this program, but it may suit you just fine. Try to talk to other investors in your area to find out what their experiences have been with the local bureaucrats.

Personally, I want tenants who have to earn their rent payments by working. These tenants, in my opinion, are more responsible and desirable. They know how hard they must work to make those monthly payments, and they appreciate the money and time I've invested in their rental homes.

Adequate Incomes and Good Credit

How do you decide if a tenant's income will be sufficient to cover the rent yet leave enough for the tenant to pay other expenses? I like the rent amount to equal less than thirty percent of the tenants' monthly income, but I can be flexible if they have little other monthly debt that must be paid. I may let the rent go as high as forty percent of their income if they don't have car or student loan payments.

Be careful when you have a couple applying to rent your property who don't have enough income to qualify, but one spouse is unemployed and supposedly looking for a job. They'll want you to evaluate their ability to afford the rent based on the not-as-yet established second income. I've been burned by this before, because the wife never did bother to get a job. And instead of paying all the rent, the wife gave me stories. In the end I was relieved just to get her and her family out of my house at a loss of thousands of dollars in unpaid rent.

This isn't to say that some people won't actually get a job. But be cautious. Unless someone is unemployed because he or she is following a spouse who got a job transfer, and this person was employed before the move, I wouldn't count this hypothetical income when deciding how much rent they can afford.

Sometimes people are self-employed. This makes it almost impossible to verify their incomes. Even if you get them to show you their last tax return, you will know they did their best to minimize the income they reported. So what do you do? Sometimes I require a larger security deposit. Or if they can show proof of substantial liquid assets in a brokerage account or bank account, and their credit is excellent, that may make me comfortable about accepting them.

I always check a tenant's credit. The best way to see if someone will pay their rent, and pay it on time, is to look at their credit record. Many companies exist that provide credit checking services for property owners (they will also usually provide you with a rental application to use). Look in the phone book under "Credit Reports" or "Employment Screening and Tenant Verification." The credit reporting company will have forms for you to complete in order to be allowed to use their services. Do this well in advance of advertising for tenants. When you get a rental application, you want to be able to get the credit check run quickly.

The credit reporting company I use lets me fax in the rental application in the morning and calls me back with the results late that afternoon. If prospective tenants have a great financial track record, I will probably accept them, even when I can't verify their incomes.

I do, however, look out for tenants with high credit card balances, car payments, and student loans. They may have managed to juggle all their bills until now, but I don't want everything to go delinquent while they are living in my property. Someone who declares bankruptcy can prolong an eviction, and in the meantime I may not get any rent.

In the past I've accepted tenants with a bad credit history. If the blotch on the credit history came with a good story, such as a past lapse of health insurance combined with a health problem, I'd try to verify the story. In one case the prospective tenants said the wife's Cesarean delivery had not been covered by health insurance. Their credit report showed a write-off from a doctor and a hospital two years ago, and they had a two-year-old child. Since their other bills were current, I decided to accept these applicants. Without good credit, they wouldn't be able to buy a house so I hoped they would be reliable, long term tenants.

Most tenants I accepted who had credit problems were among my worst tenants. These tenants were the ones who had the most difficulty paying the rent, and they didn't keep the properties as clean. Any pets who caused problems always were owned by people who had some sort of credit problems when I accepted them. Because of these experiences I've gotten tougher about taking tenants with any credit blotches, even ones related to business failures or medical costs. I'd rather drop the rent if necessary to find someone with clean credit.

While you may be more inclined to make exceptions for minor credit problems, especially if your rental market is soft, please take it seriously if a past landlord has reported late rent payments or an actual eviction. You may get excuses from the tenant, but you paid for a credit report to protect yourself from tenants who don't pay. My sister once had an applicant who had been evicted twice in the previous thirteen months, but the tenant claimed it was an error on the part of the credit bureau. Shelley expressed sympathy and invited the tenant to reapply after the tenant's credit report had been corrected. Until then, the tenant's application was declined.

If you do decide to reject a potential tenant based on a bad credit report, then the Fair Credit Reporting Act requires you to do the following. You must give the applicant the name of the credit reporting agency, explain that the credit agency didn't make the decision to reject them (you did), and let them know they have the right to get a copy of their credit report. They may then dispute the report (not your decision not to reject their rental application), and present their side of the story by adding a consumer statement to the credit report.

If you have any questions about what you must do in this situation, ask the company who ran the credit report for you to give you guidance. Remember that these requirements are designed to alert consumers to their credit reporting rights. They do not mean that you must accept people with bad credit as tenants.

The Wheedlers

Bad tenants don't accept no easily - otherwise they would never find a place to rent! Indeed, I've learned that one tip-off for a bad tenant is someone who talks too much, who always has a story to explain everything. These people can be incredibly nice, but they are often a landlord's tenant nightmare.

Let me say it again; if someone babbles it probably isn't just a personality trait. They've learned to distract and disarm people by talking. If you can't get hold of their past two landlords to check references or if they have anything questionable about their credit report, watch out! It's very difficult to tell these people no because they just keep pushing, looking for your weak spot. For example, they may tell you how their last landlady has incurable cancer. That's why she's been forced to sell her rental property, making her beloved tenants move, and that's why she's hard to reach on the telephone - she's busy dying.

You may be thinking, hah!, I wouldn't fall for that type of nonsense. But I did, in the fall of 2001, despite my years of experience. The potential tenant's credit had some blotches, but she was so friendly, so open, willing to move in soon, and it was the middle of November. I decided to give her a chance.

After she moved in, the rent went delinquent immediately. When I told her she needed to pay her rent with good as cash funds instead of checks, as per her lease, she blithely ignored me. Bogged down with other tenant problems (every year seems to have its theme, and 2002 was the year of tenants not paying the rent for all kinds of reasons), I stumbled along with her for months as she caught up on her past due rent before presenting me with yet another bad check.

Looking back I see that I should have turned down her application. It would have been hard. She seemed so open, and she was a genuinely friendly person. But even if she had pleaded and begged and cajoled, I needed to say no. It would have been far better to have taken the risk of having the property sit vacant through Christmas. I lost several months worth of rent before I got her out of my property, and that doesn't count the months of aggravation. Dealing with her endless stories wore me out emotionally. If I had been a beginning landlord, she might have driven me right out of the business.

Watch out for the wheedlers!

Maintaining a Property

When you're evaluating whether or not tenants will maintain a property in good condition, you can ask about their home maintenance skills. You can look at the way they dress, the way their car looks, and how their children behave. If the kids are sliding down the banisters while you are showing the house, and the parents don't seem to notice or care, this is going to be a problem.

I love renting to previous homeowners. They come complete with a toolbox, hose, lawn mower, and plenty of experience fixing the little things. By the way, I don't provide snow shovels, hoses, and lawn mowers to my tenants who rent houses. That's their responsibility if they want to live in a single family house. This saves me a bit of money, but far more importantly I'm not responsible for maintaining and replacing these items. That's important because being a landlady already involves plenty of hassles without me also getting calls about leaky garden hoses. Not to mention I'm not as liable if someone hurts themselves using equipment they, not I, own.

Long Term Tenants

A long term tenant is much better than a short term tenant, but it's not always easy to predict how long someone will rent from you. Even young couples who you think would want to buy their own home may take years to do it. Other couples happily break their leases early and sacrifice part of their deposit to buy a home.

I have found no consistent pattern except for two exceptions. If people say they are under contract to buy a new house which will be done in four to eight months, they will be moving soon. People with a questionable credit history, however, will usually renew their leases because they need time to repair their financial reputation. However, these are usually the tenants who have been paying their rent late to you, and you don't want them to stay!

My advice is to avoid the very short term tenants who are closing on a house in a few months. Only take them if you are getting desperate for someone with good credit, you are heading into the winter holiday season and just want to get past Christmas, or the tenant will pay an extra 15-20% rent premium to make it worth your while.

Questionable Credit Versus a Soft Heart

Potential tenants with questionable credit are a calculated risk. They already have marred credit records so they don't have as much to lose by incurring another ding from you, but they could turn out to be long term tenants because they can't qualify to buy a house. A long term tenant translates into less time, money and energy managing your properties, so that can be valuable.

Yet I've gotten much pickier over the years about accepting tenants with not so great credit records. As I settled down to edit this chapter for the second edition of this book, I looked back at all my tenants. The ones who couldn't keep their credit clean couldn't keep my houses clean either. They were the ones most likely to bounce a rent check or lose their jobs. They let their pets cause damage to the houses and the yards.

Even though most of them did pay the rent eventually, I can't emphasize enough how much more trouble they caused than the rest of my tenants combined. I've concluded that people who have trouble paying their bills are generally people who have trouble planning for anything - emergencies, someone to water the lawn when they are on vacation, or how they'll pay their debts including their monthly rent.

If you decide to consider tenants with so-so credit, I recommend requiring a significantly higher security deposit. Of course, these are the people who are the least likely to have the extra cash. And shouldn't we give people a chance, help them recover from whatever disaster they say caused their bad credit? Wouldn't we want help if our spouse divorced us and left us with three kids, or the small business we owned went bankrupt, or someone in our family got cancer?

This is where it can be difficult to be a good landlord. If you are a basically nice person, it is VERY hard to tell these people no. But if you want to be a landlord for long, you must. Otherwise their problems will become your problems as they fail to pay the rent or accidentally damage your properties. Between the financial hits you suffer while they are your tenants and the demoralization of facing a filthy vacant house after they leave, you will soon be selling your rentals.

If you feel that badly for prospective tenants who don't meet your standards, it's probably better just to hand them money rather than rent to them. Do you feel sorry enough for them to give them $500? $1,000? Or more? Honestly, it is better to give them that money up front and find a better tenant than it will be to take them as tenants. Because if you accept them, they will cost you hundreds if not thousands of dollars in unpaid rent and damages, and even more in terms of enthusiasm and time.

I recommend that you keep charity and business separate if you want to stay in the rental business for more than two years. I make money as a landlord, and I give money to charities. One of my favorite charities provides transitional housing for families in need, and helps low-income people with heating bills and food. This approach works for me.

And if somebody gives you grief about not giving hard luck tenants a chance, ask if they would like to co-sign the lease and provide the extra security deposit. Then if the tenants don't pay promptly or damage the property, you can immediately go after the co-signor, and it will be up to them to hassle the tenants to get reimbursed. Hmm, not interested. That's what I thought.

Accepting Pets

I allow pets on a negotiable basis since it gives me a much broader pool of tenants. Only once did a pair of tenants allow their dogs to do substantial damage to one of my properties (and, yes, their credit report had a few problems when I accepted them). I believe my overall good fortune has been due to selecting good tenants. Responsible people who pay their bills and take pride in their personal living environment do not allow their pets to destroy a house.

I want to know the ages of any pets. Puppies make puddles, and old dogs become incontinent. Unfixed animals, whether feline or canine, get into trouble. Even an unfixed female cat may spray in the house. I want animals who are middle aged for their breed and who don't have the ability to reproduce.

I also watch out for tenants who talk about their pets as beloved members of the family. I have eight cats, and I adore them, but I know they are pets. I would be appalled if someone could tell I owned even one cat because they could smell something unpleasant in my house (and, no, I don't disguise odors with artificial air freshener - I expect my cats to use the litter boxes which my husband and I empty regularly). Some people are inordinately attached to their animals, and will forgive them any wrong, including damaging my properties. I don't want to rent to people who coo when they talk about Fido or Fluffy. They are probably very caring people, but not the best tenants.

If a tenant has any type of credit problem, then no pets. In my experience, a tenant's credit score correlates perfectly with how well they control their pets. Less than sterling credit usually equals less than spotless house cleaning, and I don't want to vacuum up a year's worth of dog hair or replace two-year-old urine-soaked carpet when these tenants move out. I've been there, done that, and don't intend to do it again.

The Trouble with Smokers

I'm tough when it comes to smokers. Smoke makes its way into the carpets and the drapes. It discolors the walls and ceilings. Once a property has been rented to a smoker, especially a heavy smoker, nonsmokers may not be willing to rent it until the drapes and carpets have been cleaned and the walls repainted.

If a smoker tells me he or she only smokes outside, I don't believe them. The weather gets cold. It gets hot. Sometimes it rains or snows. Why will these people worry about my no-smoking rules when it's unpleasant outside? Every smoker I know gets tempted to break this agreement, even when married to a disapproving spouse who will find out as soon as she or he comes home and smells the telltale smoke.

Fortunately, few people smoke in my tenant price range. As a real estate broker, I noticed that the less expensive a house was, the more likely it was for the owner to smoke. If I owned smaller, less expensive units, I would probably have to allow some smokers. As it is, my ads state pets negotiable, no smokers. I'd rather deal with a bare spot in the lawn than the persistent odor of smoke.

Argumentative Tenants

You will talk to some strange people when you advertise a property for rent. Back before I became quite clear on my tenant selection guidelines, I had a man call on a rental house who told me he had an unfixed dog. Whoops. I told him the animal would have to be neutered. Okay, said the prospective tenant. He'd do it after he moved here.

I told him it would have to be done within thirty days, not totally happy with the idea of letting him move in with an unfixed dog. Did I really want to risk fighting with him if he later changed his mind? Plus, it was a bulldog. The owner said it was as gentle as could be, but bulldogs were named that because of their ability to take down bulls. My alarm bells were starting to ring.

Then the prospective gentleman told me he was moving to Colorado because he was going to start his own business. "Wonderful," I thought, "the guy doesn't have a stable source of income." And then he added that he needed three bedrooms so his live-in girlfriend's parents could visit. Why? Because they helped her out financially and in return they expected a bedroom they could stay in.

You can guess how thrilled I was at this point. Rather than bluntly turn the guy down (I knew I wasn't going to accept him), I explained that if I did decide to rent the property to him, I would need the security deposit up front, in good-as-cash funds. This would be necessary if he wanted me to hold the house for him until he took possession in two weeks.

This guy was already reminding me of a smarmy salesman with his I'm-your-pal attitude, and now he complained that I was nicking him too much. Why couldn't I just take an out-of-state check? He wouldn't be home for a week, and therefore couldn't go to his bank for a cashier's check until then.

I wrapped up our conversation fairly quickly. This prospective tenant didn't understand that it was my valuable property we were discussing and therefore I made the rules. All my requirements were legal and consistent, and I wasn't going to be badgered into changing them for his benefit. I told him that perhaps he could find some other property owner who was more flexible and reasonable than I was. I was relieved to say a firm good-bye and hang up.

As soon as you find yourself talking with someone who wants to argue about your rules, you know you have a problem tenant. Most people will respect your positions when you explain them. Why would I want to risk keeping a property vacant for two weeks at a cost of $620 in lost rent while I waited for an out-of-state check to clear?

Most people understand that you need your deposit in good-as-cash funds. If they are flying home the next day, they can overnight you a cashier's check or wire you the money directly into your rental checking account. Or they can get a cash advance on their credit cards from a local bank. Reasonable people understand that you need your deposit as soon as possible, or else you'll have to rent to someone else.

There is a certain type of person who slides through life by haranguing other people into bending the rules. Then these people take advantage of this kindness by trying to bend the rules even further. After my sister told her prospective tenant with the two recent evictions no, the woman called frequently over a two week period trying to wear Shelley down into taking her as a tenant despite her crummy credit.

While this type of prospective tenant is rare, you should know how to recognize one and be ready to tell them you will not rent to them. If they are hard to handle during the interview process, imagine what it will be like arguing for your rent every month. Accepting this type of tenant can produce great horror stories to tell other investors, but in the meantime he or she will make you regret ever buying a rental property. Remember that what you want is just as important as what some tenant wants, and since you have the power to choose, say good-bye to unpleasant people.

Perfect and Good Enough Tenants

Some property owners I know spend weeks looking for the perfect tenants. My time is too valuable for that. I look for good enough tenants. The first person who meets my requirements gets the property. Maybe somebody else won't cause a two week vacancy because their move date matches my property's availability date. Maybe somebody else has a higher paying job, or wants to rent for two years instead of only one. Then again, maybe this somebody won't show up and I'll regret not taking the good enough tenant.

If it's important to you to have numerous applicants to choose among, you should set your rents a bit below the market rate. The more aggressively you discount your rents, the more applicants you will have in a short period of time, and the choosier you can be.

The market for rentals changes constantly. If the market in your area gets soft, I do recommend lowering your rent rather than dropping your standards for an acceptable tenant. A reduced rental amount is worth it in exchange for high quality tenants. But remember that a good enough tenant doesn't mean the first person who says "I'll take it" when they see your property.

Once when I advertised a house for rent, I had six sets of people look at it over the weekend. My current tenant showed the property since I was out of town (though I was regularly checking my messages and calling back the people who wanted to schedule a showing).

One set of tenants announced on Saturday that they would take the property. Although the husband said he was a nonsmoker, he smelled of smoke, and the family owned a fifteen-week-old Rottweiler puppy. On Sunday a young man with a temporary job announced that he and his roommate wanted to rent the house. He was glad the landlady had a no smoking policy because he wanted her to make sure his roommate kept his agreement to only smoke outside.

Three other tenants said the house wouldn't work for them, and the last set was noncommittal. This family had particularly impressed my tenant. The children were well-behaved, the parents did not smell like smokers, and overall they seemed like pleasant people.

Even though I felt pressured to accept an application from one of the two sets of prospective tenants who said they wanted the property, I told them no. Both were probably going to smoke in the house, and then I'd have the hassle of evicting them before they turned the house yellow and stinky.

Since the one man had stated he didn't smoke, I didn't address that issue. Why argue about whether or not he really did smoke? I told his wife that a puppy didn't go well with the new perennial flower garden I was putting into the backyard (fifteen feet by fifty-five feet). This reason was true as well, and had the advantage of being irrefutable.

I was prepared to run my ad again, but luckily the noncommittal tenants called back. They had decided they wanted the property. Their credit wasn't perfect, but it came with a good story that checked out. They wanted to rent for two to three years while they got their finances in order, and then buy a house. Because the father was allergic, they would never be getting a cat or dog.

I accepted these tenants. They weren't perfect because of the marred credit. They turned out to be cheerful, sweet-hearted slobs who helped teach me that not-so-good credit equals a dirtier house, yet overall they were good enough tenants who stayed in the property for more than two years. The other two sets of tenants were not good enough.

Making someone unhappy by telling them no is unpleasant, but it's a short term type of pain. Better that than a long term pain in the form of a bad tenant. So be brave and say no to the not good enough tenant. Your reward will be getting the type of tenant you want, the kind who makes your life as a landlord as easy as it can be.

Option to Rent

Sometimes tenants will want to rent a property that you already have rented to someone else. As soon as it becomes available, they want to be the first in line. In order to ensure that this is the case, they may want to sign an Option to Rent agreement.

I was very surprised the first time this happened. An elderly woman who had recently lost her husband wanted to live near her son. This man owned a house behind one of my rental properties. He had seen my rental sign when I last rented my house. What could be more perfect for his mother than to live across the alley? He wanted to make sure she had the legal right to be the first to apply when the current tenants moved out.

Because the property wouldn't be available for half a year, I wasn't comfortable approving an application right then. Too much could change in that time period. So we drew up an Option to Rent agreement. In exchange for a fee that would be refundable if I later turned down the tenant's application, I agreed that this woman would have the first chance to put in an application for the property.

We defined the requirements she would have to meet to be accepted as my tenant such as a credit score above 625, and income/asset requirements. We stated how I would notify the applicant about the rental availability and how much time she would have to apply for it before I would be allowed to accept competing applications. I also said she could cancel the option to rent agreement and receive a refund of her deposit at any time - after all, that would leave me exactly where I usually was, looking for a tenant when my tenants gave notice. I wouldn't be hurt. Indeed, the main reason I did the Option to Rent agreement was to set the lady's mind at rest. I was thrilled to have a tenant lined up so far in advance.

Renting Multiple Properties

One of the advantages of owning a number of properties in one neighborhood is the chance to rent two or more properties by running one ad or putting up one "For Rent" sign. I will often have people call who want a bigger house or one with a later possession date than the house I'm advertising. If I have houses with leases ending over a succession of months, some callers can be switched to the next available house.

Because the Stapleton neighborhood is relatively expensive, it doesn't generate good cash flow. This means it isn't as attractive to landlords. Not to mention that many of the builders refused to sell to landlords the first two years. So the rental market for houses in this neighborhood is relatively tight due to a limited number of them. People who want to live here have to be diligent to find a rental home as opposed to a townhome or apartment (the master builder constructed hundreds of apartments). During the spring and summer, people who want to rent houses jump on any sign. Sometimes I rent two houses when I stick a sign in a yard. When prospective tenants have flexible moving dates, I rent them houses that won't be available until four months into the future.

It's very relaxing to have tenants lined up so far in advance. It also reduces vacancy. But to enjoy the same type of situation, you need to mention the possibility of other houses to callers. Most of the time they won't be interested, but it's lovely when it works out for everyone involved.

Fair Housing Laws

Federal, state and local laws exist which place restrictions on how property owners select tenants. These laws are designed to eliminate discrimination against certain classes of people.

State and local laws go beyond the federal laws by adding protected classes and providing for other tenant protections and benefits. For example, the city of Boulder prohibits discrimination based on sexual orientation, thereby adding a protected class, and the city also requires 5% interest to be paid on security deposits, which is a benefit for tenants.

The federal Fair Housing Act prohibits discrimination on the basis of race, color, religion, sex, national origin, disability and familial status. All residential property must comply with a limited number of exceptions.

For example, if you own a four-plex and live in one of the units, the other units are not covered by the federal law. Also, if a single family home is offered for sale or rent **by the owner**, discrimination is allowed 1) if the owner does not use the services of a rental or real estate agent or anyone in the business of selling real estate; 2) the owner does not own or have an interest in more than three single family homes; and 3) the owner does not engage in any illegal advertising.

These amazing exceptions, I believe, were allowed under the assumption that small time property owners could not be expected to comply with the Fair Housing Act due to lack of education and awareness. Many states such as Colorado have enacted laws which eliminate these exceptions (Colorado only allows familial status to be used as a basis of discrimination in the previously described small property owner situations). In addition,

Colorado law applies to all property, including commercial property, whereas the federal law applies only to residential property.

There are two key things you can do to stay on the right side of the law. First, obtain something in writing from your state department of housing which details your state's fair housing laws, and also check with the housing departments of the cities where you own or plan to own rental property.

Second, be consistent in how you treat potential tenants. When people call on ads, ask everyone the same questions and give everyone the same additional information (this is where your written lists come in handy). Be careful not to inadvertently get into trouble.

An example of accidentally making yourself liable to accusations of discrimination could occur in the following way. Some tenants in a protected class (which includes everyone) call about your property. Let's say they have a dog and you tell them you don't take pets.

Three weeks later the property is still vacant, and you decide to accept pets after all. You rent to someone with a dog. This person is not in the same protected class as the first set of tenants who liked your property. They see the dog, and accuse you of refusing to rent to them because of who they are, not because they own a dog. After all, you accepted a different dog owner as a tenant.

How do you protect yourself in a situation like this? By asking for everyone's name and number when you turn them down due to some requirement that could change. They smoke? Tell them you currently hope to get a tenant who does not, but you would like to take their name and number in case you change your mind. Ditto for income requirements, pet ownership, house maintenance skills, anything that you hope to get in a tenant but may not insist upon.

You can also protect yourself by keeping records of your previous tenants. Supposedly you are blind when it comes to the protected classes, but wouldn't it be nice to produce a list of past tenants who lived in your properties with children if you ever are accused of discriminating based on familial status? You get the idea. Don't throw out those old leases; keep them in a file somewhere with the original applications attached (do black out social security numbers to prevent identity theft).

If you ever have any questions about fair housing laws and how they might apply in a particular circumstance, call your state's department of fair housing. It may be called something very different so you may have to do some sleuthing. Other common names are the Civil Rights Commission, the Open Housing Commission, or the Department/Commission of Human Affairs or Human Rights. The staff should be able to answer your questions and provide information on your state laws.

Or call your real estate attorney for guidance. An attorney who specializes in real estate law should be very familiar with the current status of housing law in your state, county, and city.

Chapter Nine

Day to Day Details

This chapter is a collection of tidbits which can make your life as a property owner run more smoothly.

Property Insurance

Getting good insurance policies on your rental properties will protect you against losing your investments. Since insurance is regulated by the states, the insurance available where you live may not include some of the coverage I'm about to suggest. The two states where I own properties, Texas and Colorado, handle property insurance very differently.

Even if you don't have a mortgage and therefore no mortgage company insisting that you have insurance, you should definitely insure your properties. I remember reading about a landlord in San Antonio, Texas, who stopped paying for insurance after she paid off her two rental houses. The next year she lost both houses in a flood. You want to insure your properties against all the usual risks such as fire and flood and tornados. The coverage is well worth the cost.

Policies with different levels of coverage are offered for rental properties. Check with your insurance agent for information on the types of policies available in your state. I believe it is worth it to pay extra to get a more comprehensive policy rather than the most basic policy that will satisfy your lender. You want a policy that covers as many possibilities as is reasonable, in particular something called All Risk insurance.

The name All Risk isn't entirely accurate because some claims are disallowed. But this type of policy will cover tenant vandalism to a property. Vandalism, or malicious mischief, is not strictly defined. But it is an intentional act, one of reckless disregard for the property. If your tenant maliciously trashes your property, you can file a claim. The insurance company will pay to fix the damage, cover your lost rent for up to twelve months while the repairs are being done, and last, go after your tenant to be reimbursed.

What type of tenant damage is covered by All Risk insurance and what is not? Despite what some landlords would like to believe, All Risk insurance does not mean any damage done by a tenant is vandalism. For example, let's say you rent a house to students who proceed to retrofit your refrigerator to hold a keg and damage the appliance in the process. And all winter long these tenants leave a dog in the basement on multiple occasions past the animal's ability to hold its urine. Plus they host numerous parties. This results in the carpet eventually acquiring a collection of stains and the walls getting large indentations from the friendly but rambunctious wrestling matches that serve as entertainment.

While certainly these tenants are careless and their security deposit is not going to be returned, these tenants aren't vandals. They didn't intentionally mean to cause damage. Additionally, they trashed the property over time in multiple events. Even if the damage could be classified as reckless disregard for the property, because it was done bit by bit each event is a separate claim. Each claim means that you need to pay your deductible again.

In this situation an insurance company is likely to say that your damaged house is the result of on-going property management neglect rather than tenant vandalism. You should have noticed the damage earlier, and either stopped it from continuing to happen or evicted the tenant. Even if you get the insurance company to pay, filing too many claims may lead to your insurance being cancelled on all your properties.

In contrast, let's say you have a tenant who stops paying the rent. He strings you along with stories until finally you file for eviction. You tell the tenant that you intend to collect on the unpaid rent not covered by the security deposit by taking him to small claims court. Your tenant freaks out. He's not paying the rent because he lost his job, his marriage is going south from the financial strain, and now you are promising to drag him into court.

You become the lightning rod for all his frustration and anger, and before he moves out he does as much damage to your property as he can. Holes are punched in the walls so he can pull out the electrical wires and cut them, cement is poured into the toilet, the doors are torn off the cabinets and broken, and the carpet is slashed.

This is the type of situation that All Risk insurance is designed for. While you could have been more understanding and agreed to forget the unpaid rent if the tenant would quickly vacate the property in clean condition, you have been a diligent property manager who has been monitoring your properties. The damage done to this property is clearly malicious and substantial, and done in one concentrated burst of activity. It's worth it to file a claim for something like this.

Renter's Insurance

Some property owners require their tenants to get renter's insurance and provide proof that they have done this. If you require a certificate of insurance, you can have it set up so you'll be notified if the tenant cancels the coverage. My insurance agent thinks that making a rental insurance policy a requirement is a good idea, but currently I only recommend it to my tenants. I have so many other requirements that I hesitate to add one more, not to mention I hate the idea of the additional work required to check tenant compliance.

I explain at the time the lease is signed that renter's insurance is a relatively inexpensive policy that protects the personal belongings of the tenant. For example, if my tenant's Christmas tree catches fire in the family room, and most of the tenant's furniture in that room is destroyed, the damage to the house will be covered under the landlord's insurance policy. The damage to the furniture will not be covered. This is because the owner's landlord policy only covers the house, not any of the contents.

For a cost of under $200 per year in most areas of the United States, tenants can purchase a renter's insurance policy that will provide coverage for their personal possessions. Some insurance companies such as Farmer's Insurance will automatically include a $100,000 liability policy as part of the renter's insurance.

This liability policy protects the tenant in case they accidentally damage your property. Instead of losing their security deposit plus possibly more, they can file a claim and only have to pay their deductible. Going back to the example of the Christmas tree fire, your insurance company could decide that your tenants' negligence, perhaps by placing a candle close to the tree, led to the fire and the resulting damage. In that case the tenants' liability policy will hopefully cover them. Otherwise, they may be facing a very large bill presented by your insurance company.

Most renter's insurance policies will also provide for additional living expenses. For example, if that Christmas tree fire damages the house badly enough to force the tenants to move out, most renter's policies will provide money to pay for a short term rental while the house is being repaired. Things happen, and your tenants could be one of those people being interviewed on the ten o'clock news. Wouldn't it be good if they could tell the reporter that they were going to be put up in a hotel suite by their insurance company instead of camping in their relatives' back yard?

If you explain to your tenants how much protection they can get for a small annual payment, they will probably want renter's insurance. Even if they have few valuable possessions, they may be reassured to know that if they accidentally damage your property, they'll only have to pay a deductible. And if they lose their home, a hotel will be paid for by someone else. Do, however, make it very clear that they must rely on their insurance agent's explanation of the coverage they are buying. Many items can vary from deductible amounts to the limits and kind of coverage and benefits.

Best Rental Months

Hopefully, your old lease will end during one of the popular rental months. June and July are the best months, but May and August are close runner-ups. Next best are April and September. The worst month of all is December. Almost no one chooses to move at this time of year. Calls from prospective tenants will be few and far between.

When you sign a lease, try to get the last month to land in the spring or summer. I've done leases shorter or longer than a year in order to do this. However, if you are still at the point of acquiring properties, realize that some lenders will want to see leases of one year or longer on all of your properties. A shorter lease may cause you problems when you apply for your next loan.

Whether short or long leases are better is a matter of opinion. On one hand many tenants will honor a longer lease. At the least, if they break it early, you can use their security deposit to cover the lost rent until you re-rent the property. In return, though, you are also stuck in a long lease. If your tenants are doing something you hate, you may not be able to get rid of them until the end of the lease.

For example, say your tenant never waters the lawn. Week after week it's you who is out there moving the hose. The lease says the tenant is responsible, but an eviction judge might not consider this a significant enough breach of the lease to justify an eviction. A tenant's right to keep his or her home is very powerful. In other words, if you try to evict the tenant for not watering the lawn, the judge may not rule in your favor.

Or you may have a tenant who always pays the rent late. In Colorado, even if you have to start an eviction proceeding each and every month in order to get your tenant to pay the rent, as long as the tenant does pay by the third business day after you post the eviction notice, you're stuck accepting the rent plus any late fee. It may drive you crazy and it may be a waste of your time, but you'll have to do this every month they are late with the rent until the lease ends. Make sure your late fee is big enough to compensate you for your time.

Reserve and Maintenance Funds

Every property owner should have a property reserve fund. This money will allow you to sleep easily because if a furnace needs to be replaced, a tenant evicted, or a long vacancy endured, you will have cash available to cover these costs.

Your reserve funds should be kept in an account which is separate from your personal savings. Its sole purpose is to be used as short term operating funds for your real estate investment business. Resist the urge to borrow from it to pay for other expenses, or the money won't be there when you need it.

When I started out as a landlord, my reserve fund consisted of $2,000 for each property until I reached $5,000 in my savings account. At that point I stopped adding any additional money because the majority of my properties produced cash flow. Because I have 1031 tax deferred most of my properties in the past few years to increase my leverage, my mortgage payments are roughly twice as large and most of my properties produce negative cash flow. Repair costs have also risen because of inflation.

So I've increased my target for my reserve fund to $10,000. That way if two or three properties go vacant at the same time and one needs new carpeting and another a new paint job, I'll be fine. Having this reserve fund gives me peace of mind. It also allows me to maintain high standards for prospective tenants. I don't find myself getting desperate to fill a vacancy.

You may want to keep more or less money in your reserve fund depending on your financial circumstances and the price range of your properties. If you are investing in an expensive part of the country and have mortgage payments which average $2,000, you may want to adjust your reserve fund balance upwards. Conversely, if you are investing in an inexpensive area and your mortgage payments are under $1,000, $5,000 in your fund may seem excessive.

Another factor is your cash flow situation. If you have good monthly cash flow from your properties, it won't be as important to have a large reserve fund. Before I did my first major wave of 1031 tax exchanges my monthly cash flow could cover two vacancies out of five houses. Now that I've leveraged myself thin again, I'm at break even if every house is rented. This is another reason I increased the amount I want to have stashed away in my reserve fund.

Keep in mind that besides protecting yourself against a string of expenses hitting all at one time, you also need to save for anticipated expenses such as new carpet and paint, replacing a roof or furnace, or installing air conditioning. This money needs to be available **in addition** to your normal reserve fund. Refurbishing a fourteen-year-old house with new carpet, vinyl and interior paint can easily run over $7,000. Your reserve fund can cover the vacancy cost while you get the work done, but you need a maintenance fund to pay for the materials and labor. Saving for maintenance costs on a monthly basis is usually easier than coming up with the total amount all at once.

It's fine to blend your two funds together in one rental savings account, but make sure it's big enough (or will get big enough by the time it's needed) to cover both the unexpected as well as the expected expenses.

Happy Tenants

You'll make your tenants happy by doing two things: respecting them as the people who are helping you to achieve your financial goals, and by keeping your properties in good to excellent condition. Always call your tenants before you come by to make repairs or to show a property to new prospective tenants. It is their home. You should get your tenants' permission whenever you want to enter their home, especially if they won't be there when you come by the property.

Whenever you have contact with your tenants, you should ask them if they are having any problems with their homes. Some things that bother them may not be solvable. You can't do much about the yappy neighbor's dog who barks at them whenever they sit outside. But at least you can be sympathetic while you explain that there isn't much you can do.

I like to give tenants a small gift when they re-sign a new one year lease. A pretty gift basket with a note thanking them for being such great tenants is a good way to communicate how glad you are to have them in your property. After all, these people are paying off your mortgage for you (and I assume you wouldn't have renewed the lease unless they've been good tenants).

In the spring, I try to come by each property at least once to do a spring weeding and to trim the bushes and trees. Many tenants help me or provide refreshments. They generally appreciate the improvement in their yards and do their best to maintain them the rest of the year.

This also gives me a chance to visit with my tenants. Once they know me as a person they are more likely to be good tenants. It's much easier for people to cause problems for a stranger rather than for someone they know. You'll be rewarded if you get to know your tenants on a casual basis. Your tenants will treat you and your property with more respect.

Maintaining Your Properties

Your goal should be to keep your properties in salable condition at all times since you never know when you may decide to sell them. Deferred maintenance can be overwhelming when it must be handled all at once. Because a house is so large, something always needs a little attention. This makes perfection unreachable, but it is worthwhile as a goal.

Tenants will usually perceive your efforts as a benefit to them. Even when you are making improvements such as landscaping the backyard in order to raise the value of the property, they will feel that you are doing the work for their increased enjoyment. Many times tenants will even volunteer to help you. They are happy to live in a nicer environment, and your property is maintaining or increasing in value. It's a win-win situation.

You should keep a careful eye on your houses. Touch up the paint on the south and west sides. Watch the trim and keep it painted. These areas are the first ones to lose their paint coverage, so if you spend a little extra time painting them yourself, you can postpone hiring a painter to repaint the entire house. Never let your paint job get so old that it fails to protect your siding. Installing new siding is expensive!

When you bought your properties, you should have hired a professional to inspect them. Maintaining your properties means having an inspector come back every two to three years to inspect the properties again. The inspector will alert you to incipient problems. You'll know when sinks are about to rust out, a hot water heater is set to go, or a damp crawl space is indicating drainage problems.

You can take care of these problems before they become emergencies. This means you can handle these items at your convenience. Periods of vacancy are perfect for doing any interior maintenance. Even if you have very long term tenants who never complain about anything you should still have the properties inspected, then schedule the maintenance work to be done when it's least inconvenient to your tenants.

The repair work you need to do may be as minor as re-caulking the bathtub tile or something as major as replacing the furnace because the heat exchanger cracked. You may also want to provide new furnace filters each fall as a reminder that you expect the tenants to change them on a monthly basis.

Major Repairs and Maintenance

I usually wait for vacancies to do major interior work unless the tenants are very long term. But long term tenants rarely ask for much maintenance work. So unless damage is being done to the property, I wait until tenants move out before I touch up the paint, replace any carpeting or vinyl flooring, or install new counter tops.

Whenever I do any of these projects, I don't do them piecemeal. New carpet in the living areas usually means new carpet in the bedrooms as well. Most investment books will say it's okay to have different colors of carpet in different rooms, but that's not what you'll see in new homes. Buyers of houses do not like a hodgepodge of carpet, and neither do desirable tenants. At least match the carpet as closely as possible!

When it comes to choosing a carpet color, do not automatically choose a boring beige. Vacant houses with beige carpet, white walls, and off-white blinds are depressingly bland whether you're trying to sell them or rent them. It's okay to add color in the carpet, a wallpaper border, or in the drapes. Window valances are inexpensive and can be removed if a tenant doesn't like them.

A cut berber carpet is one of my favorites. It looks luxurious and the mixture of three to four different colors hides everyday wear and tear quite well. If you want a more standard plush carpet, always get trackless and look at colors such as a grayed blue or muted rose. If you must get a beige, get a warm one with tones of pink instead of yellow. Taupe is far superior to a boring tan.

I aim for a moderate price range on my carpets, neither the cheapest nor the most expensive. I want something nice enough to attract tenants who want a lovely home, but not so expensive that if it's damaged it will be financially very painful. I plan and budget for replacing carpet every twelve to fourteen years. Sometimes it lasts longer, but I don't count on it.

The price level of your properties will have a big influence on how much maintenance you need to do. The inexpensive properties tend to get the most wear and tear. Higher end tenants are usually between homes that they own, and they tend to take more care of where they live.

New Property Options

If you are buying a new property, keep in mind that the builder typically makes money on the options. One builder wanted to charge me $5,000 to upgrade the carpet in a rather large house. I checked with my regular carpet supplier, The Carpet Outpost in Boulder, and learned I could rip out the builder's standard carpet and replace it with a comparable upgrade carpet for $2,500. Because carpet is so easy to replace, I chose to have the builder install the standard carpet. I'll get a few years wear out of it, and then I'll select something nicer and more durable.

The problem with this approach, of course, is that I'll have to pay for that new carpet out-of-pocket. The expense won't be rolled into the mortgage. This really came home to me one summer when I had a couple of high efficiency air conditioners installed on brand new houses. They cost me almost half of what the builders would have charged, but coming up with that much cash at once took a major chunk out of my savings fund.

However, any option that causes the house to be built differently is better handled by the builder. These types of changes cost too much when done after closing. So I will pay the extra cost for a door to the master bathroom and the hardwood floors that require all the door frames to be higher to provide extra clearance. Depending on how hectic my schedule is, I'll cough up for stuff like the deck, too. Even though this is something I could hire to have done later, sometimes it's just best to have it completed at the time of closing so the property is ready to rent.

After all, I don't begrudge the builder some profit; I know the base price is a bare bones price that's kept low to attract home buyers. But I do think twice about paying for options such as carpet upgrades, air conditioners, decks, and a paint color that's different than the builder's standard beige. I do a little price comparison shopping before recklessly rolling the cost of all the extras into the mortgage.

Yet at the same time, I tend to splurge on tile or hardwood floors, granite tile counters, and upgraded cabinets. Here's how I look at it. If I put in $30,000 of upgrades that make a house special, that will raise the monthly payment by about $150 depending on current interest rates. Considering that at least half of that $30,000 went to purchase the minimum amount of upgrades to make the house attractive to tenants, that means only $75 is going beyond what the average buyer is choosing. (It's a good idea to ask the on-site sales people what options are being chosen by almost every buyer to get an idea of what people in this neighborhood consider standard.) Here's the question to ask; is it worth it to you as an investor to pay that extra $75 per month?

If you can get $1,795 in rent instead of $1,725, that's pretty much break even. But what if you can only get an extra $25, or nothing extra at all? Is it still worth it? Remember to consider your vacancy costs. When I was buying new houses at Stapleton, I knew the rental market was soft. My asking rents ranged from $1,525 to $1,975. One week's vacancy would cost me on average $450 in lost rent.

Looked at it in this way, it made sense to upgrade the tile with accents in the master and secondary bathrooms. I paid for the rounded wall corners, built-in microwaves, fireplaces, tile or hardwood floors for the main levels, upgraded toilets and fancier faucets. And because it keeps tenants happy, larger than standard water heaters so they wouldn't run out of hot water.

Besides charging competitive rents, I believe the fact that my houses are loaded with extras that many home buyers skimp on makes them easier to rent. By spending a relatively small amount of money compared to the purchase prices, I made these houses special. Almost every prospective tenant comments on the finishes, and rarely do I have to show a property more than once to rent it. I save time and optimize my rental income by minimizing vacancy while tenants get to enjoy a fabulous home. That's win-win.

Refrigerators, Washers, and Dryers

If you own small units such as condominiums or apartments, you will typically be expected to provide all appliances. But if you own rental houses, many tenants own at least their own refrigerator and washer/dryer set. I learned very quickly that it was a real pain for me to remove my appliances so tenants could replace them with their own. In my market I can still be competitive without including these appliances as part of my lease, so I don't. It saves me a lot of hassle. As a landlord who hates getting emergency phone calls, this policy works very well for me. If the refrigerator isn't keeping food cold enough, or the washing machine is making a funny sound, I don't hear about it. These are the tenants' problems.

If you've purchased a property which came with appliances, you can exclude these items on the lease. State clearly that they are not included as part of the property, but that you will leave them as a convenience for your tenants if they would like to use them. If your tenants should ever decide they don't want them (for example, because they stop working), they should notify you and you will have them removed. Make it very clear that any appliance maintenance is not your responsibility. If tenants want a broken appliance repaired, they may do so at their own expense.

My properties do come with dishwashers and stoves since these items are rarely owned by tenants. If a heating element goes out, most tenants are willing to buy a new element and install it themselves. I tell them to send me the bill for the part so I can reimburse them. However I never allow tenants to deduct expenses from their rent due. Doing that messes up my records, and keeping track of rents paid and tax deductions is a big enough bother as it is.

Vacancies

Your vacancy rate will go through cycles. Why? Because for a given property you may go through two or three tenants before you find a tenant who sticks. This person, for whatever reason, does not move on. Instead of having to look for a new tenant each year, you will instead give modest rent raises to your current tenant. Besides a bit of routine maintenance, you'll hardly spend any time managing this property.

Yet even long term tenants will eventually move on and you'll have to start the renting process over again. You'll go through another quick succession of tenants before you find the next long term tenant. In the worst case scenario all of your long term tenants will move in the same year, creating a glut of work in a short period of time, but other years (wonderfully easy years!) no one will move.

Do talk to your tenants on a regular basis about their plans so you know when to expect vacancies. That way you can make room in your schedule to handle repairs and to show the property. The longer notice you receive, the less likely you'll experience any vacancy.

After you've owned your properties for awhile, you may discover that you have to re-lease fewer than half of them each year. If your average tenant is staying for two years, you can allow up to one month of vacancy each time a tenant moves out and still only average one half month of vacancy per property per year. You'll have plenty of time to make repairs and interview new tenants.

Frequently I experience no down time between tenants. My lease allows me to show a property more than six weeks before the lease ends. As long as my current tenants keep a decently clean house that shows well, new tenants will sign a lease before the old tenants move out.

Other times I purposely create a vacancy. If I know that I plan to repaint and replace the carpeting and vinyl flooring, then I don't bother to advertise the property until I've made the improvements. Of course, I also raise the rent substantially. Tenants will pay a premium for brand new carpeting and paint.

Prepaid Rent

Years ago a student asked me about whether or not to accept prepaid rent, in his case the rent for the entire year of the lease. I was surprised that a tenant would want to do this, but sure, why not? The only consideration I can see is how this affects your taxes. You must declare rent as income when it is received, even if some of it is being paid for rent due the following year. Depending on your tax situation, moving income from one tax year to another could be bad or good.

You also have to be a good money manager. Some landlords might be tempted to spend that prepaid rent, and then have trouble making the mortgage payments later on. When one of my tenants prepaid six months of his rent, I put it into my savings fund. Then each month I transferred his rent payment from my rental savings account into my rental checking account.

Hiring a Property Manager

I think it's best to manage your own properties if possible. Why? First, because you'll certainly qualify as an active investor who can take advantage of the tax savings due to the depreciation of your properties. If you do hire a property manager, you should make sure you still meet the requirements of being an active investor. You should help set rent rates and approve tenants in order to qualify by the Internal Revenue Service guidelines. This is an area where you should check with your accountant for specific advice on the precise definition of an active investor.

But the biggest reason not to hire a property manager is the cost. Let's say your property rents for $1,000 a month and after paying your mortgage payment which includes taxes and insurance, your cash flow is $250 per month. You still have to pay for average maintenance costs of at least $100 per month. A property manager may charge you 10% of the monthly rent, or $100. $250 per month gross cash flow minus $100 for maintenance and $100 for property management leaves you with a net cash flow of $50 a month, or $600 per year. If you have half a month of vacancy per year at a cost of $500 in lost rent, you'll net only $100 a year in cash flow. Putting less than $10 a month into your pocket when it could be eleven times that amount for a small amount of work seems silly to me.

The exception would be if you're earning a great deal more per hour doing something else. In that case your properties are probably long term investments rather than a source of cash flow. Then it does make sense to pay someone else to handle the daily chores of property ownership.

You Can Manage Your Own Properties

I've had people tell me they aren't like me. I may be brave enough and smart enough to manage tenants, but they are not. This is not true. For starters, I'm not always self-assured. Calling a tenant about a problem is not fun! I'll postpone doing it or promise myself a treat after I get it done. Occasional uncomfortable situations are part of the price I, and you, have to pay in order to maximize the financial benefits of owning rental properties.

I bet you are perfectly capable of managing your own tenants. You'll have to learn on the job, but that's okay. If you know how to generally get along with people, you'll do fine. The key is to be pleasant, but firm. You will do your best to make a tenant happy, but only if what the tenant wants will make you happy, too. Never let a tenant run rough-shod over you. What you want is as important, actually I think more important, than what the tenant wants. After all, you have a lot more at risk than they do. They are talking about a temporary home - you are investing for your financial future.

If something a tenant pushes for makes you feel uneasy inside, tell them you'll have to think about it and get back to them. Don't let them pressure you into a fast response, unless they want it to be no. Sometimes I have to think something through or talk to other investors before I know how I will respond. It is always scary to have to tell someone no, but sometimes that's the way it is. Explain why you are saying no. Most people will accept your answer. If not, I suspect it's because they are being unreasonable, not you.

If you end up with tenants who are downright disagreeable, you may want to suggest that they move out before their lease is up. This happened to my sister once. The tenants were always mad at her about this or the other thing. Nothing made them happy, and lots of stuff that tenants usually appreciate such as Shelley doing maintenance work on the yard made them unhappy. She offered to let them break their lease early without penalty and was glad when they accepted. This was the first set of tenants she ever actively disliked, and she didn't mind going through the bother to find new tenants.

Fortunately most people are pleasant and enjoyable to know. You will be exposed to people you never would have met through your normal circle of friends and family. Your life will broaden in ways you didn't expect. Most tenants will recognize a great landlord when they meet one, plus they won't enjoy discord either, so they will go out of their way to get along with you.

Keeping Tax Records

I've used both Quicken and QuickBooks to track my rental income and expenses. To make doing my taxes simple, I use the same subcategories as the Internal Revenue Service does on their Schedule E. That way I can print out a profit and loss report with expenses ready to insert in the correct Schedule E blanks. The only extra category I use is HOA fees (homeowners association fees) which I write into one of the blank lines provided on the Schedule E.

Chapter Ten

The Lease

Most of the clauses you put in your lease won't apply to the majority of your tenants because they will not be late with the rent, acquire five dogs, park broken down cars on the front lawn, and eventually abandon the property full of junk that they claim was valuable after you've had it hauled to the dump. But just in case you let an undesirable tenant slide past your credit check and interview, you need an agreement in writing that specifies what is okay, what isn't, and what happens to resolve problems.

I'm not a lawyer, and even if I were housing laws vary across the country. Therefore none of what I say in this chapter can be taken as legal advice. It's words of experience from another investor. I'll tell you about the clauses I've chosen to include in my lease, and why I've put them there. Use them as a starting point to create your own lease.

You can get additional information from books such as *Every Landlord's Legal Guide* by Nolo Press. This book comes with a disk of more than a dozen real estate forms you can use such as a rental application and lease. It also provides charts of rental laws for each state. For example, while Colorado doesn't require any minimum notice from a landlord to enter a property, other states require up to 48 hours notice. The books also lists state web site addresses for state landlord/tenant statutes.

Another source of lease information is the National Association of Apartment Owners. This group includes many small investors who own single family residential properties instead of apartments. Local chapters often put on programs with speakers on a variety of topics pertinent to the small investor.

You should hire a lawyer who is familiar with the rental laws in your state and city to check your lease to make sure it complies with your local law requirements and also that it best serves your interest as a property owner. Do make it clear to the lawyer you hire that you have a budget. You don't want your lease rewritten in legalese. Instead you want him or her to red-flag anything that could be a significant problem or point out a clause you should add to your lease.

In the long run, developing a relationship with a competent real estate attorney is well worth the investment of time and money. Investors complain to me that attorneys cost too much. Yes, they do charge a substantial hourly fee, but they can also prevent you from making costly mistakes. To get your money's worth, your lawyer should specialize in real estate. A general all-purpose attorney will not be able to give you the best advice.

If you budget a couple of hundred dollars per year to be spent on legal advice then you won't hesitate to call your attorney to double-check your actions. Being frugal is wise, but sometimes it's smart to spend a little money.

When you meet with tenants to have them sign the lease, I highly suggest that you go through your lease clause by clause with them before you let them sign it. This is your last chance to discourage the bad tenants who managed to slip through your earlier tenant checks. Good tenants will not object to a strong lease, but bad tenants may suddenly realize that you will expect them to abide by each and every lease clause. If they balk at this point, consider it good riddance of potentially bad tenants.

Because you will probably modify your lease over time, I recommend that you type your lease into a computer so it will be easy to change. I am constantly fiddling with my lease to make it work better for me. You can be sure that some of the following clauses will have undergone minor revisions between the time I wrote this book and when you read it. Certain tenants are skilled at educating me about the loopholes in my lease.

General

This lease is between _____, *property owner(s), and* _____, *tenant(s). It is understood that this agreement is between the owner(s) and each tenant individually and severally. This means that in the event of default by any one tenant, each and every remaining tenant shall be responsible for timely payments of rent and all other provisions of this lease. Use of the singular word 'tenant' shall apply to each named tenant. Use of the word 'owner' shall apply to each named owner.*

When you rent to more than one tenant over the age of eighteen (or twenty-one depending on your state laws), you want every adult to sign the lease. By making each tenant individually responsible for the rent, you are better protected. If sometime in the future you have trouble collecting the rent or a judgement against your tenants, you will only need to find one tenant who has money in order to collect. It will be this tenant's problem to locate the other tenants for reimbursement.

Sometimes two or more single people will want to rent a house together. When you explain to them that they are all individually liable to pay the full rent amount, they may not like this. Why should they pay for Sam's share if Sam disappears or refuses to cough up his portion of the rent?

I'll tell you why. Because they know Sam a lot better than I do. If they don't trust him, then I don't trust him, and they aren't renting this house from me. Everybody signs, or nobody moves in.

Another example would be a married couple who rents your house. If one spouse signs the lease, then later separates from the other spouse and moves out, you would have someone living in your property who has not signed a lease with you. This may cause problems if he or she stops paying the rent and you want to evict him or her. It's best to have both spouses sign the lease.

Leased Premises

The owner hereby leases to tenant the property located at
_____ *which shall include the*
following: _____ .

This clause seems clear cut, but you need to pay attention to the inclusions. Items you would never think to list may turn up missing when your tenants move out. Do you have a built-in microwave? List it. Write down its serial number if you want to be 100% exact. Describe the fancy light fixture in the dining room, the drapes and blinds, the computerized thermostat, the keychain remote to the garage door opener, and anything else that could be easily taken and/or replaced with something less valuable.

A common problem is disappearing drapes. The tenant doesn't intend to steal your drapes. She or he doesn't even like them. The drapes are taken down and replaced with something purchased by the tenant. When the tenant moves, the new drapes go with the tenant. But somehow the old drapes have either been lost or damaged by being stored improperly. The tenant doesn't say anything and hopes you won't notice, or else the tenant plans to say you never had those drapes in the property in the first place. Play it safe. List and describe the drapes in your lease unless they aren't valuable to you.

Lease Term

The term of this lease shall be from _____ *, 20_____ at*
12 o'clock noon to _____ *, 20 _____ at 12 o'clock*

*noon. **Forty-five (45) days prior written notice to terminate** is required from either party at the end of the lease. Otherwise lease shall continue on a month-to-month basis except for new terms and conditions which tenant has notice of and agrees to by the payment of rent. After either party gives notice of termination, the owner shall have the right to hold open houses for replacement tenants or buyers from 11:00 a.m. to 1:00 p.m. each Saturday until lease terminates. The owner shall also have the right to schedule individual showings during the day or early evening with four (4) hours notice to the tenant. If the lease becomes month-to-month basis, termination by either party still requires **forty-five (45) days** written notice to terminate.*

I suggest that you specify the exact hour a lease ends. I like using 12 o'clock noon because one tenant can move out in the morning while a new tenant moves in that afternoon. Both pay you rent for that day. I'll admit this doesn't happen often, but it's nice when it does. My lease specifies that the tenant needs to give written notice to terminate the lease. Otherwise the lease will continue on a month-to-month basis.

Despite this, I don't rely on tenants to remember this requirement. About two months before the end of their lease I'll talk with them about their plans. But in case I forget, it is their responsibility to notify me if they want to terminate our agreement. If they move out at the end of their lease period without giving the required notice, I can charge them for the vacancy costs I incur before I get the property re-rented.

Remember that any time you charge a tenant for causing you a vacancy, either by breaking the lease early or by neglecting to give you the required notice that they are moving at the end of the lease term, you must make a good faith effort to re-rent the property quickly using your normal advertising methods. If you are lucky enough to re-rent the property immediately, you can't charge your old tenants for vacancy costs you didn't actually incur. However you may charge them for a portion of your advertising expenses. For example, if they break their lease at the half-way mark, you could charge them for half the advertising costs.

When my tenants sign the lease, I tell them I understand that they may need to break the lease early. They may be transferred or lose a job. (Or a couple may get divorced, but I don't mention this to the tenants even though I've had it happen - that seems too negative a thing to say!) Unforeseen stuff happens, and I tell the tenants to tell me as soon as they realize there is a problem. I will work with them to get the property re-rented as quickly as possible so I won't have to charge them for any vacancy.

Obviously, the more notice the tenants give you, the better, and in general you'll find new tenants faster if the old tenants move out during the spring or summer months. For most properties, unless they go vacant around the winter holidays, you can re-lease a property for the same rent. But if you own a property in an area which has a strong seasonal rental market such as a ski resort area or a college town, you may not be able to get normal market rent if a property goes vacant at the wrong time of year.

For example, Boulder is a college town. Students flood the city in July and August looking for places to live. If someone signs a one year lease with you, but then breaks the lease in January, you may not be able to release the unit for its full rental rate until the following summer. So any loss in rent, that is the difference between the monthly fall rent rate you were receiving and the lower rent you can ask for in midwinter, can usually be charged to the tenant who breaks the lease early. So if your rent was $1,200 and you have to reduce it to $900 to rent the property off-season, you could charge your old tenant $300 for each remaining month covered by that tenant's lease.

Even if you don't rent to students or other seasonal tenants, the fact that other property owners in your area do could become a problem for you. This happens in Boulder County. The summer rents are abnormally low because many students have left the city. When these rents are raised in August, many students who were paying the low summer rates refuse to move or to pay the winter rent rate. By the end of August the sheriff may have a three week waiting list to send deputies out to handle evictions. A property owner who does an eviction at this time of year gets in line with the student landlords to schedule an eviction date.

You can find out about local idiosyncracies like this by calling the court that handles evictions in your area. Ask if there is a time of the year when a lot of evictions happen. Then make sure your leases don't end at that time. Your tenants may still choose that month to stop paying rent, especially if they are professional scam artists, but you've done your best to protect yourself.

HINT: Some people recommend attending eviction court to find properties at good prices. Property owners may be emotional at this time and willing to sell to anyone who will make their problem go away. If the discount is good enough, you may want to become the new owner and handle the eviction yourself.

If the owner is still thinking that he or she wants to keep the property, give the owner your card. If the tenant has trashed the property, you may get a call later after the owner has a chance to see the damage. I've never personally used this technique, but if you like fixer uppers, you may find a good deal this way.

Rent

The total rent for the term of this lease is $ _____ . The first rent payment of $ _____ is due on _____ , and must be in the form of a cashier's check or money order. If the payment is made by a cashier's check, landlord reserves the right to confirm its validity with the issuing bank before accepting it as payment. If received at owner's option in the form of a personal check, acceptance of the check and possession shall be contingent on the check first clearing the tenant's bank. This lease will not become a legal contract until the first rent payment or the security deposit has been received and cleared the bank. Until that hap-

pens the owner reserves the right to cancel this lease. Owner also reserves the right to refuse payment if it is made after the agreed upon due date. In these cases, the lease will not be binding on either party.

After the first payment, rent is payable in monthly installments of $ _____ on the _____ day of the month, and shall be made payable to _____ unless tenant and owner otherwise agree in writing. Rent received early will not be deposited by the owner before the due date. After the first month personal checks will be accepted, but if a check bounces or does not clear the first time it is deposited, the owner has the right to demand that that month's rent and subsequent rent payments be made by cashier checks or money orders. If the owner exercises this right by notifying the tenant, then the tenant will no longer be allowed the privilege of paying the rent by depositing it directly into the owner's bank account. After losing this privilege, payments made directly to the owner's bank account are not allowed by this lease, and any such payments will not count as paying the rent nor will they halt any eviction from proceeding.

The owner also has the right to begin eviction proceedings as soon as a rent check bounces without waiting for it to clear if the bank has resubmitted the check. Owner has the right to insist on good as cash funds delivered to the owner to replace the bounced check amount. If the tenant has been allowed the privilege of paying the rent by depositing it directly into the owner's bank account, the tenant agrees that making another deposit to replace a bounced check is not allowed by this lease, and that any such payment will not count as paying the rent nor will it halt any eviction proceedings.

The tenant shall incur a late fee of $30.00 per day for each day the rent is not paid in full. If the owner agrees to accept less on any occasion, this shall not be construed as changing the terms *of the lease. A charge of up to $35.00 may be imposed for any tenant's check returned to owner because of insufficient funds or nonexisting account, whether the check is for rent, security deposit, or any other payment. The imposition of such charge shall not preclude a claim for treble damages under C.R.S *p27 94 21* 13-21-109. Any late fee and return check charges shall be reasonable estimates of the administrative costs incurred by the owner. Tenant agrees that such costs are difficult to ascertain and that the amounts set forth above are a reasonable measure of liquidated damages.*

I include the total rent for the entire lease period to make it crystal clear that my lease is not a month-to-month lease - it is for the entire lease term. I insist that the first month's rent and security deposit to be in good-as-cash funds. Can you imagine what a financial disaster it would be to let a tenant move in only to discover later that he or she gave you a bad check? You would have to evict these tenants with no money to cover the lost rent. Sure, you could get a judgement against the tenant, but you may not be able to collect.

When tenants have trouble coming up with the entire first month's rent plus the security deposit, they may ask you to let them make a partial payment with a second payment coming halfway through the month. If this happens, and you want to rent to these tenants, make sure your lease shows you've been paid your security deposit in full and that it is the rent that has not been paid in full. If the second payment of the rent doesn't appear, you can start eviction proceedings immediately and have a full deposit to protect you.

Accepting a partial security deposit and full rent doesn't work as well. If the second payment toward the deposit doesn't show up, an eviction judge may think that's not as serious of a problem as nonpayment of rent. The judge may order you to agree to a payment plan from the tenant because judges don't like people to be forced out of their homes. While this attitude toward unpaid rent versus unpaid security deposits may or may not be true in your state, I think it's safer to get the deposit up front. Of course, it's better not to accept partial payments in the first place, but if the rental market is soft you may need to be flexible.

Many leases will say the rent is due on the first, but it's not late until five days later. This has always seemed ridiculous to me. If the rent is due on the first but is not late until the fifth, then when is it really due? On the fifth. My rent is due on the first of the month for all my properties. If someone would prefer a due date of the fifth because that's when he or she gets paid, I'm not usually receptive. If they live from paycheck to paycheck, they probably aren't my ideal tenants anyway.

Also, since I collect the rent and pay the mortgages on many properties, it can get confusing to keep track of who has paid me rent and who hasn't, and which mortgage companies I still have to pay. I want my money on or before the first so I can deposit it at the same time and get my checks out on time to the mortgage companies. If any rent is missing, it's obvious, and I can call my tenants promptly to find out what's happened.

I want to receive my first month's rent in good as cash funds. One of my students told me about a scam artist who passed the credit check by providing a stolen identity, and paid the first month's rent and security deposit with a fake cashier's check. Whoa! This experience taught me to call the issuing bank to verify that a cashier's check is good before letting a new tenant have possession. This means tenants can't give me a check after hours or during the weekend and expect to move in right away. Good tenants usually have no problem getting a check to me during the work week.

Once I had an out-of-state tenant sign a lease who was sup- posed to overnight me the cashier's check as soon as he and his wife arrived home from their house hunting trip. I had done this many times before with tenants moving to my state without a problem. But these tenants never did give me a check. First the family supposedly had a medical emergency that required them to fly out of state again as soon as they got home. Then he told me he had sent the check, but strangely FedEx never delivered it. Then he said he had it at his new Denver office, but when I showed up in person to get it, he couldn't find it. The whole situation was extremely bizarre.

As this process dragged on for weeks, I repeatedly offered to let the gentleman out of the lease. He insisted he and his wife still wanted the house. Yet until the move-in date came and went without payment of rent, my lease wasn't clear that I had the right to re-lease the property to someone else who might actually pay me. Bad as the situation was, I didn't want to make it worse by having two tenants for one house so I waited. After this experience, I added the sentence that said the lease wasn't a contract until I had received the first month's rent or security deposit.

Many tenants think their rent check should arrive exactly on the due date. Heaven forbid that it should arrive early! They don't want to pay their rent until the last possible moment. I point out to them that the lease says I may not deposit a rent check before its due date, then I tell them to send me the rent a week early. They'll avoid late charges (and I'll have the peace of mind that comes from a pile of rent checks waiting to be deposited).

Another option that is extremely popular with my tenants is for me to give them deposit slips for my rental checking account. My bank has branches that are conveniently located close to my rental properties. When my tenants belatedly realize it's the first of the month, they can dash over to deposit their rent. All I have to do is call the automated account information system to verify that my rents have been deposited.

Remember, if you use this method of accepting rent, you must charge different rents for all your properties so you can tell who has or has not deposited their rent. Otherwise if two tenants each owe you $1,200 in rent, but only one deposits a payment, how will you know who you need to call for the missing $1,200? The automated system will probably tell you only the amount of the deposit, not who made it. Tracking down the information will take time, and I prefer to handle delinquent rent problems promptly.

This method of accepting rent also presents another problem. I had a pair of tenants who bounced a rent check every few months. My lease required them to pay the past due rent with a cashier's check or money order, but didn't explicitly deny them the right to make a deposit directly into my bank account. Even though their replacement payments always turned out to be good, I saw the potential for a serious problem. If instead of good as cash funds they had deposited another personal check that also bounced, I wouldn't know this for another ten days as notice slowly made its way to me from my bank. Two bounced checks multiplied by ten days each meant a tenant could potentially live in one of my houses for most of a month before I could start eviction proceedings.

Because many of my tenants, and I, love the convenience of rent deposits made directly to my rental checking account, I wanted to keep this payment option. To protect myself, I made it clear in my lease that this was a privilege that could be removed. I also explicitly stated when I reserved the right to begin eviction proceedings for nonpayment of rent. Fortunately I discovered this hole in my lease and fixed it before I suffered any monetary loss.

Late fees and the laws governing them vary by state. A little research should easily bring you up to date on what is required in your locale. I tend to be forgiving if the rent is one day late occasionally. I can almost guarantee late rent on the first of January or the first of July. The holidays distract everyone, and I'm okay with that. As long as tenants usually pay on time or early, I don't charge a late fee. But if someone starts to make a habit of paying late, I want to get paid for having to call them in order to get my rent.

However, just because I don't charge a late fee one time doesn't mean that I want to lose the right to charge it if the rent is late the next month. Be careful about following all the terms of your lease; if you ignore something a few times, a judge may say that you've changed the terms of the lease based on your actions.

Payment of Rent by Check

If the tenant decides to mail the rent check, tenant agrees to always write on back of check "Payable only to account XXXXXXXXX" to reduce the risk of possible mail fraud. Otherwise loss due to theft of the rent check shall be the responsibility of the tenant. Direct deposit into this account can be made by tenant at any XXXXX bank branch only if the tenant is allowed to pay rent by personal check. If tenant is required by the owner to pay rent by cashier's checks or money orders, payment must be sent directly to owner at the provided mailing address. If tenant has been denied the privilege of making direct deposits, but does so anyway, rent shall be considered not paid, and owner has the right to begin eviction proceedings.

If you or your tenants prefer that checks be sent in the mail, you should protect yourself against mail fraud. In the rural area where I live a ring of thieves hired teenagers to steal checks out of mailboxes and then cash them. In a case like this, who would be liable for the lost money?

I didn't want to find out. I told my tenants I had a new rule. All checks must say on the back "For Deposit Only" with my account number. This means a bank must deposit the checks into my account only. If a bank should ignore this requirement and cash a stolen check instead, the bank would be liable.

Incidentally, I discourage tenants from paying their rent in cash directly to me. If convenience stores keep less than $40 cash in their registers, why would I want to have $1,000 or more in my pocket? I know a landlord who lets his many tenants pay him in cash at his office on the first of every month. If I were the receptionist, I would not be very happy about holding that money. We're talking about thousands of dollars. Numerous ex-tenants know how this landlord is paid, and they could have told their friends. I think this landlord is asking for trouble.

If you don't allow tenants to make deposits directly to your rental checking account, you don't need to detail when that privilege is revoked. I decided to make it very clear whether rent had or had not been paid because I had a tenant who bounced checks, or didn't pay on time, and then made a direct deposit. Because our lease didn't spell out that this was not allowed, it put me in a difficult position. Had I or hadn't I received the rent? She would tell me that the new money was in the form of a money order instead of a personal check, but I had no way to quickly verify if that were true. In the future when tenants didn't pay the rent, I wanted to make sure I could start an eviction without waiting for the latest rubber check to bounce.

Bills Immediately Due and Payable

Tenant acknowledges that owner may be billed by the city for tenant's failure to remove snow from public sidewalks within twenty-four hours or failure to maintain yard in a condition to satisfy city or homeowner association requirements. Owner may also be billed for unpaid water bills or may incur charges related to the repair of damage caused by the tenant. If the owner bills the tenant for reimbursement of these fees, that bill shall be payable within ten days. If any bill is not paid to owner within ten days of receipt by tenant, tenant will have breached this lease and eviction may occur at the owner's option. Tenant agrees that the owner is not obligated to use any portion of the security deposit to pay these fees and expenses.

It's possible that a tenant will cost you money while occupying your property. You'll want to have the right to be reimbursed promptly for any out-of-pocket expenses without having to rely solely on the security deposit. Otherwise it is possible that by the end of the lease the tenant will owe you more than what you've received as a security deposit. Water bills can add up fast! A clause like this allows you to demand your money immediately while you still have a full security deposit.

Utilities

The tenant shall be responsible for all utilities or services connected with the property including any transfer fees except for:
_____ . *The tenant shall arrange for such utilities or services and for billing directly to tenant to begin upon commencement of this lease. The party responsible for any particular utility or service shall not be liable for failure to furnish the utility or service when the cause of such failure is beyond that party's control. Optional services such as cable and community pool passes are also the responsibility of the tenant. However, the owner is responsible for payment of any homeowner association fees even if they include some utility fees.*

I prefer my tenants to pay for all their utilities. I don't want the hassle of paying multiple bills each month for each of my properties. I used to reimburse tenants for water bills in excess of $20 because I wanted them to keep the lawns well-watered, but tracking how much I owed each tenant was a pain.

Now if I see that a lawn is turning brown, I water it myself and call the tenants when I get home. I politely remind them that it costs a lot of money to resod an entire lawn, and it would require all of their security deposit. I suggest that paying a slightly higher water bill may be more affordable. I also give them a way to save face by saying I understand it's hard to keep up with the watering in a dry state like Colorado, but please keep an eye on the grass. It shouldn't make crunching sounds when they walk across it.

One thing to keep in mind is that in many states unpaid water bills are a lien against the property. In Colorado, for example, if a tenant doesn't pay the water and sewer bill, a lien will be created. When that property is sold, the lien will have to be paid in order for the buyer to get clear title.

Luckily, most water departments have space in their computers for two names and addresses, one for the tenant and one for you. Make sure they have your information! This way you will be notified if the account goes delinquent. If this service isn't offered in your area, you may have to call to check every few months to make sure your tenants are paying. The Bills Immediately Due and Payable clause of my lease allows me to force a tenant to reimburse me promptly.

Most public service companies will also list both the tenant and the property owner in their billing systems. This is great because even if you forget to have the utilities switched to your name when old tenants move out and new tenants aren't moving in immediately, the public service company will begin billing you automatically when the old tenants' service terminates. But do check the thermostat settings as soon as possible - you don't want to pay to keep an empty property toasty warm in the winter or frosty cold in the summer. Also remember to get your name removed when you sell a property.

I pay for all homeowner association fees. They also can be a lien against the properties. Unlike gas or electricity, the HOA fees are not directly tied to any usage by the tenants. They wouldn't be inconvenienced by not paying these fees, whereas the tenants care a lot about running water and power. So I consider these fees a cost of owning a property just like paying the mortgage.

Use

The property shall be used as a residence with no more than _____ persons, and for no other purpose without the prior written consent of the owner. Occupancy by guests without prior written consent staying over ten (10) days within one calendar month will be considered to be a violation of this clause. If it is determined that one or more additional tenants have occupied the pre-

mises, such unauthorized tenants shall cause the rent for the premises to increase by $5.00 per day for each unauthorized tenant for each day exceeding the allowable ten (10) days. Owner may, but is not obligated to, give written consent to allow the new tenants to continue occupying the property with an additional security deposit of $ _____ and with the increase in rent as described above as well as having the new tenant sign the lease. A newborn or adopted child shall not be deemed an additional tenant.

There are no clear federal guidelines for property owners to use when setting a maximum number of people to allow in a given property. Sometimes there are local regulations such as the one in Boulder which says only three unrelated people may live in a rental unit. If a regulation like this exists in your area, you'll probably be okay if you comply.

Many areas don't have an occupancy regulation. What do you do then? Can you say only so many people per square foot or one person per bedroom? Following arbitrary rules like these may get you into trouble. For example, a single parent has sued and won the right to live in a one bedroom unit with a child of the opposite sex. Though HUD, the federal department of housing, uses square foot guidelines, they have said that these guidelines are not for general use.

Some groups such as Oxford House have sued municipalities over laws which restrict the number of unrelated people in a house. Oxford House rents houses with numerous bedrooms and subleases them to groups of recovering alcoholics. These people often need inexpensive places to live because their past problems with alcohol have damaged their finances. Oxford House also believes they need group support to stay sober. Recovered alcoholics are considered handicapped; this means they are a federally protected class. You can see the conflicting issues here.

In addition some areas of the country which have experienced large influxes of Hispanic immigrants have enacted laws restricting the people who may live in a home to immediate family members. Uncles and aunts and cousins are not allowed. Suits have been filed that these limitations are discriminatory because, intentionally or unintentionally, Hispanics with broader definitions of immediate family were being disproportionately affected by the new regulations. So again, local laws can conflict with a federal anti-discrimination law. Landlords can get caught in the middle.

If you want a way to restrict how many people can live in your property, you should definitely discuss your options with a lawyer. And whatever rules you decide to use, be consistent. You don't want to get into trouble for treating some people differently than others.

House and Neighborhood Rules

If this property is part of a multiple unit building or complex, tenant agrees to comply with all regulations now or hereinafter made by the owner or the building complex management relating to the leased property and any common grounds. The regulations, if any, shall be attached to this lease. If this property is located in a neighborhood with covenants, tenants agree to follow these covenants and are liable for any penalties if they do not. A copy of the covenants is included with this lease. In addition tenants agree to abide by any federal, state, or local laws.

If you own a condominium, duplex or apartment building, you want your tenants to obey the community rules. Even single family homes are subject to covenants and city regulations. For example, if the homeowners association or the city decides to hire someone to weed your property's yard because your tenants haven't, you want to make it clear that the tenants are financially liable for this bill.

When I reach this part of the lease, I mention those rules which I think are most likely to cause problems. For example, many of my properties are in cities where snow must be shoveled off sidewalks within twenty-four hours or the city will charge the property owner to have the city do it instead. I remind my tenants to make arrangements with a neighbor or friend if they plan to be out of town during the winter.

Pets

No pets shall be brought on the property without prior written consent of the owner. Any damages caused by pets shall not be considered normal and reasonable wear and tear whether or not the tenant has obtained written consent to have that pet. Tenant agrees to pay any additional security deposit or monthly rent increases charged as a result of having a pet. Such extra charges shall not be construed as waiving any right owner may have to damages or security deposit(s) as a result of damages to the premises caused by pets.

Some landlords charge an additional security deposit for pet owners. You want to make sure that all of the security deposit, however, is available to cover damages caused by a pet. I typically write in a description of any approved pets here, including their names. I also ask if I may give dogs a biscuit when I see them - I want tenants' dogs to like me, not bite me.

Motor Vehicles

*No more than three vehicles, including motorcycles, are allowed to be parked in the property's garage and in front of the property on a regular basis (**occasional** guest vehicles are excepted). If the property has garage space, it must be utilized for at least one of the vehicles - no more than two vehicles may be parked on the street or in the driveway. No trailers, campers, boats, or any other like possessions are allowed to be parked at the property. No vehicle shall ever be parked off paved surfaces.*

Any staining to the concrete floor of the garage or to the driveway from leaking vehicle fluids shall not be considered normal wear and tear. All vehicles parked on the street must be in running condition and properly registered with the state. Violation of this lease clause is grounds for eviction. If this clause is violated twice, tenant agrees that the owner has the right to evict without giving the tenant a chance to comply a second time.

My lease didn't have this clause until 2002 when I finally had a tenant who used his garage for storage, and everywhere else for cars that didn't run, his friend's trailer, and his motorcycle. It looked like a junk yard! That's not the image I want my properties to present. Pride of ownership encourages everyone in a neighborhood to maintain their properties, and unfortunately this process also works in reverse. I want my properties to appreciate in value, and that means I want the neighborhood to attract buyers who care about their homes' appearances. These desirable potential neighbors will not buy the house that goes for sale across the street from a house that looks like a disaster.

Subordination

This lease shall be subordinate to all existing and future mortgages and deeds of trust upon the property. If a mortgage holder becomes the owner of the property by foreclosure, tenant agrees to be bound by this lease to the mortgage holder.

In case a future lender requires that a lease must be subordinate before you can refinance, you'll want to have this clause in your lease. You want to make sure you have the option to refinance your properties without having to get your tenants to sign a subordination release. Most tenants would cooperate, but what if you've got one who's ornery and decides you should pay them to sign a release? It's better to avoid this potential problem.

Entry and Inspection

Tenant shall permit owner or owner's agent to enter the premises at reasonable times and upon reasonable notice for the purpose of making necessary or convenient repairs and/or improvements, or to show the premises to prospective tenants, buyers or mortgagees. Reasonable notice shall be defined as at least four hours notice in non-emergency situations. Entry times shall be limited to 9:00 am to 7:00 p.m. unless tenant agrees otherwise. In addition tenants shall have the right to change the locks, but must provide the owner with copies of keys at time of installation.

When a tenant rents a property, he or she has a leasehold on that property. This means that you have to obtain the tenant's permission in most situations in order to enter the property. In general, you should not enter the property without giving prior notice to your tenant unless it is a bona fide emergency.

One landlady told me how she and her husband dropped by a rental property they owned. I don't know whether or not they gave notice to their tenant, but they did enter the property. And what did they find? A leaking pipe under the kitchen sink. Water on the loose can be extremely damaging, so they immediately proceeded to work on fixing the leak.

The tenant returned home before they had finished the repair and told them to leave. They refused to go because their lease allowed them to make repairs. The tenant called the police, and to their surprise, the property owners were escorted out.

Even though they had the right to evict their tenant for breaking a key clause of the lease, they didn't have the right to enter the property in the meantime. Their two options were to reason gently with the tenant or to proceed with an eviction to enforce their right to enter the property for the purpose of doing repairs.

I do allow my tenants to change the locks because it is a legitimate security concern that the previous tenants and their friends may have made copies of the keys. However, tenants tend to forget the requirement to provide new keys to the property owner. They mean to do it, but never get around to actually sending a key. You may want to check your keys each time you visit your properties to make sure they still work.

Indemnification

*Owner shall not be liable for any damage or injury which is incurred by tenant or any other person or damage to tenant's personal possessions on the property or in common areas thereof. The tenant shall not hold the owner liable for any injury or damage resulting from worn or defective wiring or by the breaking, freezing or stoppage of the sewage or plumbing; furthermore, tenant agrees to assume the risk of injury to tenant, tenant's family or guests arising from slipping or falling in the common passageways, parking lot or other general areas, sidewalks, decks or driveways whether or not these areas are kept free from snow, ice and water. The tenant agrees to indemnify and hold the owner harmless for and against any and all liability arising from injury during the term of this lease to person or property, caused wholly or in part by any act or omission of tenant, or of tenant's guests, employees, or assigns of tenant. **Tenant acknowledges that tenant is responsible for obtaining renter's insurance to cover tenant's personal belongings and temporary replacement housing if property becomes uninhabitable. Tenant also acknowledges that some renter's insurance includes liability coverage for the tenant in case the property is accidentally damaged by the tenant or by the tenant's family or guests.**

This is another clause which may or may not protect me in court depending on the circumstances, but I figure it's best to include it. Of course, if I've done something negligent such as fail to have an older furnace inspected, and my tenants suffer from carbon monoxide poisoning, I may be liable no matter what I put in the lease. This clause is designed primarily to protect me from liability for foolish or careless behavior on the part of my tenants and their guests.

Renter's insurance is prudent for both you and your tenants. For more information on this topic, refer to Chapter Nine, Day to Day Details.

You should also give thought to liability insurance for yourself. Even if you try to be the best and most conscientious of all property owners, things happen. Some real estate experts will tell you to incorporate or form trusts to protect yourself. After talking with a couple of lawyers I've decided it's currently more cost effective for me to have good liability insurance policies. You should talk to some experts and explain your situation, and see what their advice is.

In addition to the landlord liability insurance included as part of my landlord property coverage for each rental house, I have also purchased an umbrella liability policy. My decision to handle potential liability in this manner is a personal one, and you should make your own inquiries before deciding what approach would be best for you.

Possession

Possession is contingent on the first month's rent and security deposit being received in good funds or clearing the tenant's bank if accepted in the form of a personal check. If the owner is unable to deliver possession of the property at the commencement of this lease, the owner shall not be liable for any damage caused thereby, nor shall this agreement be void or voidable unless possession is not delivered within five (5) days of the commencement of this lease. Tenant shall not be liable for any rent until possession is delivered. Tenant may terminate this agreement if possession is not delivered within five (5) days of the commencement of this lease unless tenant has caused denial of possession by failing to pay amounts due in verifiable Colorado good funds. If tenant has made a partial payment of the first month's rent and the se-

curity deposit, tenant remains liable for the rent even if posses-
sion is denied for failure to pay the remainder of the amount due.

    I'm always amazed when tenants breeze right by this clause despite my explanation of exactly what it means. If my old tenants don't move out on time, my new tenants are still bound by the lease they've signed with me. And I'm not liable to cover their hotel costs or any other damages they may experience while waiting the five days!

    Even if a tenant did protest, I would never allow myself to become liable for any of their expenses should I be unable to deliver possession. I do intend in good faith to provide possession per the lease we signed, but whether the current tenants move out when their lease is up is beyond my control.

    However, I would be willing to change the five days to zero if a prospective tenant insisted. I wouldn't be risking much. After all, if we had a problem most tenants would have difficulty finding another rental property quickly. Before they found something else, the old tenants might have moved out. Since the new tenants would have already gone through the application process with me, it would probably be faster and easier for them to resign a lease with me even if the old one had expired due to lack of immediate possession.

    I never give possession to tenants before I have their security deposit and first month's rent in good as cash funds. It's not enough to deposit a personal check into my account unless it's paid at least a month in advance. If I accept a personal check at the time someone takes possession, I may get a notice from my bank two weeks later announcing that the check bounced. At that point my tenants would have lived in the property free for half a month, and I would have no security deposit to cover my losses while I evicted them.

    Often I will sign a lease with only the security deposit paid to hold the property, especially when the tenant and I sign the lease more than a month in advance of the tenant taking possession. Yet I do not have to give the tenant possession until I receive the first month's rent in an acceptable form.

Usually I require tenants to pay me the security deposit and first month's rent with a cashier's check. This can be a problem if they have flown into town to get a rental in advance of a move to the area. Here's how I handle that situation. As soon as I've run a credit check on them and have notified them that I've accepted them, I expect the tenants to two-day airmail a cashier's check to me. Or they can do a direct deposit from their bank account into mine. I need to promptly receive the security deposit to hold a property for someone.

Sometimes tenants rent a property based on seeing pictures or having a local friend look at it. In that case, I'll fax a lease for the tenants to sign. They can airmail it back with their cashier's check. That way we can handle everything over the phone lines or through a shipping service. Remember to review the lease with your new tenants over the phone. You always want to make sure they understand what they are signing.

Default

If the tenant fails to pay rent when due, or breaches the terms of this lease in any other way, then after written notice of such default given in the manner required by law the owner at owner's option may terminate all rights of tenant per this lease. If the tenant abandons or vacates the property while in default of paying the rent, the owner may consider any personal possessions of the tenant left on the property to be abandoned and may dispose of them in any manner allowed by law. In the event the owner reasonably believes that such abandoned possessions have no value, they may be discarded. All possessions of the tenant on the property not excepted by law are hereby subject to lien in favor of owner for the payment of all sums due under the terms of this lease. If the owner asserts dominion over any possessions con-

sidered abandoned, owner shall be considered to be without knowledge that tenant does not intend to abandon these possessions unless tenant gives owner written notification. Owner shall give tenant a written list of all items, excepting trash, over which dominion has been asserted if tenant makes a written request.

What happens when you evict a tenant for not paying rent, and that tenant still has a bunch of stuff in your unit? Do you have to store it? Can you sell it? How can you protect yourself against being sued later for throwing out a supposedly valuable antique when all you saw was a broken lamp?

Laws vary state by state on how default situations can be handled. You should check with your real estate attorney to find out your state's laws, but you'll want to address in the lease whether you may throw the stuff away or sell it. A house full of stuff is unrentable, so you need to make sure you can get rid of it somehow. Storing it may not be a good idea. Besides costing you money, the tenants may claim their property was damaged while in your care and possession. These types of arguments with tenants will cost you in time, enthusiasm, and possibly money. Try to limit them by covering the what if questions in your lease.

Real Estate Agent

Tenant acknowledges that the owner or owner's spouse is a licensed real estate agent in the state of _____ , and can be assumed to have an above average knowledge of real estate matters. The owner rents properties with the expressed intent to make a profit.

If you are an agent, you may rent a property to some clients while they are looking for a home to buy. This could get you into trouble. If you work for them as a fiduciary agent, does that mean their interests must come first? Is it okay for their agent to make a profit by renting them a house? To prevent any misunderstandings, it's best to include a clause like this one which clarifies your relationship and your responsibilities to your client.

Security Deposit

The tenant shall pay the owner the sum of $ _____ as a security deposit to secure the performance of this lease. Of this amount, $ _____ has already been paid, and its receipt is hereby acknowledged. The remainder shall be paid by: _____.
The security deposit shall be paid by cashier's check or money order. If in the form of a personal check, acceptance of the check and possession of property is contingent on the check clearing the bank first. If payment is made by a cashier's check, owner reserves the right to confirm its validity with the issuing bank before accepting it. This lease shall not be binding on either the owner or the tenant until the security deposit has been received and accepted by the owner. Landlord reserves the right to refuse to accept payment if made after the agreed upon due date.

The security deposit may not be used by the tenant in lieu of rent. The owner shall within sixty (60) days after the termination of this lease or the surrender and acceptance of the premises, whichever occurs last, return the security deposit to the tenant or provide the tenant with a written statement as to why any portion of the security deposit was retained. The owner shall be deemed to have given prior notice for the retention of any of the deposit by mailing the statement to the last known address of each tenant. Any refund shall be divided equally between each tenant signing this lease unless the tenants provide the owner with a written agreement signed by all tenants that states otherwise.

*At the expiration of the lease term, the tenant shall surrender the property, including any furniture, appliances, outside area, yards and driveways required to be maintained under this lease, in as good state and condition as received, **including a professional*** *truck mounted cleaning of all carpeting with a receipt provided to owner*, and shall pay the owner a reasonable charge for the costs of any cleaning as may be necessary to fulfill this duty if such cleaning is not performed by the tenant. The tenant expressly agrees that the security deposit secures the performance of this maintenance and cleaning obligation, and that the deposit may be used at the option of the owner to pay such charges, including reasonable labor.

The owner has the option to use the security deposit during the term of this lease to fulfill obligations of the tenant under this lease. The owner also has the right to turn the security deposit over to a new property owner if the property is sold during the lease term.

I point out to my tenants when we review the lease that the security deposit is not the same as the last month's rent. Some landlords recommend that the security amount never be the same amount as the rent in order to make the difference clear.

When refunding security deposits, you will be under pressure from the tenant to return the full amount as soon as possible. I've done this twice in my life, and both times I regretted it. Additional expenses or damage to the property later became apparent. Since I had already returned the deposits in full, I had to swallow the expenses without compensation. It wasn't worth the time and aggravation to try and get my ex-tenants to pay.

In Colorado landlords automatically have by law the right to hold security deposits for up to thirty days. This time period can be lengthened to a maximum of sixty days if this is put into the lease. You should put the maximum amount of time allowed in your lease even if you don't always need it. Keep in mind that laws governing stuff like this is liable to change, and it's up to you to be aware of current requirements.

I assure my tenants that I will refund their deposits as quickly as possible, but I warn them that I put sixty days in my lease for several reasons. First, it may take time to discover how much it will cost to repair certain types of damage. And second, I may have a personal emergency that prevents me from assessing any damage and its cost immediately. For example, when their lease ends I or a close family member may be sick and in the hospital.

If I have tenants who are planning to buy a house at the end of their lease, I may agree to do a walk-through of the rental property before they go to the closing on their house. If everything looks okay, I may, at my discretion, refund part of their security deposit immediately. But I will never refund the entire amount until after they have moved out. I've been burned twice; I don't intend to get burned a third time.

Always provide a detailed written list of any charges you are making against a tenant's security deposit. Usually you will not be allowed to charge for your own time spent fixing or cleaning the property unless you provide for this in the lease. A friend of mine does exactly this, setting a charge for his time of $20 per hour.

Typically I handle most light cleaning myself without charge. If the property needs a deep cleaning, I hire a cleaning service. Their fee can be charged against the security deposit so it doesn't cost me any money, and I can't be accused of inflating the time in order to profit personally.

To prevent an argument with the tenant about the condition of the property, you should do a walk-through with the tenant after the tenant has moved out and you've had a chance to assess the damages. If you live in a water lien state, be sure to check the water bill due on the date the lease ended. And, incidentally, don't forget to get all the utilities switched back into your name if you don't have it set up to happen automatically.

When you have a new tenant moving in as soon as the old tenant moves out, you'll have to do your walk-through that same day. Overall, it becomes difficult to determine who was responsible for what damage when you don't experience any real vacancy for years in a row. In situations like this, I tend to be fairly lenient. How can I complain about $200 in damages when I haven't had any costly vacancies in a long time?

The distinction between normal wear and tear and damage can be a matter of opinion. Once, when my father was at small claims court waiting for his case to come up, he observed as the judge decided a case between a tenant and landlord. The landlord had withheld money from the security deposit because the dining room carpet had red stains. The tenant claimed this was normal wear and tear when living with children. The landlord said she should have protected the carpet or else not served colored drinks to her children.

In this case the judge agreed with the landlord, but I can easily imagine the decision going the other way. Since many states provide for expensive penalties against a property owner who wrongfully withholds money from a deposit, I am very careful in this area. If you are really paranoid about tenants falsely claiming that the property was in bad condition when they moved in, you can take pictures of your new tenants standing in the property after they sign the lease, or you can videotape them as you go through the house with them. Comment verbally on the condition of each room if your machine handles sound. A videotape like this would be strong ammunition in the court room.

Currently I'm not this cautious. I've had tenants damage blinds and lose drapes. I've had them destroy a small area of grass in the backyard where they set up a playhouse for their kid. And some tenants have left my houses in less than pristine states of cleanliness. It's amazing what I've found underneath stoves. But unless the problems start to add up to a significant amount, at least $200, I rarely deduct anything from the security deposits.

I can be especially forgiving if the tenants have fixed other problems the house had for which they were not responsible. In one of my houses a railing pulled away from the wall because the house shifted slightly, and I was very glad to have the tenant figure out how to solve that problem. I was then willing to overlook some minor damage caused by that tenant's cat and child.

On the other hand, most tenants won't fight about a few deductions. As long as they get back most of their money, they aren't interested in arguing with you any more than you want to argue with them. So I'm getting pickier as the years go by. I'm tired of cleaning and fixing the same house for the sixth time - I want to get paid for my trouble. Plus little expenses multiplied by dozens of tenants over many years eventually adds up to thousands of dollars.

When you do return the security deposit, it's important to give it to the right person. You may not know your tenants are getting a divorce, but if you return the deposit to one spouse, the other may not get his or her share. Or if you have two or more singles sharing the rental, paying one of them may not be a good idea. If someone else doesn't get her or his money, you may wind up paying twice. It will be your problem to recover the extra money from the first person you paid. Good luck. It's better to avoid this possible problem by cutting separate checks to roommates or a check made out to both spouses (use *and*, not *or*, between their full legal names so both have to sign the check to cash it).

One place where my lease explicitly defines how clean the property should be is for the carpets. I provide properties that have clean carpet when tenants move in and I expect the carpets to be in the same state of cleanliness when they move out. I do not want the tenants to rent a carpet cleaning machine from the local supermarket. A truck mounted system does a far superior job, and that's what I expect. It's a good idea to remind tenants about this requirement when either you or they give notice to terminate.

The last paragraph of the security deposit clause states that I may use this deposit to cover any tenant obligations. This means that the deposit covers unpaid rent as well as any damage to the property.

Assignment and Subletting

Tenant shall not assign this agreement or sublet any portion of the property without prior written consent of the owner.

I insist on choosing my own tenants. While I will consider new tenants who are recommended by old tenants who want to break a lease, they must meet my standards. I want to interview them and run a credit report. The one exception I may make occurs when not all of the old tenants are leaving.

For example, three young men rented one of my properties. As I expected, one of them eventually fell in love and wanted to set up a new home. The lease term would not be over for many months, but he had a friend who wanted to take his place in the house and on the lease. I signed a new lease with the two remaining tenants plus the new tenant without running a credit check on him. Since the other two had been good tenants for over a year and a half and each would remain fully liable for the total rent, I felt my risk was low.

Maintenance, Repairs or Alterations

The tenant acknowledges that the property is in good order and repair unless otherwise indicated in this lease or in an attached inspection report. Tenant shall at tenant's expense maintain the property in a clean and sanitary manner including floor and wall surfaces, appliances, and the yard and shall surrender the property at the end of this lease in as good condition as received, ordinary and reasonable wear and tear excepted. Installing wall bolts for shelving units, installing drapery rods, or inserting ceiling hooks is expressly prohibited without written permission from the landlord. Tenant acknowledges that repairs may have to be made to the property during the tenant's leasehold, and tenant is not due any decrease in rent if repairs are made within a reason-

able time period by owner. Tenant shall be responsible for all repairs caused by tenant's negligence and by tenant's family or guests. Tenant shall not paint, paper or otherwise redecorate or make alterations to the property without prior written consent of the owner. Tenant shall be responsible for the following mainte-nance: _____ .

My tenants are responsible for watering the lawn and gardens, shoveling snow from the public sidewalks, and basic weeding. I do try to visit each of my properties in the early spring when the weeds are first taking off. I'll spend half a day working on each yard, getting it into good shape.

Besides showing my tenants how I expect the yard to look, I get a chance to study the exterior of the house. Does the deck need to be stained again? Should I touch up the paint on the house trim? Do any of the bushes or trees need pruning? The better maintained my properties are, the more pride the tenants will have in their homes. They'll take greater care of my house, and this results in a higher property value for me.

While there, I ask to use the bathroom. On my way to the toilet I examine the interior. Do I see a problem? Smell something I shouldn't? I also ask the tenants if anything has broken. It may be something they are willing to live with (especially if they are the ones who caused any damage beyond normal wear and tear), but I don't want to be swamped by a huge pile of fix it tasks when their lease ends. It's better to keep up with maintenance.

Yard Maintenance

Tenant is responsible for mowing and watering the lawn, and watering other landscape plants. Tenant must follow local watering restrictions, and is liable for any fines for violation. Tenant is also responsible for weeding any rocked areas in the yard. Tenants are not allowed to apply pesticides or herbicides to the yard without the written consent of the owner. Otherwise tenant is liable for the costs incurred in decontaminating the soil. Under NO circumstances barring an emergency shall the tenant prune, cut down, or destroy any plants on the property. Otherwise tenant shall be liable for any cost incurred for replacement plants and installation.

While I require tenants to maintain the yard, including watering it, I want them to understand it is their responsibility to follow water department rules on when and when not to water, how much, and what.

My concern about the improper use of poisons is based on a neighbor's experience. I once lived across the street from a house that used to be owned by a man who worked for a local city. His job included spraying weeds. He brought home some serious herbicide which needed to be diluted, but he applied it full strength to his yard. Then he sold the house. Trees in that yard and in neighboring yards started to sicken.

What did the new owner have to do when he determined what the old owner had done? The yard's dirt had to be removed to a depth of four feet and disposed of as toxic waste. While this example may be extreme, nationwide homeowners and tenants misuse and overuse both pesticides and herbicides. Toxic waste situations are not good for property values. Tenants must get written permission from me to use any poisons on my properties.

Regarding my concern over pruning, I once bought a house partially because I loved the front yard. In particular I was enamored of some bushes. One day when I came by, I was shocked to see those bushes trimmed to the ground. I kept my cool fairly well when I knocked on the door and asked my tenant what had happened. It turned out he didn't want the bushes blocking the front window, but I learned my lesson. Landscaping affects the value of a property to a great extent, and I want to be the only one who makes major pruning decisions.

Smoking in the Property

No smoking by the tenant or the tenant's guests or family is allowed inside the property. Any damage caused by smoking, including the smell of smoke and discoloration of paint, shall NOT be considered normal and reasonable wear and tear. Tenant acknowledges and agrees that smoking inside the property is grounds for immediate eviction at owner's option.

Smoking discolors the paint and makes the carpet and drapes smell. If the majority of your prospective tenants are smokers, this clause may make your properties too difficult to lease. And new tenants won't object to a smoky property if they also smoke; they'll never notice the smell.

But if nonsmokers make up the majority of your tenant pool, it makes sense to avoid smokers. Nonsmokers won't be interested in smoky properties so it will be harder to re-rent your properties. And smokers cause damage. Counters and tubs get burn marks, and sometimes so does the flooring. Paint gets yellowed and drapes and carpet pick up the smell of smoke. This equals more time and money invested in maintenance. Balance these potential problems against your available tenant pool when you decide on your smoking policy.

Severability

The unenforceability of any clause of this lease shall not effect the enforceability of any other clause or clauses.

Severability comes into play when someone, presumably a judge, decides one clause or section of a clause in a lease is not legal. If this happens to you, you'll want the rest of the lease to remain in force.

Waiver

Any waiver by either party, or any breach of any clause of this lease, shall not be considered to be a continuing waiver of a subsequent breach of the same or a different clause of this lease. Any acceptance of a partial payment of rent by owner shall not be deemed a waiver of owner's right to the full amount thereof nor a waiver of owner's right to begin eviction proceedings.

You may decide to ignore a clause of your lease. Perhaps a new pet shows up or a girlfriend moves in. Since the property is being well maintained, you look the other way. Whatever clause it is that you decide to ignore, you want the rest of the lease to still be in force.

In case a tenant is late with the rent, you may want the option to accept partial payment while making it clear that the rest of the rent is still due and its nonpayment is cause for eviction. Laws regarding how evictions are handled vary state by state, and you should check with a lawyer before taking partial rent.

Attorney's Fees

If either party to this lease prevails in any legal action brought by either party to enforce the terms hereof or relating to the property, the prevailing party shall NOT be entitled to reimbursement for all costs incurred in connection with such action including reasonable attorney's fees. Each party will be responsible for their own costs including attorney's fees.

I used to have this clause award attorney's fees to the prevailing party since I thought it would deter a tenant from dragging me into court. But on second thought, I don't always agree with the verdicts of judges. It would be bad enough to lose a case where I thought I was in the right; I don't want to add insult to injury by making myself liable for my tenants' costs if they win. So I have each party pay for their own costs, win or lose. At least that way I can limit how much I choose to spend on a case. I'd hate to be responsible for some tenant's inflated bill.

Some property owners may consider making only the tenant liable for the winner's legal costs. That way if the tenant wins a case, the owner won't have to pay for the tenant's costs, but if the owner wins, the tenant must reimburse the owner's costs. While this may seem to be a clever approach, judges don't like leases that fail to treat parties equally. A judge may say that whoever wins will have costs reimbursed if the property owner tried to reserve that right solely for himself or herself.

Notice

Any notice required by this lease from either party may be given by mailing the notice to tenant at the property and to owner at _____ . *Notice to one tenant shall be deemed notice to all tenants. A change of address to be used for notification purposes shall be effective only if notice is given in writing.*

It may seem silly to send a notice to your property after a tenant has moved out, but you need to have somewhere to send notices to your tenants. It is the tenant's responsibility to provide a forwarding address to the post office.

Additional Terms and Conditions

Use the blank lines of the additional provisions clause to cover requirements that are unique to one of your properties or a special concession you've granted to a particular tenant. How many blank lines you insert is up to you. However, if something needs to be listed for every property you own, you'll save time creating a standard clause inside your lease to cover that issue.

Entire Agreement

The foregoing ___ number of pages constitute the entire agreement between the parties and may be modified only in writing signed by both parties. The following exhibits, if any, have been made a part of this agreement before the parties' execution hereof: _____ . The undersigned tenant(s) hereby acknowledge receipt of a copy hereof.

Dated this day of _____ , 19 ____ .

Owner: _____ Owner: _____

Owner's contact information: _____

Tenant: _____ Tenant: _____

Tenant's contact information: _____

You should mention how many pages are in your lease so a tenant can't say you've inserted a page he or she never saw before. In addition, it's a good idea to have the tenants initial all other pages to prove that those are the pages they read and those are the clauses they agreed to abide by when they signed the lease.

I've also begun to add a Move Out Requirements exhibit as part of my lease. Certain problems such as numerous burnout bulbs, no toilet paper, and dirty baseboards have become my pet peeves when tenants move out. As the years go by, I'm sure you'll develop a list of things that drive you crazy, too. This type of exhibit is one way to prevent yourself from going nuts. Specifically listing items instead of merely requesting "clean" increases the odds that the tenant will handle them properly. And if not, then the financial penalties have been agreed to in writing.

Move Out Requirements

This property was cleaned before you moved in. When you move out, it should be as clean. Every light fixture has a light bulb of the correct wattage in every socket. Any burned out bulbs should be replaced when you move out.

1. If the house is dirty you will be charged $20 per hour for the owner's labor to clean, or market rate for a cleaning service.

2. Any missing, burned out, or incorrect wattage light bulbs will be replaced at a charge of $1.00 per bulb.

3. At least 1/2 roll of toilet paper will be left in at least one bathroom, or tenant will be charged $2.

4. Clean up of any pet feces in yard will be charged at $40 per hour.

5. Any cleanup of feces, urine, or other disgusting substances in house will be charged at $50 per hour.

6. Lawn will be mowed within three days of move out if tenant moves between the months of April and October. Otherwise tenant will be charged a flat $50.

Some areas seem to be consistently forgotten by many tenants. Below is a reminder list.

1. Baseboards and windowsills. Use a vacuum's soft bristle attachment and/or a damp (not wet) sponge to clean them.

2. Carefully pull the stove out and clean the sides of the stove, the wall behind it, and the floor. Also remember to clean the inside of the stove.

3. Clean stove pans or replace them.

4. Clean glass in light fixtures.

5. Dust heating vents.

6. Clean out window or sliding glass door tracks using vacuum and/or wet sponge.

7. Vacuum window screens.
8. Clean inside of all windows within six feet of floor level.

My lease is by no means exhaustive. Its length is a compromise between caution and my desire not to scare off prospective tenants. It is constantly evolving as my tenants teach me where I need to be more specific. Your lease will also change as you learn what does and does not matter to you. The area of the country where you live may also dictate adding clauses to handle special local circumstances. Any lease is a work in progress, evolving as you gain expertise in your rental market.

Chapter Eleven

1031 Tax Deferred Exchanges

The Congress of the United States has done several things to make investing in real estate attractive from a tax viewpoint. Besides allowing small investors to depreciate their properties, the government has also provided a way for investors to switch their investments from one property to another on a tax deferred basis.

Section 1031 of the Internal Revenue Code (IRC) and regulations issued by the Treasury Department have established and clarified the tax exchange rules which allow investors to sell one or more properties and to buy replacement properties without triggering the usual capital gain tax consequences of a sale. Properties involved in a 1031 tax deferred exchange must be "like kind" which means real property for real property. Land, apartment buildings, houses, attached housing such as townhomes and condominiums, and commercial properties such as office buildings and strip malls are all considered real property.

This provision in our tax code gives real estate investors a great opportunity to improve their portfolios of investment properties. If you think that you could make more money or save time owning a different property, you can sell the one you have and buy the better one without losing part of your investment to the tax man, although you will still have to pay typical closing costs.

Compare this to what happens when you invest in the stock market. Let's say your stock rises dramatically in value, but you think it won't do as well in the future. If you sell it, you'll have to pay taxes on your gain before you can reinvest what's left of your money.

The sale of investment real estate works differently. If you correctly follow the 1031 exchange rules, you can buy and sell properties without triggering any federal taxes due. In addition most states will consider 1031 tax deferred sales non-taxable events. Nevertheless, due to the differences between state tax laws, you should check with your accountant to verify how your state views 1031 tax deferred exchanges.

Personal Residence Versus Investment Property

The rules for doing a tax deferred exchange for investment properties are different than the tax free rules for selling a personal residence. A personal home tax exemption happens almost automatically. As long as your gain is $250,000 or less if you are a single person, or $500,000 or less if you file a joint tax return, and you have owned and used your home as your primary residence for at least two out of the last five years, you won't owe any capital gain taxes. And even if you only partially meet these requirements, you can still avoid paying some of your capital gain taxes in some cases.

If you want the sale of your investment property to qualify for a 1031 tax deferred exchange, however, you will have to meet a number of completely different requirements. If, like most investors, you are not exchanging one property directly for another property, you must hire what is called a "qualified intermediary" to hold your money between the time you sell one property and buy a new property. This intermediary will help you complete the required paperwork and make sure you follow the rules correctly.

Sometimes you will have used a property over time as both a principal residence and as an investment property. You may have moved out of your home and turned it into a rental property, or vice versa, you may have moved into one of your rental properties. Or you may have a home that includes office space or a rental unit. Examples of how the tax gains in these types of mixed situations are handled appear later in this chapter.

If you don't comply exactly with the Treasury regulations, your exchange may not be considered valid. Then you will owe capital gain taxes even if you have reinvested your money into another real estate investment.

Why You May Want to Sell Your Property

Some people think they will never do a 1031 tax deferred exchange. They intend to buy their target value of properties and hold these properties until the loans are paid off. They want to avoid the costs of selling a property which may include sales commissions, potential vacancy, and miscellaneous closing costs. These buy and hold investors also want to avoid the hassle of selling.

Despite the disadvantages inherent in selling an investment property, many situations might arise which would make a 1031 tax deferred exchange desirable. You should be familiar with how the rules work because if you are a real estate investor for very long, you will likely encounter a situation where you'll want to use a tax deferred exchange.

Despite the costs involved in selling a property, sometimes it makes more sense to get out of a specific investment and into a different one. Perhaps the neighborhood where your property is located has become undesirable, causing you a number of difficulties. Vacancies may have become harder to fill or you may be concerned about your safety when visiting the property.

You may decide that another neighborhood in your city offers more potential for appreciation. You may believe that this increased appreciation will cover your selling and exchanging costs plus give you something extra. Or you may want to increase your leverage by investing the equity from one property into something more expensive.

Even if you still like the neighborhood around your property, you may decide to move to a different city or state. Americans are a mobile people. If you buy properties in Illinois, then decide to retire in Oklahoma to be near your relatives, you will have a problem. Either you must hire a property manager to take care of your investments for you when you move, or else you will need a way to take your investments with you.

Some people exchange in order to consolidate their real estate holdings. Let's say you own five condominiums. You may decide to sell them and trade the equity into a small apartment complex, or, conversely, you may own an apartment house and hate it. You may want to trade into single family homes instead.

Sometimes gaining control of family property will encourage you to make a 1031 tax deferred exchange. After his grandfather's death, a friend of mine and his sister were left with joint ownership of some farm land in Missouri. Since the property was producing a cash flow rate of return which was less than 2% per year, the siblings decided to sell the property.

Because of the way the grandfather had structured his estate, actually putting his grandchildren on the title to the land many years ago, the grandson's taxable gain in his inheritance was almost the full value of his share of the property. If he sold it in the normal fashion, he would owe tens of thousands in taxes.

Instead he used a 1031 tax deferred exchange so he could avoid paying taxes at the time of sale. He reinvested his share of the sale proceeds in a single family house in Colorado. This house was located close to his personal home so it would be easy for him to manage, and it promised a much higher rate of return.

If you own properties with a partner, you may reach a point where you would like to discontinue the partnership. Whether you sell out your interest in the joint properties to your partner, or together you decide to sell the properties on the open market, you'll want a way to take your full equity with you without letting the tax man take a bite. Even if your partner plans to keep his or her share in cash and pay taxes on it, you can still use a 1031 tax deferred exchange to shelter your share of the proceeds.

Another reason you may decide to do a tax deferred exchange is because you need to pull money out of a property, but you can't qualify to refinance. Or the refinance won't pull out as much cash as you need. You could sell the property, deduct the selling costs, pay taxes on the money you take out, and reinvest the rest on a tax deferred basis. This way you can postpone paying taxes on the money you want to keep invested in real estate.

Don't rely blindly on an attorney, certified public accountant, or title company employee to explain the 1031 tax deferred exchange rules to you correctly. Unless this person has been trained in real estate tax laws and specializes in exchanges, he or she may not understand all the rules.

For example, a real estate broker in Colorado needed to sell his four-plex in order to get some much needed cash. The broker didn't need all of the proceeds from the sale, but when he checked with an attorney, he was told 1031 tax deferred exchanges are an all or nothing deal. The attorney said if the broker kept and spent any of the money, he wasn't allowed to reinvest the rest on a tax deferred basis. THIS IS NOT TRUE.

The broker could have used an exchange to protect some of his money. Unfortunately, he was given incorrect advice and didn't do a 1031 tax deferred exchange. He paid taxes on the full amount of gain, leaving him with less to reinvest after he took out the amount he needed to cover his immediate cash requirements.

A parent may exchange properties for the purposes of estate planning. If a parent owns one large apartment building and knows that his two children cannot agree on anything, he may decide to sell his building and exchange the proceeds into two buildings. Then he could leave one building to each child separately, preventing future co-ownership squabbles.

Or someone with a large apartment building may want to liquidate his or her investment over a period of time. By exchanging into many smaller properties, this investor can sell one unit at a time as funds are desired.

These are just some of the reasons why people who want to stay invested in real estate may find themselves exchanging property. The main objective is to keep your hands on as much of your money as you can. If you pay some of it to the government you will have less to reinvest. Less to reinvest means you will have to wait longer before you achieve your financial goals.

Taxable Gain

The reason to do a 1031 tax deferred exchange is so you can defer paying taxes on your gain in a property or properties. Obviously you must have a gain to protect from taxes before it makes sense to participate in an exchange. If you have a small gain, the costs of a 1031 tax deferred exchange may be more than you could save in taxes. And if you have a loss you certainly don't want to pay for an exchange.

A simple exchange of one property for another costs $500-$1,000 for the intermediary's services. If you are exchanging from one property into two or more properties, the fee will go up $250-$500 for each additional property. If you want to do a reverse exchange where you buy the replacement property before you sell the relinquished property, the fees may be several times more. You may also be charged miscellaneous fees for items such as long distance phones calls, faxes, overnight services, and copies. Get a complete list of probable costs from whomever you plan to use as your qualified intermediary so you can accurately estimate the total cost of doing an exchange.

Since you will decide to do an exchange only if the amount you'll save from taxes will be more than the cost of doing the exchange, you must first determine how much your potential tax liability will be. Calculating the amount of taxable gain for a property can get complicated. You will need to know several numbers: your projected selling price, your selling costs, and your adjusted basis in the property. Let's look at these three areas.

Selling Price

You probably have a good idea of your property's value. You've been receiving flyers in the mail from real estate agents who have sold other properties in the neighborhood and you've been calling on "For Sale" signs to find out asking prices. Agents can show you the sold prices for properties like the one you want to sell. And you can always pay for an appraisal. Keep in mind that in a rising market your property may be worth more than recent sales, and in a soft market you will probably get less than recent comparable sales prices.

Selling costs

Selling costs involve a number of fees such as real estate commissions and title insurance. Most agents will do a net sheet for you which lists all of the costs which will have to be subtracted from your sale proceeds. If you don't plan to use an agent, a title company or a lawyer who specializes in assisting For Sale by Owners may give you an idea of what fees to expect. Any exchange costs you incur can also be deducted as additional selling costs.

Your "amount realized" is what you get after subtracting the selling costs from the selling price. Many sellers will then subtract the balance of any loans on the property to get their net proceeds. These sellers think that the amount of money they walk away with at closing is their taxable gain, but actually the tax law ignores loans. We'll see why later in this chapter.

For now, to find out your taxable gain, subtract the selling costs from the anticipated selling price, but then also subtract your "adjusted basis" in the property instead of your loan balances. The resulting number is the gain on which you will potentially owe taxes.

Adjusted Basis

Your adjusted basis is the purchase price you paid plus the closing costs for that purchase plus the cost of capital improvements you made while you owned the property, minus the depreciation you took over the years.

Adjusted basis = Purchase price + purchase closing costs + capital improvement costs - accumulated depreciation

Let's say you purchased an investment house ten years ago for $100,000 and you paid $2,000 in closing costs. Your beginning basis in the property was $102,000. You've owned the property for ten years.

Based on the tax assessor's valuation when you bought the property, you decided ten years ago that 85% of the property's purchase price came from the value of the improvements, not the land. Eighty-five percent of $100,000 (we'll ignore the fact that some closing costs may also be depreciated) was $85,000. Dividing $85,000 by 27.5 years gave you a $3,000 annual depreciation expense.

Since you've owned the property for ten years, the $3,000 annual depreciation adds up to a total depreciation expense of $30,000. Your beginning basis in your investment property was $102,000. Subtracting the $30,000 you've taken in depreciation gives you $72,000. If you've made no improvements to the property, your adjusted basis is $72,000.

Purchase price	**$100,000**
Closing cost	**$2,000**
Beginning basis	**$102,000**
Yearly depreciation	**$3,000**
Ten years of depreciation	**$30,000**
Adjusted basis (beginning basis -	
ten years of depreciation)	**$72,000**

But let's say your agent tells you that all the houses that are comparable to the one you own have decks. In order to make your house competitive, the agent recommends that you add a deck before you put your property on the market. You agree to do this and the new deck costs you $3,000.

By installing the deck you've made a capital improvement to the property. This means that you have increased your adjusted basis. Because the deck is brand new, you haven't had time to start depreciating this improvement. Therefore you should add the full cost of the deck to your adjusted basis. $72,000 + $3,000 = $75,000. This amount is your new adjusted gross basis in the property.

Adjusted basis	**$72,000**
Capital improvement (new deck)	**$3,000**
Adjusted gross basis	**$75,000**

You sell the property for $140,000. To determine your taxable gain in the property, you subtract your selling costs and adjusted basis from the sales price.

Sales price	**$140,000**
Selling costs	**$10,000**
Adjusted gross basis	**$75,000**
Taxable gain (sales price - selling costs	
- adjusted basis = $140,000 - $10,000	
- $75,000)	**$55,000**

Loan Amounts and Taxable Gain

But what about any loans on the property? Let's say you have a loan with an $80,000 balance. Subtracting the closing costs of $10,000 and the loan balance of $80,000 from the sales price of $140,000 produces a net to you of $50,000. So isn't the taxable gain only $50,000, not $55,000?

Sales price	**$140,000**
Closing costs	**$10,000**
Loan balance	**$80,000**
Net proceeds (sales price - selling costs	
- loan balance = $140,000 - $10,000	
- $80,000)	**$50,000**

However, guided by current tax law, the Internal Revenue Service doesn't care about loans. Whether you purchased the property with all cash or with a loan doesn't matter to them. The loan balance is treated essentially the same as cash both when the property is acquired and when the property is sold. It is ignored.

Normally this treatment of the loan balance isn't a problem. Hopefully you've been paying down your loan as fast as you've been depreciating the property, and your net proceeds and your taxable gain will be close to the same number. This means that the tax you think you'll owe on the net proceeds will be close to what you do owe on your actual taxable gain.

Let's give our example a new twist. What would happen if you had refinanced your property after owning it for eight years? You purchased your investment property for $100,000, but after owning it for eight years the value had increased to $130,000 with a loan balance of $75,000. You refinanced the property to pull out some of your equity.

Your bank was willing to give you a loan equal to 80% of the new value of $130,000, or $104,000. When you paid off the old loan balance of $75,000 plus $2,000 in closing costs, you walked away with $27,000.

New loan	**$104,000**
Closing costs on new loan	**$2,000**
Old loan	**$75,000**
Cash out (new loan - closing costs on new loan	
- old loan = $104,000 - $2,000 - $75,000)	**$27,000**

Did you have to pay taxes on this $27,000? No, because refinancing a property isn't considered a taxable event. Continuing with our example, you sell your property in the tenth year for $140,000. By this time the new loan's balance has been paid down to $100,000. When you subtract the selling costs of $10,000 and the new loan balance from the selling price, you get net proceeds of $30,000.

Sales price	**$140,000**
Selling costs	**$10,000**
Loan balance	**$100,000**
New net proceeds (sales price - selling costs	
- loan balance = $140,000 - $10,000 - $100,000)	**$30,000**

Since you receive only $30,000 when you sell your property, it may seem unfair to have to pay taxes on a gain of $55,000. Remember, though, you pulled $27,000 out of the property two years ago. The Internal Revenue Service didn't tax you on that money then, but you will be taxed now based on your capital gain in the property.

Overall, the fact that the Internal Revenue Service doesn't tax you on money you pull out of a property through refinancing is actually an advantage for the investor. It's always better to pay taxes later rather than sooner as long as you remember that the tax bill will come due the day you sell the property. You must make sure you'll have enough money to pay your delayed taxes or else use a 1031 deferred tax exchange to reinvest your proceeds. Oddly enough, it is possible for an investor to get in a situation where he or she can't afford to sell a property.

In a worst case scenario it's possible to sell a property and end up owing more in taxes than you receive at the closing. Let's take a look at our example again, but this time we'll say you have owned the property for twenty years. That means you've depreciated your basis in the property by another $30,000. Taking the beginning basis of $102,000 and subtracting twenty years worth of depreciation gives you an adjusted basis of $42,000.

Beginning basis	**$102,000**
Twenty years of depreciation	**$60,000**
Adjusted basis ($102,000 - $60,000)	**$42,000**

If you add the deck just before you sell the property, your adjusted basis in the property will become $45,000.

Capital improvement (new deck)	**$3,000**
New adjusted basis ($42,000 + $3,000)	**$45,000**

You've owned the property for an additional ten years and its value has increased to $200,000. Your selling costs are now $15,000. Subtracting the selling costs and the adjusted basis from the sale price gives you a taxable capital gain of $140,000.

Sales price	**$200,000**
Selling costs	**$15,000**
Adjusted basis	**$45,000**
Taxable capital gain (Sales price -	
selling costs - adjusted basis = $200,000	
- $15,000 - $45,000)	**$140,000**

But half a year ago you refinanced the property with an 80% loan-to-property value loan, giving you a new loan balance of $160,000. After paying off the old loan balance of $58,000 plus closing costs on the new loan, you walked away with $100,000 cash. Now you sell the property. Subtracting the selling costs and the loan balance, $159,000, from the selling price gives you net proceeds equalling $26,000.

Sales price	**$200,000**
Selling costs	**$15,000**
Loan balance	**$159,000**
Net proceeds (Sales price - selling costs	
- loan balance = $200,000 - $15,000	
- $159,000)	**$26,000**

Since your taxable gain is $140,000 you must pay taxes on that amount. This $140,000 in gain will be taxed at two different rates. Since you have depreciated the property by $60,000, $60,000 of your total gain is considered recaptured depreciation, and under current law is taxed at a maximum federal tax rate of 25%. You will owe $15,000 on this portion of your gain (this exception to the maximum capital tax rate of 15% is a surprise to some investors).

The remainder of your gain, $80,000, will be taxed at whatever capital gain tax rate applies to you. Assuming that you will incur the current maximum regular capital gain tax rate of 15%, you will owe an additional $12,000. Your total federal taxes due will be $27,000.

Tax on gain attributed to depreciation	
(25% of $60,000)	**$15,000**
Tax on balance of capital gain	
(15% of $80,000)	**$12,000**
Total taxes due ($15,000 + $12,000)	**$27,000**

Here is where you could land in hot water. Your proceeds from selling the property will be $26,000, but you could potentially owe taxes of $27,000. Looking only at the federal taxes due, you will have to come up with an extra $1,000 at tax time. And if your state is among those that tax capital gains, you could owe additional thousands for state taxes. If you spent or reinvested in illiquid assets the entire $100,000 you received when you refinanced, you may not be able to afford to sell your rental property.

You can't count on a real estate agent to point out a problem tax situation like the one in this example. An agent's job is to sell your property and to tell you what you will net without taking into consideration your tax liability. You'll need to talk with your accountant to discuss the tax angles. The moral of this story is to check your numbers on a refinanced property with a view toward taxes before you decide to sell.

Of course, if you are doing a 1031 tax deferred exchange, you will avoid the immediate problem of owing more taxes than you will net in proceeds from a sale because you'll be able to continue deferring your tax liability into the future.

If you've had an accountant doing your taxes for you, you don't have to calculate your taxable gain yourself. Call your accountant and ask what your current basis is in the property you want to sell. If you've been doing your taxes yourself, you'll have to do your own basis calculations. At the very least you may decide to hire an accountant to double-check your figures.

To Exchange or Not to Exchange

Let's say your taxable gain when you sell a property will be only $4,000. If your combined federal, state, and local taxes are 20%, your tax burden will be $800. After considering the costs of doing an exchange plus the costs and hassles involved in the additional accounting work, there would be no financial advantage to doing an exchange.

However, if your gain will be $50,000, a 20% combined tax bracket would mean a tax bill of $10,000. If you plan to reinvest your proceeds in real estate, you most likely should be doing a 1031 tax deferred exchange. The cost of hiring a qualified intermediary will be far lower than your potential tax bill. The money you save can continue to compound and grow for your benefit instead of going to Uncle Sam.

The Rules for 1031 Tax Deferred Exchanges

To have your sale of a relinquished property (or properties) and purchase of a replacement property (or properties) qualify as a 1031 tax deferred exchange, you must follow some rules listed in the tax code. The basic rules are easy to understand and we'll cover them first. If you want to do a more complicated exchange, the first set of rules may not work for you. However, the law provides for exceptions, and we'll look at those as well.

To start with you must exchange "like kind" property. This means you must exchange any kind of real property for any other real property. You can exchange a piece of vacant land for an apartment house, an apartment house for ten condominiums, or three houses for a small commercial strip mall. Depending on the state, other assets may be considered to be real property. For example, in Colorado water rights are real property. If you get tired of tenants and think that the value of water is sure to sky-rocket with the next drought, you could use a 1031 tax deferred exchange to switch your property investments into water rights.

The second basic requirement of a 1031 tax deferred exchange is that you may not receive the proceeds from the sale of your property. Someone else must hold the funds until they can be reinvested into a replacement property. You must hire a qualified intermediary to fill this role; your exchange will not be valid if you simply ask your real estate agent or a title company to hold the money for you. Legally you could demand your funds from anyone except a qualified intermediary. If you have this right then you have what is called constructive receipt of your funds.

A qualified intermediary, on the other hand, can and will legally refuse to give you your funds for a restricted period of time. You grant this power when you sign the paperwork authorizing the person or company to act as your qualified intermediary. This written agreement with the intermediary prevents you from taking possession of or exercising control of your money except as provided for by the tax law. If you eventually decide not to complete a 1031 tax deferred exchange, the regulations specify when the intermediary may return your funds to you.

Selecting a Qualified Intermediary

Finding a qualified intermediary can be as easy as looking in the phone book, but a recommendation is the better route. At this time no federal requirements, and very few state requirements, exist to govern who can or cannot call themselves qualified intermediaries. Anyone from an attorney to a real estate broker to a title or escrow company may offer to act as a 1031 tax deferred exchange intermediary.

However, there is a rule that disallows anyone who has acted in an agency position for you within the last two years to act as your qualified intermediary. For example, your real estate agent or personal lawyer would be disqualified if they have worked for you within the last two years.

You do not have to hire someone locally to act as your qualified intermediary. Many 1031 tax deferred exchange specialists offer national service. Paperwork is faxed or overnighted, and money is wired from one account to the next. Questions can be asked and answered over the phone.

Tax exchanges may be done only with properties located inside the United States and the US Virgin Islands. Why? Because a 1031 tax deferred exchange allows you to defer federal taxes. As long as your investments stay in the United States, the Internal Revenue Service knows it will be paid taxes when and if you do sell a property without exchanging it. Money shifted into investments outside of the United States may be gone for good without any eventual receipt of taxes by the Internal Revenue Service.

You will want to investigate the person or institution you hire to act as your intermediary. You'll want someone with experience, and you'll want someone you can trust with your money. While it is possible to set up systems to protect yourself against the possibility of the intermediary stealing your funds such as requiring your signature to release funds, these options add costs to your basic exchange fee. In any case, you'll want to hire someone with a sterling reputation since it's possible for an intermediary to be in control of several million dollars of other people's money at any given time.

The cheapest way to avoid exposure of your money to theft is to schedule the closing date for your relinquished property and the closing date for your replacement property for the same day. Then the intermediary can arrange for your funds to be sent from one closing directly to the next closing. (You must hire an intermediary even if you are doing back-to-back closings unless you are actually exchanging your property for the seller's property, something which occurs rarely.) Having both closings on the same day allows you to neatly avoid the issue of the intermediary holding your funds for an extended period of time.

Yet scheduling both closings together can create problems of its own if you are exchanging into several properties. Logistics may prevent you from having all of the closings occur on the same day. Even if you do schedule all of your closings perfectly, problems may occur. You may have trouble with your loan on the replacement property, and therefore the second closing will have to be postponed while you make the lender happy. Someone else involved in one of the transactions could become ill or die. The possibilities are endless.

A workable alternative is to protect yourself by hiring someone trustworthy and with a good track record. You can and should check on what the intermediary is doing to safeguard funds in-house. If you are hiring a company to act as your qualified intermediary, at least two people in the firm should have to sign to release funds. Client funds involved in exchanges should be kept in an account segregated from the company's operating funds, and an outside certified public accountant should be doing or at least checking the financial record keeping.

Identifying Your Replacement Properties

You must identify, that is provide a list of your potential replacement properties, within forty-five days after the sale of your relinquished property. This identification must be in writing and delivered to your qualified intermediary.

You will have to comply with certain restrictions when you identify your replacement properties. You must identify specific properties. It is not sufficient to say you will buy something located in a certain city or county or neighborhood. You must identify individual pieces of property by their specific street addresses (legal descriptions are not required).

Though you have forty-five days to identify the properties you may buy, you should try to identify them much sooner. You may identify them even before you close on your relinquished property. You should be looking for your replacement properties as soon as your relinquished property goes under contract.

Since you can change your list of identified properties up until the forty-five day deadline, you'll want to give yourself time to have each identified property inspected before the deadline expires. If the inspector finds major problems, you may redo your list and substitute a different replacement property for the one you decided was unacceptable. By identifying early you've given yourself the flexibility to change your mind.

How Many Replacement Properties

You must comply with rules which restrict the number of properties you may identify as potential replacement properties.

If you identify three or fewer, you will qualify for a 1031 tax deferred exchange even if you eventually buy only one or two of these properties. If you identify more than three replacement properties, you must satisfy one of two additional requirements.

The first exception is when you identify replacement properties with a combined fair market value which equals or is less than 200% of the fair market value of your relinquished property.

Fair market value of replacement property = (less than) 2 X fair market value of relinquished property

Let's say you sell a house for $150,000. You want to buy four condominiums each worth $50,000 as your replacement properties. All properties are priced at fair market value. Will you be in compliance with the first exception to the rule which allows you to identify only three potential replacement properties?

4 X $50,000 = $200,000
2 X $150,000 = $300,000

The answer is yes. Because the fair market value of your identified replacement properties is less than twice the fair market value of your relinquished property, this identification would be valid, even if you don't buy all four of the condominiums.

The second exception allows you to identify more than three replacement properties even when the combined fair market value of these properties exceeds the maximum allowed by the first exception. If you identify properties worth more than 200% of the fair market value of your relinquished property, you must close on enough identified properties to allow you to acquire 95% of their value.

Let's say you sell a house worth $200,000. If you identify four replacement properties worth $110,000 apiece, the total fair market value of the replacement properties is $440,000. Since this is more than twice the fair market value of your relinquished property (2 X $200,000 = $400,000), you must purchase properties worth 95% of the total identified replacement properties' value in order for your 1031 tax deferred exchange to be valid.

95% of $440,000 = $418,000

Since each property is worth $110,000, if you fail to buy even one, you will not have purchased 95% of the value of the identified replacement properties. Then none of your purchases will qualify as 1031 tax deferred exchanges, and you will owe tax on your entire gain from the sale of the relinquished property.

Does this mean you should never identify replacement properties worth more than 200% of the value of your relinquished property? Not at all. Remember, if you've identified three or fewer properties, the 95% requirement doesn't apply in the first place. Even if you only close on one property your exchange will still be valid (though you may not have managed to defer all your taxes if you failed to reinvest all of your proceeds from the relinquished property - this is covered later in this chapter).

If you have identified four or more replacement properties, then you still have a safety plan. If you schedule all of your closings for the replacement properties within the forty-five day identification limit, you'll know if any deal falls apart in time to redo your list of identified properties. You will, of course, remove that problem property from the list. The safety key is to schedule all of your closings within the forty-five day identification deadline.

180 Days to Close

No matter how many replacement properties you have identified, you have up to 180 days after selling the relinquished property to buy them. The actual guidelines say you have 180 days after the sale or until the filing of your next federal tax return, whichever occurs first, to buy your replacement properties. Sometimes, depending when you sell your relinquished property, you will have to file a tax extension if you want to use the maximum of 180 days before you close on your replacement property.

Though it's generally best to close on your replacement property or properties as quickly as possible after the sale of the relinquished property, you may need the full 180 days. You may be under contract to buy a new property, and it will take time for it to be built. Or a seller may insist on a later closing date for tax purposes. Having 180 days to close on your replacement property gives you valuable flexibility.

Reinvesting All of Your Proceeds

If you want your exchange to be 100% tax deferred, you must comply with more requirements. You must reinvest all of your cash into the replacement property. In addition your replacement property must have a value equal or greater than the value of the relinquished property. If you do take some cash out and don't reinvest it, or if your replacement property is worth less than the relinquished property, you will owe taxes on that money.

Let's say you sell a property for $200,000 after deducting selling costs and your taxable gain is $100,000. You have depreciated the property by $40,000. This means that if you didn't do an exchange, $40,000 of your gain would be treated as recaptured depreciation and taxed at 25%. The remaining $60,000 gain would be taxed at your maximum capital gains rate.

If you buy a replacement property for $180,000, $20,000 of your gain will not be deferred. The IRS will apply the highest applicable tax rate to this recognized gain, that is 25% for recaptured depreciation instead of your maximum capital gains rate.

If you buy a replacement property for $150,000, then the highest applicable tax rate will apply only to the first $40,000 of your recognized gain. The remaining recognized $10,000 gain will be taxed at your maximum capital gains rate.

In these examples an exchange will still make financial sense because you are deferring taxes on $80,000 or $50,000 of gain, but you must make sure you structure the purchase so you have the cash to pay the taxes you will owe. The easiest way to do this is to not reinvest all of your equity into your replacement property. Reduce it by the amount of taxes you'll need to pay, and set that cash aside for tax day.

The same type of tax consequences result if you take out any cash when you do an exchange. Even if you buy a replacement property worth more than the relinquished property, taking out cash is a taxable event. The Internal Revenue Service will calculate taxes due first at the highest rate that could apply which is the 25% on gains attributed to depreciation. Any cash you receive in excess of the depreciation you've taken on the relinquished property will be taxed at your maximum capital gain rate.

Minimizing Additional Cash Invested

When you exchange properties, you may want to fix up the property you are selling. Rather than investing additional cash into the property by paying out of pocket for the fix up costs, I make a point of using contractors and suppliers who will agree to be paid out of proceeds at closing. That way I can use the equity from the property to pay some of the major bills.

For example, one property I sold in the spring of 2004 needed new carpeting and a new roof. I paid for the carpeting by getting a line of credit from the carpet store. I paid the minimum $100 payment each month until the property sold and instructed the closing agent to pay off the balance from my sale proceeds. For the new roof, I used a contractor who had done work for me before. He agreed to be paid when the house sold.

You may need to invest additional money into a replacement property. If it is an existing property, you may want to increase the purchase price and have the seller agree to replace or repair items before the closing. If the seller insists that the earnest money be increased by a matching non-refundable amount to cover the risk that you don't purchase the property, it may be worrth it to you in order to minimize the extra cash out of pocket.

If you are buying a new home as a replacement property, you'll have to decide between saving money by purchasing some items after the closing versus rolling their cost into the purchase price. For example, when buying new houses I discovered I could save almost $2,000 per unit by having air conditioning installed by an independent contractor instead of the builder. Yet that meant having to come up with over $3,000 additional cash out of pocket per house. If you have the cash, then save the money. But for many investors, you may have to pay the builder's premium on some expensive options in order to minimize your cash outlay after closing.

Carrying Over Your Basis

When you do an exchange, you'll have to file the IRS form 8824, Like-Kind Exchanges. This form allows you and the IRS to calculate any recognized gain from the exchange that is taxable now, the deferred gain (or loss), and the basis of your replacement property or properties. Filling out this form can be tricky; I strongly recommend hiring someone who has experience with this form to help you. Otherwise you may discover many years in the future that you did it incorrectly and not be able to rectify your mistake. Misstating your basis as being smaller than it really was could cost you thousands in taxes in the future, so it's important to fill out this form correctly.

The Reverse Exchange

You may locate the property you wish to buy before you sell your relinquished property. In this case you could do what is known as a reverse exchange. This type of exchange got its name because your intermediary buys the replacement property (using funds provided by you) before you sell the relinquished property. The intermediary holds the replacement property until the sale of the relinquished property occurs, and then transfers title to you as part of a 1031 tax deferred exchange.

For many years title holding/reverse exchanges were not directly addressed in the tax code, exposing these exchanges to the risk of being challenged by the IRS. Yet many investors were doing reverse exchanges. Finally the IRS issued safe harbor rules for reverse like kind exchanges effective on or after September 15, 2000.

When you buy a replacement property in advance of selling a relinquished property, the replacement property must be held in a "qualified exchange accommodation arrangement." This "QEAA" must meet the following six requirements.

First, the title to the property must be held by a qualified "exchange accommodation titleholder." In addition this "EAT" must be subject to federal income tax from the time the property is purchased to the time the property's title is transferred to you.

Second, at the time the EAT takes title to the property it must be your bonafide intent that the property is a replacement or relinquished property that is being purchased or sold as part of a tax deferred exchange. This requirement only becomes a problem if you don't complete an exchange, and the IRS has reason to believe you never meant to complete it.

Third, you and your EAT have up to five business days after the EAT takes title to a property to complete an agreement in writing that specifies that this property is being held by the EAT as part of a 1031 tax deferred exchange for your benefit. The agreement must specify that the EAT will be treated as the owner of the property for all federal income tax purposes. This must be reflected in actuality by how the parties involved in the reverse exchange report financial information on their tax returns.

Fourth, you must identify the relinquished property within forty-five days of the EAT taking title to the replacement property. This is the same as a straight forward exchange when you have forty-five days after selling a property to identify the replacement property. As soon as the EAT buys a replacement property on your behalf, the clock starts to tick for you to identify the property or properties you will be selling.

The implication is that all of the other rules that normally apply to a straight forward exchange identification apply to a reverse exchange, too, but this is not explicitly stated. It appears that you may identify up to three possible relinquished properties to be sold without having to sell all of them. Or identify more than three relinquished properties as long as the replacement properties are worth no more than twice the value of the total value of the identified relinquished properties. Or identify four or more relinquished properties as long as you sell enough of them to equal 95% of their total value. However, whether or not to assume that these rules apply is up to you and your qualified EAT. Hopefully more explicit regulations will have been issued by the time you need these questionable areas clarified.

Fifth, within 180 days of the EAT buying your replacement property for you, you must complete the reverse exchange by taking title to the replacement property. Be careful, because this time period can be reduced. If the due date of your federal income tax return for the year in which the transfer of the relinquished property occurs comes sooner than 180 days, the exchange must be completed by then. This rule, similar again to what happens when you do a straight forward exchange, may make it necessary for you to file for an extension in order to have enough time to complete an exchange.

Sixth, the combined time period for the relinquished property and the replacement property to be held in a QEAA cannot exceed 180 days.

During the time period that the EAT owns the replacement property, the IRS does allow you to lease the property under lease terms that effectively shift all of the economic burdens and benefits of ownership to you. Your lease should allow you to manage the property as you see fit, including selecting tenants and making alterations. The EAT typically rents the replacement property to you on a triple net basis, meaning that you as the tenant are responsible for all expenses. An experienced qualified intermediary should be able to provide an appropriate lease agreement.

The Internal Revenue Service hasn't clearly addressed how depreciation should be handled. Does the EAT have to take, or is it even entitled to take, the depreciation deduction for the time period of its ownership of the property? Or should you take the depreciation? If you ask, your EAT can tell you how he or she has decided to handle this issue.

Because a reverse exchange is more complicated to do than a typical exchange, you can expect an intermediary to charge significantly higher fees for this service compared to a straight forward exchange. Keep this in mind when you are deciding whether or not to do a reverse exchange.

Also, financing can be tricky to arrange for a reverse 1031 exchange. Lenders do not like the idea of loaning money to you to buy a property that will be held in the name of the qualified intermediary. Often the only solution is for you to provide the intermediary with enough cash to purchase the property, and then you get a loan when you complete the exchange by buying the property from the intermediary. In the past I have raised the cash to do this by borrowing from friends and relatives as well as from my own lines of credit. Before you decide to attempt a reverse 1031 exchange, make sure you have lined up financing from a lender who has participated in these type of exchanges in the past and is comfortable with how title to the property will be held. Otherwise, you will need to line up reliable sources to loan you the necessary cash.

The Improvement Exchange

Sometimes you will want to exchange a property for one that is not already built. Or you may wish to purchase a property that needs extensive renovations, and you want to include the cost of those renovations in the exchange value of your replacement property. In situations like these you can provide a qualified intermediary with the funds to build or renovate your replacement property, either before or after the sale of your relinquished property. The tricky part is to make sure you close on your replacement property within the 180 day deadline.

Combining the Principal Residence Gain Exclusion with a 1031 Exchange

The principal residence gain exclusion allows an individual to exclude, or not pay taxes on, up to $250,000 gain realized on the sale or exchange of a personal residence. For most joint returns, the exclusion amount is twice as much, $500,000. Until recently, it wasn't clear how or if this exclusion applied to properties that were included in 1031 exchanges. Due to some clarifications made by Congress in the fall of 2004 and Revenue Procedure 2005-14 issued by the Internal Revenue Service in early 2005, several possible combinations have been specifically addressed. While the following examples cannot be relied on as specific tax advice, they will help you understand how you could combine the principal residence gain exclusion with a 1031 exchange.

Your Home Changed Into a Rental Property

When people move, they may want to turn their old home into a rental property. Assuming that they lived in the house for at least two years before they moved, if they sell it within the next three years they can exclude part of the gain using the principal residence gain exclusion. If they have additional gain, they can defer the taxes on most of this amount using a 1031 exchange.

For example, let's say you bought a house for $300,000. After living in it for two years, you move into a new house and rent out the old one. Each year you depreciate the property by $8,000. Just before three years is up, you sell the rental house for $600,000 after selling expenses. Your gain is $300,000 plus $24,000 in recaptured depreciation. As an individual, you can use the principal residence gain exclusion to exclude $250,000 of your gain from taxes. The remaining $50,000 could be shielded by exchanging it into another rental property. However, taxes must be paid on the recaptured depreciation.

Moving Into a Rental Property that Was Originally Part of a 1031 Exchange

Let's say that you and your spouse acquire a townhouse as part of a 1031 exchange. Your adjusted basis in this replacement property is $250,000, plus you had depreciated the relinquished property by $35,000. You rent this townhouse for three years, and depreciate it by $10,000 per year for a total of $30,000. Then you move into the property and make it your principal residence. You live there for at least two years before deciding to sell the townhouse for $595,000 after selling expenses.

Your gain is $345,000 plus $65,000 in depreciation. As a couple, you can typically exclude up to $500,000 in gain under your principal residence gain exclusion. However, you will have to pay the 25% recaptured depreciation tax on any depreciation taken on both this property and the original relinquished property if that depreciation was taken after May 6, 1997.

Note that normally a homeowner can qualify for the principal residence gain exclusion every two years. However, if a property was obtained as part of a 1031 tax exchange, the property must be held for at least five years to qualify for this exclusion. Which two years you occupy the property doesn't matter. You could live in the property during the last two years as in our example, or during years two and three with the property being a rental both before and after your personal residency.

Combining Home with Business or Investment Use

You and your spouse run a business out of your home. You purchased the property four years ago for $400,000. You've used 25% of the property's square footage for your office space, so the basis has been allocated as $300,000 for the residence and $100,000 for the business area. You've depreciated the business portion by $3,000 per year for a total of $12,000.

You sell the property for $900,000 after selling expenses and exchange part of the proceeds into a $300,000 office condo. The gain must be apportioned between the office and the residential spaces. Because you originally allocated 25% of your home to office space, you multiply $900,000 by 25% to get $225,000. Your original cost, or basis, for the office space was $100,000. Subtracting this from the business portion of $225,000 gives you $125,000. Now subtract the depreciation you've taken, $12,000, and you have a basis of $113,000 in the office condo.

The portion of the sale that is apportioned to the residence use is 75%. $900,000 multiplied by 75% equals $675,000. $300,000 was originally allocated as the basis for the residential part of the property. Subtracting this basis from the $675,000 gain leaves $375,000 in gain. This amount is less than the maximum $500,000 exclusion allowed per joint return, so no tax is owed on this portion.

Notice that the personal residence gain exclusion is allowed in this situation even though you have only owned the property for four years. This is because you did not buy the property as part of a 1031 exchange.

Contract Provisions

When you do a 1031 tax exchange, you will need the buyers and sellers involved in your various transactions to agree to sign the necessary paperwork. The 1031 tax expert who assisted me with this chapter, Richard Levy of 1031 Solutions, has generously allowed me to include in this book as a sample the contract language he suggests investors working with his company use in their contracts. If you are the seller, you would add the following language in the "Additional Provisions" section of your contract.

BUYER AGREES TO COOPERATE IN AN IRC SECTION 1031 EXCHANGE BY SELLER AT NO COST OR LIABILITY TO BUYER INCLUDING, WITHOUT LIMITATION, THE ASSIGNMENT OF SELLER'S RIGHTS, BUT NOT SELLER'S OBLIGATIONS, UNDER THIS CONTRACT ON OR BEFORE CLOSING TO SELLER'S QUALIFIED EXCHANGE INTERMEDIARY, (put in the name of your intermediary).

If you are the buyer, you would make the contract in the name of "(your name) and/or Assigns" and add the following language in the "Additional Provisions" section of your contract.

SELLER AGREES TO COOPERATE IN AN IRC SECTION 1031 EXCHANGE BY BUYER AT NO COST OR LIABILITY TO SELLER INCLUDING, WITHOUT LIMITATION, THE ASSIGNMENT OF BUYER'S RIGHTS, BUT NOT BUYER'S OBLIGATIONS, UNDER THIS CONTRACT ON OR BEFORE CLOSING TO BUYER'S QUALIFIED EXCHANGE INTERMEDIARY, (put in the name of your intermediary)

SELLER FURTHER ACKNOWLEDGES AND AGREES THAT, AT BUYER'S REQUEST, BUYER'S EARNEST MONEY DEPOSIT SHALL BE REFUNDED TO BUYER BY SELLER AND REPLACED WITH AN EQUAL AMOUNT OF FUNDS FROM BUYER'S QUALIFIED EXCHANGE INTERMEDIARY AT ANY TIME AFTER ASSIGNMENT OF THIS CONTRACT TO BUYER'S QUALIFIED INTERMEDIARY."

Of course, these clauses should not be construed as tax or legal advice. They are provided here to give you an idea of the wording you could use in your contracts. You should check with your own qualified intermediary for recommended language. He or she may insist on you using a different phrasing. In addition, some states now offer standard 1031 tax deferred exchange addendums to add to contracts. Using this type of addendum makes the language more familiar to the other agent involved in the transaction and reduces the possibility of someone getting confused and refusing to sign a contract that includes a 1031 exchange clause.

By including an exchange clause in your contract, you may accidentally give a seller of a replacement property or the buyer of a relinquished property a strong bargaining position. If the property is one that you have identified either as a replacement property in a forward exchange or a relinquished property in a reverse exchange, and the forty-five day identification deadline has passed, the seller or buyer may conclude that you are highly motivated.

They could be right. Paying extra or selling for less may be cheaper than paying the taxes if your exchange falls apart. If you wait until the last minute to buy or sell an identified property, don't reveal this fact. Be evasive if an agent, buyer or seller asks when a relinquished property was sold or a reverse exchange replacement property was purchased. Say it's not been long, and change the topic.

Tell your agent to protect your interests by also being evasive. Many agents get to chatting, and before they know it, they've disclosed that you sold your relinquished property more than a month ago. Whoops. Good-bye negotiating power. Do try to avoid this type of situation by placing your replacement or relinquished properties under contract and finishing the inspection well ahead of your identification deadline. You always want time to change your mind about what property is going to be bought and sold.

Summary

In general, 1031 tax deferred exchanges are easy to do. Most exchanges are forward exchanges involving only one or two replacement properties. If you do a more complicated exchange, your tax qualified intermediary will guide you through complying with the rules.

Doing a 1031 tax deferred exchange is a wonderful way to conserve your capital for reinvestment whenever you decide to sell one of your rental properties. Participating in multiple 1031 tax deferred exchanges over a span of years can allow you to postpone paying capital gain taxes indefinitely. Yet refinancing some of your properties along the way can allow you access to some of your equity on a temporarily tax free basis.

Appendix A - Cash Flow Worksheet

Use this worksheet to determine how much cash flow a sample house would produce if you owned it free and clear.

Annual Income

Projected monthly rent X number of months rented a) _____

Annual costs

Average annual maintenance	_____
Taxes	_____
Insurance	_____

Total Annual Expenses (a - b)   b) _____

Annual Net Cash Flow

Annual income - annual expenses   c) _____

Sample Cash Flow Worksheet

Annual Income

Projected monthly rent X number of months rented a) <u>15,525</u>

Annual costs

Average annual maintenance	<u>1,735</u>
Taxes	<u>1,600</u>
Insurance	<u>950</u>

Total Annual Expenses   b) <u>4,285</u>

Annual Net Cash Flow

Annual income - annual expenses (a - b)   c) <u>11,240</u>

Appendix B - Average Annual Maintenance

Use this worksheet to predict the annual maintenance costs for any given property averaged over ten years. The list of ten year expenses includes several blanks for other. Other expenses may be the cost of fencing, repairing a porch, or any other expenditure you feel a particular property will need.

Annual Miscellaneous

Small stuff such as minor repairs and ads   a) _____

Ten Year Expenses

Repaint exterior (may occur twice)   _____
New furnace   _____
New roof   _____
New hot water heater   _____
Repaint interior   _____
New carpet   _____
New vinyl   _____
New air conditioner   _____
Other   _____
Other   _____
Other   _____

Total Ten Year Expenses   b) _____

Average Annual Expenses

Total ten year expenses divided by 10   c) _____

Combined Annual Costs

Annual Miscellaneous + Average Annual (a + c)   d) _____

Sample Average Annual Maintenance

This worksheet uses the numbers from the example in Chapter One.

Annual Miscellaneous

Small stuff such as minor repairs and ads   a) ___250___

Ten Year Expenses

Repaint exterior	2,700
New furnace	1,800
New roof	3,500
New hot water heater	650
Repaint interior	2,000
New carpet	2,400
New vinyl	1,800
New air conditioner	0
Other	0
Other	0
Other	0

Total Ten Year Expenses   b) 14,850

Average Annual Expenses

Total ten year expenses divided by 10   c) 1,485

Combined Annual Costs

Annual Miscellaneous + Average Annual (a + c)   d) 1,735

Appendix C - Cash Flow per $1,000

Use this worksheet to calculate the cash flow you would receive for each thousand dollars worth of equity you have invested in a property owned free and clear.

How Many Thousands Invested in Sample House

Cost of sample house divided by 1,000   a) _____

Cash Flow per $1,000 Invested

Annual Net Cash Flow from Sample House   b) _____
Cash flow per thousand (b divided by a)   c) _____

Value of Target Properties

Target income   d) _____
Target total property value (d divided by c)   e) _____

Sample Cash Flow per $1,000 Worksheet

How Many Thousands Invested in Sample House

Cost of sample house divided by 1,000   a) _____180

Cash Flow per $1,000 Invested

Annual Net Cash Flow from Sample House   b) _11,240
Cash flow per thousand (b divided by a)   c) _62.44

Value of Target Properties

Target income   d) _60,000
Target total property value
        (d divided by c multiplied by 1,000)   e) _961,000

Appendix D - Rate of Return

Purchase price   _____
New loan   _____
Down payment (purchase price - new loan)   _____
Previous appreciation and principal paydown   _____
Total cash invested (closing costs + down payment
+ previous appreciation and principal paydown)   _____
Income received   _____
Expenses
       Taxes   _____
       Interest   _____
       Insurance   _____
       Miscellaneous   _____
       Total expenses   _____
Cash flow (income - expenses -principal paydown)   _____
Principal paydown   _____
Appreciation   _____
Depreciation   _____

Cash flow rate of return
Cash flow divided by total cash invested   _____
Principal paydown rate of return
Principal paydown divided by total cash invested   _____
Appreciation rate of return
Appreciation divided by total cash invested   _____
Tax Savings
Depreciation amount multiplied by your combined
federal, state, and local income tax percentage   _____

Total rate of return
Four rates of return added together   _____

Index 2ed

Order Form

Call 1-800-324-6415 to order by credit card. Or copy and mail this order form to: Gemstone House Publishing, P.O. 19948, Boulder, CO 80308.

Name: _____

Address: _____

_____

City & State: _____

Zip: _____

Phone #: _____

Discount schedule when ordering direct from publisher:

1-2 books	no discount ($18.95 ea)
3-4 books	20% ($15.16 ea)
5+ books	40% ($11.37 ea)

For large quantities, contact the publisher for correct discount.

Please send _____ copies of *Rental Houses for the Successful Small Investor 2ed* at $_____ each for a subtotal of $_____

Add $3.00 shipping for the first book $___3.00

Plus $1.00 for each additional book $_____

Total: $_____

I'm paying by:_____ Check

_____ Mastercard, Visa, Discover, Amex

Card #: _____ Expiration Date: _____

Signature: _____